THE STATE
OF THE STATES

THE STATE OF THE STATES

Fourth Edition

Edited by
Carl E. Van Horn
Rutgers University

A Division of Congressional Quarterly Inc.
Washington, D.C.

CQ Press
1255 22nd Street, NW, Suite 400
Washington, DC 20037

Phone: 202-729-1900; toll-free, 1-866-427-7737 (1-866-4CQ-PRESS)

Web: www.cqpress.com

Copyright © 2006 by CQ Press, a division of Congressional Quarterly Inc.

All rights reserved. No part of this publication may be reproduced or transmitted in any form or by any means, electronic or mechanical, including photocopy, recording, or any information storage and retrieval system, without permission in writing from the publisher.

Cover design: Vincent Hughes Visualization

♾ The paper used in this publication exceeds the requirements of the American National Standard for Information Sciences—Permanence of Paper for Printed Library Materials, ANSI Z39.48-1992.

Printed and bound in the United States of America

09 08 07 06 05   1 2 3 4 5

The Library of Congress Cataloging-in-Publication Data are available under 2005032284.

To my wife, Christy Van Horn, who shares my enthusiasm for the art and science of politics and government

Contents

Tables and Figures ix
Preface xi
Contributors xiii

1. Power, Politics, and Public Policy in the States   1
   Carl E. Van Horn

2. The State of State Elections   14
   Kenneth Dautrich and David A. Yalof

3. Legislators and Legislatures   29
   Alan Rosenthal

4. Being Governor   53
   Thad L. Beyle

5. State Courts in Their Political Environment   81
   Lawrence Baum

6. Accountability Battles in State Administration   101
   William T. Gormley Jr.

7. State Government Finances: A Review of Current Conditions and the Outlook   120
   Henry A. Coleman

8. State Education Policy in the New Millennium   141
   Margaret E. Goertz

9. State Welfare Policy   167
   Irene Lurie

10. State Health Policy   192
    Joel C. Cantor

Tables and Figures

Tables

4-1	Governors' Institutional Powers	61
4-2	Gubernatorial Elections, 1970–2004	66
4-3	Job Approval Ratings of Current Governors, Mid-2005	69
4-4	Gubernatorial Election Expenditures, 1977–2004	71
7-1	State Government Expenditures, Fiscal Year 2003	125
7-2	State General Fund Revenues, Fiscal Year 2003	126
7-3	Casino Tax Revenue by State, 2004	130
8-1	Economic and Racial/Ethnic Make-up of the States	144
8-2	Educational Expenditures per Pupil and Revenues by Source and State, 2001–2002	160
9-1	Welfare Caseloads and Benefit Levels, by State	169
9-2	Use of TANF and Maintenance of Effort Funds, Fiscal Year 2003	184
10-1	Essential Public Health Services	193
10-2	Medicaid Expenditures by Type of Service, Fiscal Year 2003	198
10-3	Summary of Coverage under Federal Medicaid Rules	199
10-4	State Medicaid Cost Containment Strategies, Fiscal Years 2002–2004	209

Figures

9-1	Families on Welfare	172
10-1	Health Insurance Coverage of the Non-elderly, by Source of Coverage and Federal Poverty Level, 2003	200

Preface

If state governments are the "laboratories" of democracy, as Supreme Court justice Louis D. Brandeis wrote, they have been working overtime to produce wide-ranging policy innovations that influence the lives of all Americans. States are making and implementing laws on a variety of consequential and controversial subjects, such as embryonic stem cell research, the right to die, gay marriage, and homeland security.

States are not only innovators. Since the founding of the Republic, state governments have been central to the education of children, the building of roads and bridges, the economic development of communities, and the provision of public health and safety. As federal government policymakers authorized new initiatives to help the poor or regulations to clean up the environment, states were asked to take on even more tasks.

Given the critical importance of state government to the public life of the nation, state politics and public policy have become vital subjects for scholars and should be on the "must know" list for all college and university students studying political science, public policy, and public administration.

The State of the States, fourth edition, with clear, concise, and lively chapters by leading scholars of state government and politics, provides comprehensive coverage of politics, political institutions, and public policy in the states. Each chapter describes, analyzes, and explains trends of the past thirty years and looks at new challenges facing state governments at the beginning of the twenty-first century.

Chapters on governors, legislatures, courts, bureaucracies, and campaigns and elections examine the transformation of state political institutions. Chapters on fiscal policy and the states' roles in providing education, welfare for low-income citizens, and health care for the poor and elderly reveal contemporary policy developments.

Acknowledgments

I wish to express my appreciation to several individuals who helped me prepare the fourth edition. Melissa Qualls and Scott Reynolds at the John J. Heldrich Center for Workforce Development provided helpful research assistance. Working again with CQ Press was a pleasure. Charisse Kiino and Colleen Ganey helped me through the revision and made many valuable suggestions—as did the reviewers for the fourth edition: Scott Allard (Brown

University), Jeffrey D. Greene (University of Montana), Jay Barth (Hendrix College), and Patricia K. Freeland (University of Tennessee). Joanne S. Ainsworth provided excellent editorial guidance, and Belinda Josey kept the production process running smoothly.

Contributors

Lawrence Baum is professor of political science at Ohio State University. He is the author of *The Supreme Court*, 8th ed. (CQ Press, 2004) and *American Courts*, 5th ed. (2001). Topics of his research include judicial behavior and elections.

Thad L. Beyle is professor of political science at the University of North Carolina at Chapel Hill. He has worked in the North Carolina governor's office and the National Governors Association.

Joel C. Cantor, Sc.D., is director of the Center for State Health Policy and professor of public policy at the Edward J. Bloustein School of Planning and Public Policy at Rutgers, the State University of New Jersey. His research currently focuses on state regulation of health insurance and hospitals; racial disparities in access to health care; and the supply of physician services. He received his doctorate in health policy and management from the Johns Hopkins University School of Hygiene and Public Health in 1988.

Henry A. Coleman is professor of public policy at the Edward J. Bloustein School of Planning and Public Policy at Rutgers University. He served as executive director of New Jersey's State and Local Expenditure and Revenue Policy Commission and as a senior adviser in the governor's policy office. He has also worked in the federal government at the U.S. Department of Housing and Urban Development (HUD), Government Accountability Office (GAO—formerly the General Accounting Office), and the U.S. Advisory Commission on Intergovernmental Relations (ACIR).

Kenneth Dautrich is chair of the Department of Public Policy at the University of Connecticut. His research focuses on public opinion, the media, and voting. His most recent book is *The First Amendment and the Media in the Court of Public Opinion* (2002) with David A. Yalof.

Margaret E. Goertz is professor in the Graduate School of Education and co-director of the Consortium for Policy Research in Education at the University of Pennsylvania. She specializes in the research of state and federal education policy and school finance.

William T. Gormley Jr. is professor of public policy and government and co-director of the Center for Research on Children in the U.S. (CROCUS) at Georgetown University. He is the author of several books, including *Bureaucracy and Democracy: Accountability and Performance* with Steven Balla (CQ Press, 2004).

Irene Lurie is professor of public administration and policy in the Rockefeller College of Public Affairs and Policy at the University at Albany, State University of New York. She has analyzed welfare policy for many years and recently studied the implementation of TANF by frontline workers in four states.

Alan Rosenthal is professor of public policy and political science at the Eagleton Institute of Politics at Rutgers University. He has worked with legislatures throughout the country. His latest book is *Heavy Lifting: The Job of the American Legislature* (CQ Press, 2005).

Carl E. Van Horn is professor of public policy and political science at the Eagleton Institute of Politics and chair of the Department of Public Policy at the Bloustein School of Planning and Public Policy at Rutgers University. From 1990 to 1992 he was the director of policy in New Jersey's office of the governor.

David A. Yalof is an associate professor of political science at the University of Connecticut. His first book, *Pursuit of Justices: Presidential Politics and the Selection of Supreme Court Nominees* (1999), won the American Political Science Association's Richard E. Neustadt Award as the best book published on presidential studies in 1999. Yalof has written extensively on issues in constitutional law and Supreme Court politics. His work has been published in *Political Research Quarterly, Judicature, Constitutional Commentary,* and *Presidential Studies Quarterly,* among other journals.

THE STATE
OF THE STATES

1

Power, Politics, and Public Policy in the States
Carl E. Van Horn

Today, at the beginning of the twenty-first century, state governments are at the cutting edge of political and public policy reform. State government leaders wield enormous political influence, not only over the destinies of their states, but over the future of the nation. From health care, education, and homeland security to stem cell research, the right to die, and election reform, states are leading the way.

The power, political influence, and public policy significance of state governments today could not have been anticipated in the middle of the twentieth century. Then, state governments languished in relative obscurity—overshadowed by a burgeoning national government responding to the crises of depression and war and overseeing an unprecedented period of economic prosperity. Americans turned to Washington, D.C., for leadership and for a share of rapidly growing federal programs.

The sweeping national and international events that shifted government activism to the federal level bypassed state governments. The federal government expanded way beyond the limited role envisioned by the U.S. Constitution's framers. State governments were scorned by many observers as racist, incompetent, inflexible, and politically and economically anemic.[1]

Over the last thirty years, however, profound changes have occurred—sometimes dramatically, sometimes gradually—and state government institutions have been transformed. Responding to landmark court decisions, pressing concerns of their residents, and diminished federal government activism, states pioneered solutions to the country's most difficult problems.[2] Now that states have strengthened their political and economic houses, they occupy a much more important role in American politics and public policy.

Governors, state legislators, judges, and bureaucrats are responsible for carrying out much of the nation's public business and are setting national agendas, too. Increasingly, federal policymakers expect state governments to assume full policy and administrative responsibilities. States are more committed to managing and paying for such traditional local government services as law enforcement and education.

States are also more politically significant than they were thirty years ago. Strong and effective governors have risen to national prominence, and the state capitals are now the proving ground for the presidency. Every U.S. president since 1978, with the exception of George H. W. Bush, the forty-first president, first served as a governor. Jimmy Carter (1977–1981) had been the governor of Georgia; Ronald Reagan (1981–1989) had been the governor of California; former Arkansas governor Bill Clinton served as president from 1993 to 2001; and George W. Bush, former governor of Texas, was elected to the presidency in 2000 and reelected in 2004.

The Quiet Revolution

The rising importance of state governments was produced by a quiet revolution in American politics that was not an entirely smooth one. The origins of more muscular state governments came about through changes in representation, government organization, and managerial competence that had been spawned decades ago.

Perhaps most important, landmark decisions that required legislatures to reapportion themselves changed state governments from unrepresentative, homogeneous political backwaters to more effective representative governments. The U.S. Supreme Court in *Baker v. Carr* (1962) and *Reynolds v. Sims* (1964) removed barriers to direct representation of voters and reapportioned legislatures according to the principle of "one person, one vote." The Voting Rights Act of 1965 eliminated obstacles to full political participation by African Americans.

Revamping state constitutions, restructuring institutions, and assembling professional expertise enabled state governments to design and implement far-reaching public policies. Furthermore, the policymaking circles—in legislatures, courts, bureaucracies, and governors' mansions—were no longer exclusively filled with the upper-middle-class white males that had dominated government for most of American political history.

State legislatures and administrative agencies today have greater numbers of women and minorities than twenty years ago. Women holding legislative office, for example, increased from 4 percent in 1969 to 22.6 percent in 2005.[3] In Arizona, Colorado, Delaware, Maryland, Nevada, Vermont, and Washington women hold 33 percent or more of the seats in the legislature.[4]

Women's participation in state government positions also has risen at the appointive policymaking levels. Women have been more successful in getting elected to the top position as governor. In 2005 eight women are governors.[5]

Minority participation in elected and appointed policymaking positions in state government also has grown. In 1970 none of the governors was black and less than 2 percent of legislators were black. Even so, blacks, who account for 12 percent of the U.S. population, held no governorships and just 8 percent of the state legislative positions in 2001.[6]

Hispanics increased their share of elected positions in several states where they make up a significant part of the population—Arizona, California, Colorado, and New Mexico. Arizona, Florida, and New Mexico have elected governors of Hispanic origin.

Legislators and governors from these newly empowered groups demanded greater government efforts to ameliorate social and economic problems in their communities. Elected officials' policy priorities reflect their life experiences and professional training. More teachers and working women in elected and appointed positions encouraged greater attention to family leave programs, child care, and women's and children's health care.

Although there is no doubt that business and labor groups still wield power in state politics, environmentalists, consumer advocates, senior citizens, and social policy advocates have become more influential. Citizen participation in state policymaking has exploded since the early 1970s. State agencies now routinely allow citizens to voice concerns through public boards and commissions, ombudspersons, public advocates, and public hearings. Newly active groups raise money and contribute to candidates, advertise in the mass media, and exert considerable influence over governors and legislatures.

The state initiative process—which gives voters a direct voice in making policy—has been employed with increasing frequency by political leaders, interest groups, and citizens' groups. Ballot initiatives doubled between 1976 and 1990. At times, initiatives have been used to circumvent the legislative process. In other cases, the mere threat of mounting such a campaign spurs the legislature to act.

In 2004, 162 ballot questions appeared in thirty-four states—62 proposals were launched by citizens' groups[7]. In recent years, voters weighed important and controversial proposals, including the regulation of pornography, acid rain, gay rights, abortions, drug use, and the length of time legislators may remain in office.

Political institutions have expanded their staffs in order to pursue their policy agendas and to compete with rival institutions. Governors expanded staffs overseeing the bureaucracy, monitoring developments in Washington, D.C., and shepherding legislative proposals in the statehouse. Legislatures bolstered staffs to keep a watchful eye on the executive branch and to provide more effective service to constituents.

The cumulative impact of these changes has been dramatic. State officials are far more willing and able to carry out significant responsibilities. States routinely execute complex policy initiatives: water supply and quality improvement programs, pollution prevention programs, education reform, science and technology development, and energy conservation programs.

Matching the activism of the elected branches of government, the state courts hired more judges, law clerks, and administrative officers to meet the rising demand for court review of policy and administrative cases. Courts handed down far-reaching decisions on such important policies as expanding the rights of women, gays, minorities, and criminal defendants. In doing so, state judges often relied on state constitutions to establish rights that the U.S. Supreme Court has not established by relying upon the U.S. Constitution. State courts also expanded the rights of individuals to recover for personal injuries and imposed strict liability rules for faulty products. These policy developments fostered by court rulings have met with a conservative backlash as rulings on everything from gay rights to fiscal policy are challenged by elected officials and at the ballot box.

Fiscal Squeeze Play

Over the last several decades, state government spending increased dramatically. In 1964, for example, state governments spent $24 billion; by 1990 that figure had grown to more than $350 billion; and in 2005 expenditures are estimated to be $526 billion.[8] During this same period, state spending increased at a slightly faster rate than federal government spending, somewhat faster than the rate of inflation, and considerably faster than local government spending.[9]

Finding enough money to satisfy the needs of their states—and the demands of interest groups—is a constant struggle for state policymakers. When the national economy is booming, state revenues surge and new programs are initiated. When the economy weakens, the bright outlooks are replaced by the gloomy years of budget deficits, tax increases, and program reductions. State governments do not have the same flexibility that federal policymakers have when it comes to borrowing funds for operating basic government services. All but a few states adhere to strict requirements to balance their budgets every year and to limit borrowing for capital investments in roads, highways, schools, and the like.

National policy often makes matters worse for states, because federal lawmakers often pass the buck of responsibility without passing on the bucks to handle ambitious national goals in education, health care, and programs for the poor and disabled. In recent years, with Republicans controlling the White House and Congress, federal lawmakers have cut federal taxes and increased defense spending, which has led to mounting deficits. This federal fiscal policy formula imposed additional burdens on state policymakers, because spending on domestic programs from highways to higher education was either slowed down or cut back.

Reductions in federal aid to states and local governments are wreaking havoc on state budgets. In the mid-1980s, when federal aid was cut deeply, states increased taxes to make up some of the shortfall. Now the political landscape is different, because conservative policymakers in the state capitals are less willing to raise taxes. State governments are ruled by more Republicans than Democrats—twenty-eight of the fifty governors are Republicans, and half of the legislative chambers have a majority of Republican members.[10] These officials are more likely to want to reduce government taxes and spending. In some years state tax cuts have exceeded state tax increases. As a result, states are now much less able or willing to replace lost federal revenues.[11]

The end product of large federal government deficits and mandated increases in state spending is to seriously compound the fiscal challenge for state officials. To pay for substantial increases in defense and entitlement programs, federal lawmakers have sharply cut aid to state and local governments.

Consequently, states are receiving less money from the national government and more pleas for help from local governments.[12] In 2003 federal aid was $3 of every $10 spent by the states, down from $4 of every $10 thirty years ago.[13] Moreover, federal aid has not kept pace with federal mandates to provide health care to the poor or to reform education programs.

Although their revenue-raising power has increased, state governments still struggle to balance the desire for new services with the ability to pay for them. Individual and corporate income taxes are now far more important than sales taxes and other fees. In 1967 only 22 percent of state government revenue derived from the income tax; by the 1980s it was nearly 40 percent.[14] States also have found significant new sources of revenue in state lotteries, which have been created in forty states and the District of Columbia.[15] States are still prohibited from taxing sales over the Internet—a major source of potential revenue in a service-driven economy.[16]

Most important, state fiscal policy is influenced by the tax limitation movement spawned nearly thirty years ago by conservatives seeking to curb the growth in government spending. Spurred by California's Proposition 13 in 1978, which reduced property tax revenues by 57 percent and limited future increases to no more than 2 percent annually, citizens and legislators clamped down on the rapid growth in state spending. Between 1978 and 1984, only three of the nine states that voted on Proposition 13–type initiatives approved them. But voters in eleven states accepted more moderate tax and spending limitation measures.[17] Legislatures in dozens of other states responded to the conservative message of tax and spending cuts.[18]

Today, many gubernatorial and legislative candidates run on the "no new tax" pledge favored by conservative interest groups. When the national economy weakens and state revenues fall, some elected officials break those pledges by raising taxes, or at least bend them by raising fees. For example, between 1981 and 1983 and again in 1990–1991 and in 2001, in the midst of national recessions, states imposed substantial tax increases to meet their needs and to cope with deep reductions in federal aid. States increased the sales and corporate taxes, income tax rates, and gasoline taxes and extended new user fees. In 1991, for example, thirty-four states raised more than $16 billion in income, sales, and corporate taxes and cut more than $10 billion in programs just to keep their budgets in balance. California raised $7 billion in new revenues and cut $7 billion in programs but still faced a $6 billion deficit the following year.[19]

Federal policymakers are reluctant to pay for new domestic program initiatives, because to do so would require either higher taxes or increased borrowing. Interest groups have turned their attention to state officials and have turned up the political heat on them to satisfy their demands. Unfortunately, state governments cannot "count on the federal cavalry to come charging over the hill with aid from Washington." The states are operating in "an atmosphere of fend-for-yourself federalism."[20]

Devolving responsibility to state governments was supposed to be accompanied by deregulation of federal control, but the federal government has continued to impose strict regulations. Federal mandates relating to education reform, under the No Child Left Behind Act, for example, have cost state governments hundreds of millions of dollars annually. Congress and presidents satisfy constituencies wanting more help by imposing new demands on state capitals, but they don't always authorize the resources to accompany the new tasks.[21]

The economist Richard Nathan has called the current state of American federalism the "Devolution Revolution."[22] The idea behind this revolution is simple: to reduce the size and influence of government by cutting taxes and spending and by sending federal responsibilities to the states. For the last decade, the Republican-controlled Congress has adopted budgets that have included sharp reductions in aid to the states.

Although the long-term effects of the Devolution Revolution are not yet known, we do know that such changes are already shaping state policy and politics. States are being asked to assume important new responsibilities, generally with fewer resources than were previously available to remedy problems. State policymakers have been given greater latitude to define policies and programs to fulfill broad federal objectives. The combination of constrained resources and expanded opportunities represents the upside and downside of the new American federalism.

Power and Conflicts

Reforms fashioned decades ago to strengthen state governments simultaneously encouraged governors, legislators, judges, and bureaucrats to assert power boldly. As power fragmented, state politics became more conflict ridden. Policymakers who wanted to tackle tough problems often found it difficult to find consensus for specific actions. Distrust deepened as governors, judges, legislators, and administrators jealously guarded their prerogatives.

In other words, the changes that made state governments more democratic and responsive brought some troubling consequences. With more at stake in the governance of states, everyone has a greater incentive to seek more power and control. Personal and partisan conflicts often escalate into battles for institutional control.

Reforms that fostered modern political institutions were democratic in that power was more evenly dispersed across the legislative, executive, and judicial branches. Yet, these changes came at the expense of clear lines of institutional responsibility and accountability. It is increasingly difficult for the press and public to determine which institution or individuals to hold accountable for state policies and program management.

Prevailing attitudes about the duties of legislators also changed. Modern legislators are more likely to pursue personal or district agendas than the priorities of party leaders or the governor. Legislators will champion their districts' interests even if they come in conflict with state party organizations, governors, and legislative leaders.[23] With their antennae tuned to the voters back home and campaign contributors, legislators often ignore appeals for party discipline, and it is therefore harder to get legislation approved. Intense competition is apparent in all phases of state political life from elections to state budget decisions. More legislators, judges, bureaucrats, and interest groups have sufficient clout to engage in the struggle but seldom have enough power to rule.

The desire to retain power shapes the political process within institutions, especially in legislatures in which electoral considerations are paramount. The quest for power is hardly a new phenomenon, but career politicians are more intent on winning because they are more determined to stay in office as long as possible. "Permanent" legislators are compelled to deliver benefits to their districts, claim credit for accomplishments, and attack opponents in the executive branch or elsewhere.[24] Clearly, these strategies serve their intended purpose; incumbents rarely lose.[25]

Campaigns for public office are also more intense and expensive. Costs are rising because people are willing and able to spend huge sums of money to get elected. Because the building blocks of modern campaigns (media consultants, pollsters, and television advertising) are expensive, statewide candidates—and even legislative candidates in competitive districts—must collect huge sums of money or have large personal fortunes.

The harsh reality is that candidates who cannot afford high-cost elections are unlikely to succeed in statewide campaigns or in competitive legislative districts. As a result, interest groups or party leaders who contribute money or political support or both get special attention from the candidate and from officeholders who want to keep their jobs. Educators, developers, senior citizens, labor leaders, and others are effective advocates because they supply the campaign funds or the committed volunteers that keep incumbent politicians in office or elect new officeholders.

A by-product of conflict in state politics and policymaking is an institutional arms race. Governors, legislators, bureaucrats, judges, and interest groups are employing new techniques and strategies to achieve their goals. Governors assert greater control over the bureaucracy. Legislatures step up efforts to oversee executive-branch agencies. Interest groups bypass representative institutions and go directly to the voters through the initiative process. State courts adjudicate disputes between legislators and governors and make policy independently.

Few observers of American politics are nostalgic for a return to an era when a handful of party bosses and top-ranking elected officials called the shots. But political stalemates are often caused by ambiguous authority and personal political ambition rather than by clashes over competing policy visions or political ideologies. Cross-institutional battles often muddle the policymaking process into a round-robin policy game as courts, legislatures, and governors fight with one another for control.

The more strident and negative tone of contemporary politics has engendered greater public skepticism about state officials and political institutions. The trust-in-government index developed by the University of Michigan's

National Election Studies, which has tracked opinions about public trust in government for more than fifty years, hit its lowest point during the 1990s and remains well below its fifty-year average. This index reflects a lack of public confidence in the honesty, fairness, and judgment of elected officials.[26] An obvious outgrowth of that skepticism has been the adoption of laws limiting the number of terms that legislators may serve—a policy in force in fifteen states in 2004.[27]

Divided party control of the legislature and governorship also contributes, if not guarantees, a certain amount of institutional conflict. Voters in many states do not seem to be bothered by divided control of the machinery of government. A remarkable increase in split-ticket voting has taken place in the last thirty years. Split control of state legislatures increased from four states in 1982 to twelve states in 1994, but decreased slightly to ten states in 2005.[28]

When legislators and governors clash, they often punt unresolved issues and hard choices to the bureaucracy. This policymaking-by-other-means has generated a host of commissions and "independent" authorities created through legislative and gubernatorial action. It has also drawn state judges into disputes between legislatures and governors or between legislatures and government agencies. For example, courts have ruled on the authority of governors to exercise their line-item veto and on the extent of gubernatorial appointment and removal powers.

When this happens, courts become policymakers.[29] State judges have handed down dozens of decisions in civil rights cases in which they protected the interests of minorities. But these decisions sometimes engender a backlash from legislators, governors, and voters who perceive that the courts are thwarting majority preferences. Voters and elected officials have sought to rein in the courts by amending state constitutions, passing new laws, or removing judges from office.

Bureaucracies also are embroiled in disputes over their activities, purposes, and performance. Legislatures have sharpened their oversight of agency decisions through sunset laws, which require periodic reviews of administrative rules and regulations. Governors have exerted greater control through executive reorganizations, a reduction in the number of boards and commissions, centralization of budgeting techniques, and executive orders mandating direct accountability to the governor.

In other words, the stakes are high, the competition is intense, and the lines of authority are ambiguous. Such a mixture makes state governments interesting and important governments to watch and study. It also makes life in state politics demanding and sometimes demeaning for those who serve in public life.

The State of the States

The authors of the chapters in this book are among the keenest and most experienced observers of state government and politics in the nation. Each chapter describes and assesses how states are shaping American public policy and politics in the twenty-first century. The authors offer their informed perspectives on major changes under way in state capitals and the impact of significant federal policy changes on the states. They also describe and explain the key features of state politics and government today and identify the critical challenges for state political leaders.

In Chapter 2, "The State of State Elections," Kenneth Dautrich and David A. Yalof review recent trends in legislative, gubernatorial, and judicial elections in the United States. They point out that state elections have become the "principal means by which most of the major domestic issues" are discussed and resolved. They also examine the growth and importance of statewide initiatives and referendums that give voters a direct role in making public policy at the ballot box.

Chapter 3, "Legislators and Legislatures," by Alan Rosenthal, provides a vivid portrait of the more than 7,300 individuals who serve in state legislatures, how they get elected, and how they adapt to being legislators. Rosenthal describes how legislatures are organized to carry out their responsibilities to represent their constituencies, respond to their governor's agenda, make public policy, and oversee the executive branch. He explains how and why legislators and legislatures are exercising greater influence on the allocation of money and the direction of state policy.

In Chapter 4, "Being Governor," Thad L. Beyle reviews the growing political influence of governors and the increased pressures on them to manage complex government organizations. Governors' political influence has risen because, in the last eight elections, at least one of the major party candidates for president has served as a governor before running, and four were elected president. More powerful governors have also clashed with courts, legislatures, and other members of the executive branch. Beyle chronicles how shifting federal responsibilities that have been delegated to the states are influencing the office of governor and the people who serve there.

Chapter 5, "State Courts in Their Political Environment," by Lawrence Baum, examines institutions that referee conflicts between governors and legislatures or between governors and other executive branch agencies. State courts also make policy and thus generate conflict with other government actors. Baum explains the relationships between courts and the politics and politicians of their states. He concludes that although the "autonomy of state courts has been reduced, it remains substantial."

In Chapter 6, "Accountability Battles in State Administration," William T. Gormley Jr. catalogs the controls that curb the power of state bureaucracies to make and carry out policy. As state administrative agencies take on greater responsibility for the implementation of public policy, politicians, judges, and citizens demand more accountability from administrative agencies. States have increased legislative oversight and executive management techniques and involved citizens in a wider range of bureaucratic decisions. Federal agencies and federal and state judges have also increased their control over state bureaucracies. Battles over accountability have pit state political institutions against one another in a bitter struggle over authority, with state bureaucracies as the ultimate prize.

In Chapter 7, "State Government Finances," Henry A. Coleman sketches the landscape of state fiscal policy. He explains how and why state government finances play such a central role in the U.S. federal system and why states are likely to be even more important as providers of government services in the future. He describes the fiscal crisis plaguing many states as they struggle to balance budgets while meeting the rising costs of health care and education. He also explores the impact of tax and expenditure limitation policies on state governments.

Chapter 8, "State Education Policy in the New Millennium," by Margaret E. Goertz, portrays the preeminent role that state governments have in the financing and regulation of public elementary and secondary education. Goertz argues that the intense politics of education finance and battles over educational programs dominate the state policy agenda as legislators, governors, and judges wrangle over the competing reform values of equity, excellence, efficiency, and choice. She also describes the influence of significant new federal education policy—the No Child Left Behind Act—on the performance of public schools.

In Chapter 9, "State Welfare Policy," Irene Lurie explains why the shape of welfare for the poor has commanded so much attention from state policymakers. For more than two decades, state governments have attempted to reform welfare programs, successfully convincing the federal government that states should have more flexibility to experiment with strategies for moving welfare recipients into jobs. Lurie describes swift-changing welfare policy and shifting federal and state priorities. She also traces the development and impact of a major federal welfare reform law adopted by Congress and the president in 1996—described by President Clinton as an attempt to "end welfare as we know it."

In Chapter 10," State Health Policy," Joel C. Cantor explains how health policy and spending on health programs have come to play an increasingly important role in state governments. In 2003, for example, spending on Medicaid—the federal-state health care programs for low-income people—tied with elementary and secondary education as the largest item in state budgets. Cantor also points out that state elected officials have responded to their frustration with the lack of improvements in federal health policy by enacting ambitious new programs to control health care costs, improve quality, and expand coverage for the working poor and children.

Conclusion

State governments face unprecedented challenges. Congress is cutting federal aid to the states, consolidating programs, and turning control over to governors and legislators. Governors and legislatures are seldom willing or able to raise taxes to fill the void. Interest groups—from businesses to environmentalists—are engaging in tough political battles in the state capitals. State government officials are trying to do more with less and manage problems that previously were settled elsewhere.

The intense competition in state politics makes meeting these new challenges even more difficult. Partisanship is on the rise, and elected officials are most likely to behave like free agents, which makes it harder for political leaders, such as governors, to find consensus and get laws enacted.

The rising cost of elections means that many elected officials are more beholden to contributors and less accountable to the general public. The deep public resentment of campaign spending and special interest politics helps explain why voters are cynical about politicians and why proposals to limit the terms of officeholders have caught fire in so many states.

No doubt, raising money for political campaigns diverts time from governing and compromises elected officials. Legislators and governors even hold large fund-raising events while important policy issues are under consideration. Elected officials regularly solicit and receive campaign contributions from businesses that either have contracts with the state or want to do business in the future.

These governing practices affect policy priorities and choices. As the power of well-financed special interests increases, policies serving the public interest often suffer. Policymakers concerned with their political power are more likely to serve the narrow interest or follow the safest path than deal with difficult choices. Electoral expediency can crowd out other important public values, like ethical behavior, transparency, and accountability.

The increasing reliance on statewide initiatives to resolve public policy disputes is troubling. In some of the nation's most populous states, such as California and Florida, state elected officials routinely sidestep direct responsibility for making choices by resorting to initiative campaigns. What is advertised as an experiment in direct democracy is rarely a grass-roots citizen's movement. Instead, the initiative petition drives and elections are dominated by high-spending interest groups that fund television advertising and direct mail campaigns.

Looking to the future, those who fear the enhanced power of state governments paint a grim picture. They predict that the safety net for poor people will be shredded and that incompetence and corruption will run rampant.[30] Those who embrace the larger state role foresee innovative and efficient programs operated by officials who have a better grasp of the needs of their citizens. They say states can and will assume responsibility for addressing problems where the federal government has failed.

Proponents and opponents of devolution are exaggerating the downside and the upside of the growing importance of state governments. It is unwise to pin hard-and-fast conclusions on any enterprise as complex and diverse as state governments in a nation of more than 300 million citizens. Yet, we can say that enhanced responsibility and reduced federal aid are bringing new and more difficult challenges to state capitals. As the new century of the American "experiment" begins, state governments, and those who govern them, have more power than ever. They are struggling under these new burdens to meet rising expectations and manage this new reality. State government leaders are being reminded of the old Chinese proverb: be careful what you wish for because it may come true.

Notes

1. Terry Sanford, *Storm over the States* (New York: McGraw-Hill, 1967).
2. Ann O'M. Bowman and Richard C. Kearney, *The Resurgence of the States* (Englewood Cliffs, N.J.: Prentice-Hall, 1986).
3. Center for American Women and Politics, *Women in Elective Office, 2005: Fact Sheet* (New Brunswick, N.J.: Eagleton Institute of Politics, Rutgers University, 2005).
4. Ibid.
5. Ibid.
6. David Bositis, *Black Elected Officials: A Statistical Summary* (Washington, D.C.: Joint Center for Political and Economic Studies, 2001).
7. Initiative and Referendum Institute at University of Southern California, *Ballotwatch: Election 2004 Preview* (Los Angeles: Initiative and Referendum Institute at University of Southern California, 2004).
8. National Governors Association and National Association of State Budget Officers, *The Fiscal Survey of States* (Washington, D.C.: National Governors Association and National Association of State Budget Officers, 2005).
9. Advisory Commission on Intergovernmental Relations, *Significant Features of Fiscal Federalism, 1984* (Washington, D.C.: Advisory Commission on Intergovernmental Relations, 1984).
10. National Governors Association, *Governors' Political Affiliations and Terms of Office* (Washington, D.C.: National Governors Association, 2005); National Conference of State Legislatures, *2005 Partisan Composition of State Legislatures* (Washington, D.C.: National Conference of State Legislatures, 2005).
11. Robert Rear, "Federal Impasse Saddling States with Indecision," *New York Times*, January 2, 1996, A1.
12. Richard P. Nathan and Fred C. Doolittle, *Reagan and the States* (Princeton: Princeton University Press, 1987), 62.
13. National Association of State Budget Officers, *2003 State Expenditure Report* (Washington, D.C.: National Association of State Budget Officers, 2003); "Measuring Federal Aid: Whose Straw Is Shortest?" *Governing* (September 1987): 48.
14. Advisory Commission on Intergovernmental Relations, *Significant Features of Fiscal Federalism*, 51.
15. North American Association of State and Provincial Lotteries, *Did You Know? Lottery Sales*, Willoughby Hills, Ohio, August 2005, http://www.naspl.org/faq.html.
16. Steven D. Gold, Brenda Erikson, and Michelle Kissell, *Earmarking State Taxes* (Denver, Colo.: National Conference of States Legislatures, 1987), 6.
17. Patrick B. McGuigan, *The Politics of Direct Democracy in the 1980s* (Washington, D.C.: Free Congress Research and Education Foundation, 1985), 52, 54, 55.
18. Advisory Commission on Intergovernmental Relations, *Significant Features of Fiscal Federalism*, 71.
19. Earl C. Gottschalk Jr., "Across the Country, Increased State Levies Hit Incomes Harder," *Wall Street Journal*, November 11, 1991, C1.

20. David Shribman, "Governors of Fiscally Strapped States, Seeing No Sign of Relief, Yearn for the Good Old Days," *Wall Street Journal,* August 19, 1991, 10.
21. Nathan and Doolittle, *Reagan and the States.*
22. Richard Nathan, "The Role of the States in American Federalism," in *The State of the States,* 3rd ed., ed. Carl E. Van Horn (Washington, D.C.: CQ Press, 1996).
23. See, for example, Malcolm Jewell, *Representation in State Legislatures* (Lexington: University Press of Kentucky, 1982).
24. See, for example, Joel A. Thompson, "Bringing Home the Bacon: The Politics of Pork Barrel in the North Carolina Legislature," *Legislative Studies Quarterly* 11 (February 1986): 91–108.
25. Richard Niemi and L. R. Winsky, "Membership Turnover in U.S. State Legislatures: Trends and Effects of Redistricting," *Legislative Studies Quarterly* 12 (February 1987): 115–124.
26. The National Election Studies, Center for Political Studies, University of Michigan, *The NES Guide to Public Opinion and Electoral Behavior* (Ann Arbor, Mich.: University of Michigan, Center for Political Studies, 1995–2002), http://www.umich.edu/~nes/nesguide/nesguide.htm.
27. National Conference of State Legislatures, *The Term Limited States* (Washington, D.C.: National Conference of State Legislatures, 2004).
28. National Conference of State Legislatures, *2005 Partisan Composition of State Legislatures.*
29. Dave Frohnmayer, "The Courts as Referee" (paper presented at the State of the States Symposium, Eagleton Institute of Politics, Rutgers University, New Brunswick, N.J., December 15–16, 1988).
30. See, for example, Richard Cohen, "States Aren't Saints, Either," *Washington Post Weekly Edition,* April 3–9, 1995, 28.

2

The State of State Elections
Kenneth Dautrich and David A. Yalof

At approximately 11 a.m. on November 17, 2003, the soon-to-be former chief executive of California, Grey Davis, stood among 7,500 invited guests crowded near the west steps of the state capitol in Sacramento. Also present were three other former California governors, various Hollywood celebrities, and numerous foreign dignitaries.[1] The relatively brief open-air ceremony they were attending was already nearing its formal conclusion. Arnold Schwarzenegger, victor in a historic gubernatorial recall election that had effectively ousted Davis from power the previous month, was now being sworn in as the thirty-eighth governor to lead this most populous state in the union.

What events transpired to transform Davis, the same Democratic governor who had successfully secured his own reelection just a year earlier, into the ranks of former officeholders? Certainly political circumstances had not been kind to Davis, as the state of California suffered more than its share of troubles during the previous twelve months. A state budget deficit of almost $25 billion had spurred Davis to impose an unpopular increase in the state's vehicle licensing fee, effectively tripling what was known not so affectionately as the "car tax."[2] California was also recovering from an energy crisis of its own making. In response to an energy shortage several years earlier, California officials had negotiated unfavorable long-term contracts with power suppliers in neighboring states, which did not prevent those suppliers from imposing large increases in its rates. Thus, when blackouts had occurred on Davis's watch, electricity rates were allowed to skyrocket, with some increasing by as much as 300 percent. All in all, California had cemented its reputation as the nation's most dysfunctional state in recent years, and as governor since 1998, Gray Davis shouldered much of the blame. Yet despite all the state's troubles, Davis was reelected by the voters in November of 2002, garnering 47 percent of the vote to 43 percent for his opponent, Bill Simon. How was such a dramatic political turnaround even possible?

The answer lies in the eccentricities of California state election law, including its bizarre recall mechanism, countenanced by a political system that affords each of the fifty states tremendous latitude in determining the process by which their state officeholders attain and maintain power. A veritable patchwork quilt of state election rules has taken hold in this country. Although many states authorize primary runoff elections to determine party nominees for office, only the state of Louisiana features a system of nonpartisan primary run-off elections.³ Nebraska is the only state in the union to hold nonpartisan elections for statewide office; its candidates are listed on ballots without party labels, and parties are forbidden to recruit candidates. By virtue of a voter initiative in 2004 that restored a qualifying primary for partisan races, Washington is once again the only state in the country to hold so-called "blanket primaries," in which primary voters can cross party lines and choose candidates of either party by office. And state governments vary considerably in whether issue initiatives and referendums are permitted and whether legislators are limited to the number of terms they may serve. Considered against this multitextured background, California's recall mechanism suddenly appears less bizarre. In fact, seventeen other states currently authorize the recall of statewide officials in some form, rendering the recall mechanism downright ordinary in theory, even if it is only rarely exercised in practice.

First authorized by a state constitutional amendment ratified in 1911, the recall mechanism in California allows the state's voters to remove elected officials before their terms of office expire. Previous recall efforts in California succeeded in ousting four state legislators and countless local officials from office. Moreover, every California governor since the mid-1960s has faced at least token recall efforts. Yet, because petitions for the recall of statewide officers such as governors must be signed by the number of voters equal in number to 12 percent of the last vote for that office, no gubernatorial recall in California had ever before succeeded. Nationwide, only one governor in history had ever before been recalled from office—North Dakota voters ousted their chief executive, Lynn Frazier, in 1921.⁴

Thus, in adherence to state law, opponents of Davis in 2003 had to gather 897,156 signatures on petitions to initiate a recall; given past experience, experts had estimated they would need approximately 1.2 million signatures to ensure that there were enough valid ones. Venom against Davis proved so great, however, that even that obstacle was quickly overcome; Secretary of State Kevin Shelley announced on July 23, 2003, that the recall petition contained 1,356,408 valid signatures.⁵ Once the petition requirement was certified, if a majority of California voters favored the recall on election day, the candidate with the plurality of votes at that same election would be authorized to succeed him within a few weeks. When the Hollywood actor Arnold Schwarzenegger entered the race to succeed Davis in August, numerous high-profile Republican candidates withdrew from the race and threw their support to the movie star. Finally, on election day 2003, 55 percent of those voting favored the recall; in the race to succeed Davis, Schwarzenegger received 48 percent of the votes among the field of 135 replacement candidates, making him the clear victor.⁶

Some might be tempted to write off the unusual confluence of circumstances that produced a successful recall in 2003 as simply an amusing political lesson in how success can so quickly turn into failure. Perhaps the election of wrestler and political Independent Jesse "the Body" Ventura to the Minnesota governorship in 1998 should be written off as an aberration as well;

after that election, Minnesotans would once again rely on the major parties to provide a chief executive, presumably someone with considerable experience in government. Regardless, state elections and the officeholders they produce can no longer be written off as the concern of people living in only a handful of states. With national security at the forefront of American politics, and most national reforms stymied by an increasingly polarized Congress, state elections have taken on increased importance as the principal means by which most of the major domestic issues will be ultimately resolved. Welfare has been primarily a state issue since 1996. Recent conservative Supreme Court decisions have afforded states considerable discretion to pass abortion restrictions and fund religious schools. State lawmakers today define marriage and determine whether or not it is available to homosexual couples; they help determine the price of gas independently of other states; and they pass budgets that will determine the level of social services to be provided to millions of Americans. Governors are in a position to lead state legislatures to their own preferred conclusions or to veto the legislation altogether. Are we truly confident that the best and most qualified candidates ascend to these increasingly important positions? Even more important, with threats such as recalls an ever-present reality, are state officials even in a position to serve the public effectively?

The Structure of State Campaigns and Elections

Ultimately, states are responsible for the administration of all elections that take place in the United States. Amendments to the U.S. Constitution along with several voting rights laws place some guidelines and restrictions on what states can and cannot do. States, for example, cannot deny women, people at least eighteen years of age, or minorities the right to cast a ballot. States cannot charge a fee to vote (a "poll tax" was used in some southern states after the Civil War as a way of discouraging blacks, who tended to be poorer, to vote) or require a "literacy test" (blacks also tended to have less education). But beyond these federal guidelines largely intended to promote civil rights, states absolutely control and manage elections.

As a consequence, today each of the fifty states has a different system for electing state officials. Some states require voters to be registered months before election day, whereas others (such as Wisconsin) allow voters to register when they show up to vote at the ballot box. Only North Dakota has no requirement at all for registration.[7] Some states mandate that voters register as a member of a political party, and others do not. Some states require political parties to have open primary elections for selecting party candidates, whereas others allow party conventions or caucuses to accomplish this. And as California made us well aware in 2003, some states have provisions for recall elections.

The technology used for casting a vote also varies. Some states, or even counties within states, use paper ballots. Others use levered voting machines. Still others use high-tech touch screen computers. Regardless of the technology used, there are also variations in how the candidates are presented on the ballot. Third party candidates often must achieve a minimum number of signatures from voters to get on the ballot at all (and the number of signatures varies quite a bit from state to state). Some states use the Indiana ballot format, in which the name of the political party appears at the top of the column and candidates for the various offices appear below the party label, thus cuing the voters to partisan-based voting (some states using this type of ballot include a lever or check box above the column to allow a voter to select all of a particular party's candidates in one stroke). Alternatively, other states use a so-called "Massachusetts ballot," which organizes the slate of candidates on the basis of the office they are seeking and simply supplies a label indicating the candidate's party affiliation.

Moreover, although all fifty states have a two-party electoral system, some states are so dominated by one of the two parties that "real" competition is in the primary or caucus, when the dominating party's nominee is chosen. In some states, such as Idaho, Utah, and Wyoming, Republicans dominate the state legislature. In other states, like Hawaii, Democrats are firmly in control. In still other states, such as Illinois, Michigan, and Pennsylvania, high levels of competition for control of the state legislature make the parties fairly even.[8]

Campaign finance rules and regulations make up another important difference among the states. State parties and candidates are not subject to the recent round of federal laws sponsored by Sens. John McCain and Russell Feingold (the Bipartisan Campaign Reform Act) that placed restrictions on soft money. These laws place restrictions only on soft money in federal elections. The 2002 law actually benefits state parties in that it allows for $10,000 to be contributed to state parties to support voter mobilization efforts.[9] The raising and spending of money in elections for state office are regulated by the laws of each state. Forty-nine of the fifty states allow for soft money in elections (Connecticut is the single exception). However, the limits and sources of soft money vary from state to state.

As a result of state control and management of elections, fifty unique systems for voting can be found across the fifty states. Although this configuration makes it difficult to summarize and explain how state elections work, it provides for a great deal of color, nuance, and diversity in American campaigns and elections. Despite the variation, a useful framework for beginning to understand campaigns and elections within the states includes the state political party organizations.

State Party Organizations

Whereas the U.S. Constitution makes no mention of political parties (indeed, the Founding Fathers somewhat naively planned that the federal government would not include political parties), most state constitutions acknowledge and support political party organizations. Each of the fifty states features state Democratic Party and Republican Party organizations. Although many other party organizations (such as the Green Party, the Socialist Party, and the Libertarian Party) exist in many states, all the states, similar to national politics, are dominated by competition between the Republican Party and the Democratic Party. Occasionally an independent or third party candidate might win, such as Independent Jesse Ventura's victory to become governor of Minnesota in 1998 and Gov. Lowell Weicker's successful run as an Independent in Connecticut in 1990. The Independent Angus King served as Maine's governor from 1995 until 2003. But those are the exceptions rather than the rule. Of the more than 7,000 state legislative seats, only about 20 are held by Independents or members of a third party.[10] Like the competition for federal office, candidates for state office compete in the two-party system of elections.

Candidates for federal office—the presidency or a seat in the Senate or House of Representatives—have, over the past several decades, become less reliant on the national parties to wage successful campaigns.[11] These federal races are often higher profile, attracting the attention of many donors, and often attracting wealthy candidates who can fund their own campaigns. Once in office, federal elected officials also have access to a variety of campaign resources, including the franking privilege, which allows officials to send mail to their constituents without affixing postage, and easy access to and attention from the news media.

With the exception of one state office (that of governor), most candidates for state elective offices do not enjoy these same resources. Instead, the state and local party organizations play a more important role in election politics. To be sure, in the past, state parties did exercise much more control, leadership, and discipline over the nomination process and the conduct of general election campaigns. Today, the state parties typically do not control the nomination of candidates and the conduct of campaigns. However, they do continue to play a large supportive role.[12] Specifically, there are four electoral functions of the state parties that make them very important to state elections.

First, there is fund-raising. Successful campaigns for the state legislature, governor's office, or other statewide office often require professional campaign staffers (such as a campaign manager, pollster, and media director). These campaigns also need to advertise in newspapers, on radio, and on television. Salaries to support campaign staff and money to produce and place advertising are often in high demand. The parties are highly organized for fund-raising to help support their own candidates. Although individual campaign fund-raising does occur, the state party organizations remain the primary source of funding for most candidates for state office.

A second electoral function of state party organizations is to provide campaign support services to candidates. The state parties often hire political strategists, purchase advertising, develop databases of voters, organize rallies, and fund phone bank activities, all aimed at supporting their candidates and improving their chances of electoral success. The parties also spend much time and effort organizing the get-out-the-vote activities on election day. These activities include calling the party faithful to remind them to vote and providing rides and assistance to those who need help getting to the polling place.

The third function of the state parties in election politics is the recruitment of candidates and influence over the nomination process. Back in the days of the political bosses and party machines, the state and local party organizations exerted a great deal of control over the selection of candidates who would wear the party label in the general election campaign. Laws curtailing patronage, however, weakened the power of party leaders. The professionalization of campaigns and the ability of candidates to raise funds outside of the party system has further weakened the parties' lock on the nomination process. Finally, the decades-long trend toward primary elections as the most common means of nominating candidates has reduced party influence in this area. Despite these factors, the state parties remain active in identifying candidates who they believe represent the party well and offer promising prospects at the polls.

A fourth electoral function of state parties is to provide a framework for voters to make a vote choice. In most cases in the two-party system, the general framework involves a choice between the Democratic candidate and the Republican candidate. State parties, like their national counterparts, develop a platform, themes, and messages and attempt to communicate their ideas to voters through rallies, news articles, advertising, and selecting candidates who represent the party's goals. The organized competition between the Democrats and Republicans through these and other activities provides a clear framework within which voters can decide whom to vote for.

How are state political parties organized to carry out their mission of getting candidates elected? The Democratic and Republican state party organizations across the fifty states each have a state committee, typically including those elected to represent localities plus other elected party officials, which oversees the party's activities. This committee is responsible for holding state conventions, where party members convene to develop a party platform, recruit and sometimes nominate candidates for office, and develop fund-raising strategies. These conventions are also used to coordinate the activities of local party groups.[13]

The state committees are also responsible for electing the state party chair and other officers, such as treasurer and secretary. The party chair is the spokesperson for the party and often has a great deal of influence in regard to fund-raising, spending, and the allocation of other resources to candidates. Party chairs are particularly powerful and visible when their party does not occupy the governor's office. Although the governor is the recognized leader of his or her state party, the chair of the opposing party is generally considered to be that party's leader. Each state party chair also serves on his or her party's respective national committee.

Gubernatorial Elections

The most celebrated and highly visible election for state office is that of governor. Although most states also have elections for other statewide offices (the exceptions are Maine, New Hampshire, and New Jersey), such as lieutenant governor, secretary of state, state attorney general, and state treasurer, the most prominent and powerful elective office is that of governor. It is not surprising, then, that gubernatorial elections tend to be characterized by higher levels of party competition and attract more attention than other state elections.

Party competition for the governor's office is high in most regions of the country. From the New Deal to the mid-1960s, Democrats held a discernible advantage in competing for the state's highest office.[14] Since 1966, however, most states have experienced competition in the governor's race. For example, over the past forty years, neither the Democratic nor Republican Party's gubernatorial candidates have won more than 45 percent of the gubernatorial contests in New England, the Mid-Atlantic, the Plains, and the Rocky Mountain states. Democrats for governor have been more successful on the West Coast and in southern states, winning 65 percent of the contests since 1966. The trend in the South more recently, however, favors Republicans. In the mid-western states, Republicans have won about 65 percent of governors' races over the past four decades.[15] After the 2004 elections, twenty-eight of the governors were Republicans and twenty-two were Democrats, and none was Independent or from a third party.

Along with gubernatorial elections, races for the U.S. Senate tend to be competitive and higher profile. However, unlike the Senate races, gubernatorial elections are substantively about local issues. Local issues certainly are discussed in the U.S. Senate races, but rarely are national or international issues (such as foreign policy, defense, and foreign aid) fodder for discussion or debate in gubernatorial contests. Rather, the substance of gubernatorial campaigns typically revolves around local and state issues.

Many state constitutions limit the number of terms that any particular governor might serve. So, unlike races for the state legislature, the U.S. Senate, or the U.S. House, incumbency is less a factor in gubernatorial races. Incumbents who run do tend to do well. In 2002, 75 percent of incumbent governors won reelection (83 percent in 2000, 92 percent in 1998, 100 percent in 1992 and 1996, and 90 percent in 1994).[16] But since many states limit their chief executives to two terms, governors' races are less likely to find an incumbent eligible to run. After the 2004 elections, thirty-six of the fifty governors were serving in their first term in office, and twelve were in their second term. The remaining two governors (Mike Huckabee of Arkansas and George Pataki of New York) were in their third terms.[17]

Recent trends in voting behavior and candidate behavior indicate that, like presidential and U.S. Senate elections, gubernatorial elections have become increasingly "candidate centered" and less influenced by party organizations and partisanship. In state elections for governor where there is also a presidential contest on the ballot, the level of split-ticket voting has increased over the years, indicating that party labels have become less influential and the candidates themselves have become more important. Another indicator that individual candidates are becoming more important than party labels in gubernatorial races is the increase in "partisan turnovers," where the party of the incumbent changes. About one-quarter of governor races experienced party turnovers in the mid-twentieth century, whereas in the current era the turnover rate is about 40 percent.

Candidates themselves have also become increasingly independent of the political parties. The professionalization of campaigns (which also has affected U.S. Senate, House, and many of the larger competitive state legislative and local mayoral races) has distanced candidates from their party organizations. Candidates for governor raise money independently of the party; hire their own campaign managers, media consultants, fund-raisers, and pollsters; host their own rallies; and purchase their own advertisements. The candidates generally work hand-in-hand with their respective party organization in a coordinated attempt to win on election day, but because they have their own professional campaign organizations they are less dependent on the party organization.

State Legislative Elections

There are 7,382 elected members of the fifty state legislatures across the nation. California, the largest state in population (about 35 million), is represented by a state legislature with 120 members (80 in the state house and 40 in the state senate). New Hampshire, a state that ranks forty-first in total population (about 1.3 million), is represented by a state legislature with 424 members (400 in the house and 24 in the senate). Even Vermont, ranked forty-ninth in size, has more elections for the state legislature than does California, which is nearly fifty times its size.

The wide variation in state legislative representation is accompanied by a correspondingly high disparity in the way state legislative campaigns are conducted. Many races for the state legislature, particularly in the less populous legislative districts, feature campaigns where candidates canvass for votes door to door, campaign budgets are very small, and production of lawn signs and buttons are the extent of the paid advertising. By contrast, in a state like California, where a legislative district is virtually the same size as a U.S. congressional district, campaigns tend to be highly professionalized and well funded, making use of television spot ads, strategic campaign consultants, and pollsters.

Moreover, the nature of campaigns in the 7,382 legislative elections is often dictated by the competitiveness of the particular seat. Fifty percent of these seats are occupied by Republicans and 49 percent by Democrats, giving the general impression that there is a fair amount of competition for the state houses and senates.[18] However, in the 2004 state legislative races, fully

35 percent of all contested seats ran a candidate from only one of the two major parties. In many cases, the single candidate was the incumbent running for reelection and was thus unopposed, indicating the power of incumbency in legislative races. Without any real competition, the general election campaign is rendered fairly meaningless. In many of these noncompetitive elections, the campaign is, in fact, nonexistent.

But many of the state legislative races are characterized by a high level of competition, and increasingly many of these races have become well-financed and highly professionalized. As state government has become more important in making policy, interest groups, political action committees, and national political players have placed more attention on winning legislative races as a way to influence public policy. At the same time, with a general decline in the power of party organizations, there has been a trend toward more "candidate-centered campaigns" in legislative races.[19]

State Judicial Elections

To close observers of state electoral politics, no sight proves more troubling than that of state judges actively campaigning to secure and maintain their positions on the bench. And yet state judicial elections are a modern-day reality—currently thirty-nine of the fifty states in some way elect their appellate judges. Although many states feature nonpartisan judicial election contests in which full-blown campaigns between two or more contestants are rare, thirteen states hold contested partisan judicial election contests. These partisan contests have all the hallmarks of normal elections, with judges required to raise funds and publicly tout their credentials for judicial office. Although judges and candidates for the judiciary will often discuss the merits of court procedures in general terms and their own qualifications, as well as those of any opponent, the Code of Judicial Conduct prohibits responses to candidate questionnaires involving substantive issues of law that are likely to come before the courts.

Judicial elections clearly promote greater judicial accountability to the voters than do appointive systems. In one notable example of such accountability, votes against the death penalty proved the electoral undoing of the California Supreme Court's chief justice, Rose Bird, along with two of her colleagues, in 1986. Unfortunately, these partisan elections also open judges up to the charge that certain judicial decisions were rendered to curry favor with special interests and other major contributors to their campaigns.

More common are nonpartisan judicial elections, in which party labels are shunned altogether. To get on a nonpartisan judicial ballot, candidates must gather the requisite number of signatures; state parties play little or no role in the process. The most frequently used form of judicial elections is modeled after the Missouri plan, which was first used in 1940. A screening committee composed of lawyers and judges selects a small number of qualified judicial candidates (usually three), and the governor must appoint one of them to a term on the bench. When the judge's first term ends, he or she usually stands for reelection on the ballot with no opponent specified—voters merely give an up-or-down vote for retention. If the judge fails to get a majority vote for retention, the screening committee once again meets to identify a new set of candidates for the governor to choose from.

Proponents of the Missouri, or merit, plan hail it as the best of all methods of judicial selection. With parties relegated to the sidelines, candidates can be chosen for their merits as jurists, rather than because they have dutifully served one of the two major parties in the states. Unlike federal judges, who serve for life, the requirement that these state judges must be voted into a second term makes them at least somewhat accountable to the public. At the same time, votes against retention are so rare (less than 3 percent of judges have failed to win retention elections) that judges can remain on the whole independent; rarely do sitting judges in merit plan states feel compelled to tarnish their office by engaging in partisan election tactics. Unfortunately, merit plan selection processes carry their own set of disadvantages. As the scholar Philip DuBois pointed out in his landmark 1980 study, *From Ballot to Bench: Judicial Elections and the Quest for Accountability*, the partisan politics of other systems is replaced by local bar politics in staffing the screening committees.[20] In some instances this kind of politics can be just as sordid as other systems, and those who end up on the committees may be no more qualified to choose judges for their merit than political party organizations would be. Moreover, turnout has been exceptionally low for such judicial retention elections.

Critics also claim that a vote against retention is so unlikely that judicial accountability to the public remains at best an unrealistic hope. Although statistically true, that provides little solace for the judges who do find themselves expectedly or unexpectedly in a fight for their judicial lives. In Florida, which uses a form of the Missouri plan, one Supreme Court judge only narrowly won his retention election in 1990. Critics were able to put him on the defensive for striking down a Florida law requiring parental consent for those under eighteen to get abortions.

In states where full-blown partisan judicial election contests are held, candidates raise millions of dollars each election cycle from lobbying groups with a significant interest in the process. In 1988 the candidates for the six open seats on the Texas Supreme Court raised more than $10 million. In 1986 the three endangered justices in California spent nearly $4.5 million in an unsuccessful effort to retain their seats on the state supreme court. That same year in Ohio, the two candidates for chief justice of the Ohio Supreme Court spent more than $3 million. To those who believe judicial accountability to the public is important, the high costs of electing judges is simply the price of doing business. Yet for others, judges beholden to various contributors for their help in keeping their positions on the bench is too high a price.

Initiatives and Referendums

On March 12, 2002, Governor George Pataki proposed an amendment to the New York State Constitution that would have let citizens put certain initiatives directly on the ballot for public approval. As a Republican governor in a state government otherwise controlled by Democrats, Pataki had good reason to call for the advent of such a mechanism. In fact, he had been consistently calling for the constitutional authorization of such initiatives ever since 1994, when he first ran for governor. Meanwhile, the Democratic leadership in the state legislature remained just as adamant in opposing such direct initiatives from the public. Those officials, including Assembly Speaker Sheldon Silver, noted that laws passed by referendum often contradict one another and thus risk being invalidated by the courts. Silver described it as a full employment bill for lawyers.[21] But neither side can claim pure motives in this regard; if the partisan balance of New York State politics was tipping in the opposite direction, with the legislature controlled by his fellow Republicans, Pataki might well oppose such a direct initiatives amendment, and the Democratic minority might favor it.

Initiatives and *referendums* are the formal terms describing measures that appear on the ballot and must be approved by the voters. Unlike initiatives, referendums appear on ballots only after they have first been approved by the legislature. More than eight hundred state laws have been adopted in this way, including some that have generated intense voter interest, such as women's suffrage and the elimination of poll taxes. *Constitutional referendums*, requiring that voters approve of state constitutional amendments passed by the legislature, are also common in many states. Additionally, nineteen states feature the requirement of *general referendums*, in which voters must approve all bond issues after the legislature has approved them. Finally, twenty-three states currently permit *legislative referendums*, in which the legislature offers to put a measure on the public ballot.

By contrast, initiatives are proposals that bypass the legislature and go directly before the voters. Currently, more than half the states feature initiatives of some type. Voters in eighteen states have the right to petition changes in their state constitutions without legislative approval, and eighteen states allow simple legislative initiatives that create or rewrite laws without legislative approval. Because the legislature often opposes such initiatives (indeed, legislative opposition is often the primary reason that the proposal is offered in the form of an initiative), they tend to be rejected at a far greater rate than referendums. According to one study, just 44 percent of initiatives placed on ballots between 1981 and 1992 were approved. With the stakes so high, campaign spending in favor of or against such initiatives has tended to soar in recent decades. Consider that campaign spending on sixteen California ballot initiatives in 2004 combined to top $200 million. Some campaign spending regulations that apply to candidate elections do not apply to referendums or initiatives; as the Supreme Court recognized nearly thirty years ago, speech about such measures lies "at the heart of the First Amendment.... It is the type of speech indispensable to decisionmaking in a democracy."[22]

California's propensity to hold such initiatives has been fueled by state laws that make it relatively easy to place initiatives on the ballot. All it takes is an idea and $200 to officially register to circulate an initiative for 150 days. Then just 5 percent of the number of voters from the most recent gubernatorial election (8 percent in the case of constitutional referendums) is necessary to get the initiative or referendum on the ballot, at which point a simple majority can approve it to become law. Once an initiative becomes law it is binding and can be overturned only by another duly passed initiative. California political experts agree that, realistically, $1 million to $2 million is necessary to place an initiative on the ballot, no matter how absurd or unnecessary the proposal. Horse lovers were no doubt pleased when, Proposition 6, The Prohibition of Horse Slaughter and Consumption of Horsemeat for Human Consumption Act of 1998, qualified as an initiative and was voted into law. Few at the time thought the senseless killing of horses had become a statewide problem in the 1990s—certainly it was not a more pressing concern than the looming energy crisis and other issues.

Since the late 1970s, California has become something of a hotbed of initiatives. Proposition 13, passed by California voters in 1978, rolled back property taxes and because of this lost revenue forced the state to cut government spending. That proposition became a rallying cry for antitax movements in other states and sparked interest across California to put more and more initiatives on the ballot. The most frequent topics for such propositions have been term limits, environmental laws, and affirmative action. If the public is so heated about these issues, why don't legislatures simply take note and pass these popular enactments in the first place? In regard to proposals for term limits, the desire for self-survival and a long political career is obviously a key factor in each legislator's individual calculus. Moreover, whereas the legislature is apportioned to represent residents whether or not they vote, it is primarily active and engaged voters who drive the success of initiatives. Most initiatives are too extreme to gain favor within the legislature. Still, initiatives don't necessarily make the government more democratic. Few citizens read the lengthy pamphlets or initiative texts circulated prior to a formal vote.

Term Limits

The Supreme Court's 1995 decision invalidating state laws creating term limits for representatives to the U.S. House of Representatives and Senate posed no obstacle at all to grass-roots efforts to impose term limits on representatives and senators in state legislatures across the country.[23] Thus, even as congressional term limits in twenty-three states were eliminated by the Supreme Court's holding, the term limits movement continued to pick up speed at the state level. In all, twenty-one states in the 1990s adopted the popular government reform, driven by voter disdain for state legislators. In those states the intrinsic power of incumbency—that is, the overwhelming advantage legislators enjoy to stay in office once they arrive there—was obviously diluted. In the affected states, party leaders in the legislature, whether legislative speakers or committee chairs, had a more difficult time coordinating their efforts to forward legislative agendas or override the governor's vetoes. Not surprisingly, in those states that adopted term limits, the executive branch became relatively more powerful during this same period.

Still, despite the success enjoyed by the term limits movement, the electoral power incumbents wield in all fifty state governments should not be underestimated. Incumbent governors, most of whom were already term limited prior to the 1990s, enjoy a high reelection rate. Although generally facing highly qualified and experienced challengers, approximately three-fourths of all governors who sought reelection during the last four decades have been successful. And considering only those incumbent legislators who can run for reelection, state representatives generally win reelection 90 percent of the time, with state senators trailing close behind (86 percent). That's still short of the more than 95 percent reelection rate enjoyed by incumbent members of the U.S. House of Representatives during the last four election cycles, but it confirms the premise that voter disdain for the state legislatures in general does not translate into voter dislike of their own individual legislators.

Moreover, having reached its high tide in the late 1990s, the term limits movement in the states now appears on the decline. Indeed, there is some evidence that the movement may see a turnaround just as the term limits passed in the 1990s begin to claim their first victims in state legislatures across the country. At last count, six of the twenty-one states that adopted such laws have already reversed course and rescinded term limits altogether. Even in California, the same state that "limited" its governor's second term to just over a year, term limits (six years for assembly members, eight years for state senators) are once again up for discussion. By the end of the current decade many of the gains of the term limits movement may be blunted. And as the reversal of these reforms takes hold, even the holdout states may find themselves unwilling to put their own state legislatures at a relative disadvantage to others.

Conclusion

There are some commonalties in elections for statewide office. Competition between the Democratic Party and Republican Party mostly characterizes the electoral process, although the role of the parties has somewhat diminished; all states hold regular elections for governor and state legislators; incumbents win at astonishingly high rates; and there is a general trend toward the professionalization of campaigns and toward rising costs of waging campaigns.

However, within these broad commonalities there exist huge differences across the fifty states in how elections are administered and conducted.

Among these variations are the existence and nature of term limits rules, the level of competitiveness between the two major parties, the size and significance of state legislative districts, whether or not state judges are elected, and the ability of voters to recall duly elected officials prior to their term ending. Although these differences make it difficult to summarize the state of state elections, they make for interesting stories, such as the recall of California governor Gray Davis. More significantly, the diversity of elections in state politics allows the nation to sustain its historical identity as a federalist system and satisfy the many geographic subcultures in the American nation.

Notes

1. "Schwarzenegger Inauguration draws High-Profile Crowd," in CNN.com's *Inside Politics*, November 17, 2003, http://www.cnn.com/2003/ALLPOLITICS/11/17/schwarzenegger.ap/.
2. Martin Kasindorf, "The Fiscal Train Wreck Has Arrived," USAToday.com, November 25, 2002, http://www.usatoday.com/news/nation/2002-11-25-budgets-usat_x.htm.
3. Michael Barone and Richard Cohen, *The 2004 Almanac of American Politics* (New York: National Journal Group, 2003), 693.
4. Dale Wetzel, "California Recall: North Dakota Blazed the Trail Over 80 Years Ago," *Bismarck Tribune*, August 2, 2003, 1B.
5. Gary Delsohn, "Vote on Recall-and Candidates-Oct. 7," *Sacramento Bee*, July 25, 2003, A1.
6. Margaret Talev, "It's Arnold: Schwarzenegger Coasts to Victory as Davis Is Ousted in Historic Vote," *Sacramento Bee*, October 8, 2003, EL1.
7. Janelle Carter, "Bill Won't Force N.D. to Register," *Bismarck Tribune*, April 12, 2002, 6A.
8. See Harold W. Stanley and Richard G. Niemi, *Vital Statistics on American Politics, 2003–2004* (Washington, D.C.: CQ Press, 2003), 21, for data on how all fifty states have fared with respect to party competition over the last fifty years.
9. Richard Perez-Pena, "A Federal Soft Money Ban Could Benefit State Parties," *New York Times*, March 22, 2002, A1.
10. Data obtained from the Web site of the National Council of State Legislatures, http://www.ncsl.org.
11. For a complete discussion of the reduced influence of parties in campaigns and elections, see Martin P. Wattenberg, *The Decline of American Political Parties* (Cambridge, Mass.: Harvard University Press, 1998).
12. Barbara G. Salmore and Stephen A. Salmore, *Candidates, Parties and Campaigns* (Washington, D.C.: CQ Press, 1989).
13. Malcolm E. Jewell and David M. Olson, *Political Parties and Elections in American States* (Chicago: Dorsey Press, 1988).
14. Jerrold G. Rusk, *A Statistical History of the American Electorate* (Washington, D.C.: CQ Press, 2001), 438.
15. Stanley and Niemi, *Vital Statistics on American Politics, 2003–2004*, 20.
16. Ibid., 45.
17. These data are drawn from the Web page of the National Governors Association, http://www.nga.org.
18. Drawn from an article by Tom Story on the National Council of State Legislatures Web site, http://www.ncsl.org.

19. See Salmore and Salmore, *Candidates, Parties and Campaigns.*
20. Philip Dubois, *From Ballot to Bench: Judicial Elections and the Quest for Accountability* (Austin: University of Texas Press, 1980).
21. Elizabeth Benjamin, "Senate Seeks More Hands-On Politics for Voters," *Times-Union,* April 30, 2002, B-2.
22. *First National Bank of Boston v. Bellotti,* 435 U.S. 765, 777 (1978).
23. *U.S. Term Limits, Inc. v. Thornton,* 514 U.S. 779 (1995).

3

Legislators and Legislatures
Alan Rosenthal

Power in the American political system, both at the federal and state levels, is not concentrated. It is shared by the three branches of government—the legislature, executive, and judiciary—which play distinct roles. Constitutionally the first branch, the legislature, is the most democratic, transparent, and turbulent of the three. It is the branch of government whose principal functions are representation, lawmaking, and balancing the power of the executive. It serves as the arena in which different values, interests, and priorities are expressed and where conflict takes place, consensus is built, and settlements are reached.

As one can imagine, legislatures in the fifty states are vibrant and complex institutions. Although they have characteristics in common, they differ in many respects. Even their names vary: twenty-seven are called "legislature"; nineteen, "general assembly"; two, "legislative assembly"; and two, "general court" (the official Massachusetts title is "Great and General Court). The upper chamber of the legislature is known everywhere as the "senate," and the lower chamber is the "house of representatives" in forty-one states, the "assembly" in four, the "house of delegates" in three, and the "general assembly" in one. These legislative bodies are located in state capitals that range in size, from Atlanta and Boston to Cheyenne, Wyoming, and Montpelier, Vermont. The building that houses them is known as the "state capitol" in thirty-three places, "the capitol" in one, the "state house" in twelve, and the "legislative hall," the "legislative building," the "state legislative building," and the "main capitol building" in four.

These differences in nomenclature alone are meant to suggest the variation among legislatures in so many other respects. Indeed, no two legislatures are quite alike, although they may resemble one another in some ways. Therefore, the generalizations that will be made in this chapter should be understood with the following qualification in mind: many or most, but not all, legislatures fit the pattern.

Legislative People

No one description fits the 7,382 individuals who serve in state legislative offices. These men and women vary in what motivates them, how they get to the legislature, and how they adapt to legislative life.

What Makes Them Tick

Most of the nation's legislators are men, white men, although women and minorities have made gains in past years. Women now constitute 22.5 percent, African Americans 8.2 percent, and Latinos 3 percent of legislators in the fifty states.

Let's look at a few examples drawn from the rich variety of legislators who have served or are currently serving. Each of these examples—Frank Smallwood of Vermont, Tom Loftus of Wisconsin, Harriet Keyserling of South Carolina, and Willie Brown of California—is the subject of a fascinating memoir or biography.[1]

Smallwood, a Republican, spent only one two-year term as a member of the Vermont Senate. A political science professor at Dartmouth College in New Hampshire, he lived just across the river from Norwich, a small town in Windsor County, Vermont. Before his stint in the legislature, he served on the Board of Trustees of Vermont State Colleges and chaired a commission that drafted a bill to establish a more coordinated higher education system. That bill was defeated in the legislature, which became one of the reasons he decided to run.

Moreover, Smallwood believed that "there is an important difference between studying and doing." The time had come, he thought, "for me to get off my duff and take part in the action." He wanted to see what he had to offer, whether he could make any difference, and whether Vermont was ready for creative ideas with regard to higher education, land use, and other areas.

The motivation was there, but the opportunity arose because he had been awarded a year's sabbatical leave from Dartmouth. That freed him to campaign. The Windsor County legislative district had three senate seats, and in the primary election seven candidates ran for three Republican nominations. Smallwood placed third, winning one of them. He then proceeded to win the general election.

Tom Loftus spent fourteen years in the Wisconsin Assembly, during which time he held the top office of Speaker for eight years. It would appear that politics was in Loftus's bones; the question was when he would run and for what office. Before running for office, he pursued graduate study in government and public policy at the LaFollette Institute at the University of Wisconsin, worked as a speech writer for members of the Democratic caucus in the assembly, and then became a member of the Speaker's staff. To fill out his political credentials, he also worked on a legislator's reelection campaign and for the campaign of a Democratic presidential candidate. The opportunity to run came when the assemblyman who represented the district that included Sun Prairie, Loftus's home town, decided to retire. Loftus declared for the seat and, after winning the primary and general elections, returned to Madison as a member of the legislature instead of as a staff employee of the legislature.

It was no surprise that Loftus found his way to the Wisconsin legislature, but no one could have anticipated Harriet Keyserling's election to the South Carolina legislature, where she served for sixteen years. She appeared to be totally out of place in the political culture of the South. Having grown up on the Upper West Side of Manhattan in New York City, she went to college at Barnard, where she became interested in politics and liberal causes. She married Herbert Keyserling, the son of old family friends, who was a native son of the small, conservative town of Beaufort, South Carolina, where he was a physician. She moved to her husband's town, did the bookkeeping for his medical practice, raised four children, and worked as a volunteer in the community. Keyserling organized a chapter of the League of Women Voters in Beaufort and began to observe the workings of county government.

As a league observer, she thought how differently she would have voted on some of the issues that were being decided by county government. So, with some urging from friends, she decided to run. As unlikely as it may seem, Keyserling, who in her own words was "a middle-aged Jewish woman with a New York accent," became the first woman to be elected to and serve on the Beaufort County Council. When the incumbent from the legislative district decided not to seek reelection, he urged Keyserling to run for his house seat and offered to manage her campaign. It was not an easy decision, but she finally chose to go ahead, mainly because she wanted to make a difference.

Willie Brown, who has come to be known in legislative circles around the country as "legendary," spent thirty-two years in the California Assembly, about half of which were as Speaker. The great-grandchild of slaves, he grew up in the town of Mineola in East Texas and suffered the pain of segregation and discrimination. Brown's intelligence and his will to succeed were clear early on. As a young man, he moved to San Francisco to live with his uncle and attend college and law school. He started to hone his political skills in church politics and came under the wing of Phillip Burton, an influential member of the California Assembly. With Burton's help, Brown challenged an incumbent assemblyman in a primary. He lost. Two years later, at the age of thirty, Brown easily won primary and general elections and went on to Sacramento, where he acquired and exercised power longer and more deftly than anyone else in the history of the California legislature.

At different times in their lives and for a variety of reasons, people like Smallwood, Loftus, Keyserling, and Brown choose to embark upon careers in politics. Most pursue candidacy avidly, others deliberate about whether to run, and a few back into politics. Whatever their motivations, running for public office requires sacrifice. Success is by no means assured. A candidate always risks rejection by the electorate, which can be a heavy blow to one's self-esteem. Moreover, campaigning and governing both infringe upon the income, family life, leisure time, independence, and privacy that people cherish. Therefore, it is hardly surprising that relatively few

Americans become seriously engaged in politics and even fewer seek elective public office.

Those who do choose to run for office are strongly enough motivated to compensate for whatever hardships they might anticipate. Several explanations have been offered as to why people run. A first explanation, involving psychological factors, was advanced years ago by political scientist Harold Lasswell.[2] People run for office, according to him, out of the need to nourish weak egos on a public stage. Another political scientist, James David Barber, offered an interpretation that ran counter to Lasswell's.[3] Those legislators, whom he classified as "lawmakers," ran because healthy, strong egos encouraged them to get involved in public affairs. Psychological factors can be applied to many political candidacies. Harriet Keyserling's low self-esteem played a part in her entry into politics and her subsequent political life. Willie Brown's formative experiences with racism in East Texas had much to do with his drive to exercise power. Psychological factors probably play some role in the recruitment of many people to political life.

A second explanation, one that fits many political people, involves sociological factors. As a class, legislators are not reflective of the composition of the population as a whole. By and large, they tend to be older, better educated, more successful in their outside careers, and have higher incomes than the constituents they represent. Unlike Willie Brown, who is certainly exceptional, they are likely to come from relatively advantaged backgrounds rather than relatively disadvantaged ones. A disproportionate number are products of political families, with fathers, mothers, uncles, aunts, or other close relatives active in politics, and sometimes holding public office themselves. These recruits perceive politics and politicians differently from the way ordinary citizens do. The impressions they receive from participating family members are positive, whereas the impressions citizens receive from the media and other environmental forces are negative. Those from political families appreciate the rough and tumble of democratic politics and respect the people involved. Ordinary citizens, by contrast, are cynical about the political system and distrustful of people elected to public office.

A third explanation, a rather simple one, is that people who run for the legislature and other offices want to do good. At least they want to do what they consider to be good. Americans believe that politicians are just out for themselves, not the public. For example, a survey sponsored by the National Conference of State Legislatures found that only 35 percent of people believed that elected officials work to serve the public interest, rather than their own interests.[4] Among the thousands of legislators in the states, some no doubt use their public office for private gain. A few—but only a few—are corrupt, and some can be considered ethically challenged in one way or another. But the overwhelming majority are neither corrupt nor unethical.[5] As Loftus has observed, "most people who hold elective office are there for the right reasons."[6]

What are the "right" reasons for people to run and then serve? Like Smallwood, Loftus, Keyserling, and Brown, they want to make a difference—that is, they want to make things better for their constituents and for citizens of the state. Many of them are interested in reshaping education policy, some want to develop environmental programs, others want to work on transportation, and some are concerned about improving health policy. Both Democrats and Republicans want to be elected because they believe that they can do a better job than their opponents and that control of the legislature by their respective parties will provide better policies for the state. Practically everyone who runs for office wants to help people by providing them with information, assisting them with problems they have with government, and making law in their behalf.

People in public office also derive personal satisfaction from serving. A few even benefit in their outside careers. In this respect, it is in their personal interest to serve the public. Most of them enjoy exercising power, but in their eyes power is the means to achieve meritorious objectives. Many also like the challenges of political life, in particular the game-like aspects of competing in elections and in the legislative process. They are not selfless saints.

People often charge legislators with wanting above all to get reelected and accuse them of simply "playing politics." The charge is well taken. Very few officeholders want to lose an election. They have staked too much on achieving office. Moreover, to be rejected by one's constituents is hurtful; it can leave permanent scars. Incumbents usually feel unsafe, whatever their margin of victory in the last election. They try to win over as many groups and voters as possible and try to alienate as few as possible. Anticipating what voters want and don't want is what they ought to be doing. Some might call it pandering, but herein lies the democratic connection between the representative and the electorate.

Smallwood, Loftus, Keyserling, and Brown each had political experience of one sort or another before they ran for the legislature, although only Keyserling had previously held elective office. Generally speaking, 35 percent of the nation's state legislators have held elective office immediately prior to their service in the legislature, although another 13.3 percent have held appointive office.[7] The proportion holding an elective office varies among the states. In Vermont two out of three legislators have held office prior to their election to the legislature, in Ohio one out of two, and in Maryland, Minnesota, and Washington roughly one out of three.[8]

People who manage to win come to the legislature with political views. With very few exceptions, they are either Democrats or Republicans. Of the total legislators elected in 2004, only 63, or less than 1 percent, were Independents, Greens, Progressives, or affiliated with a party other than the two major ones. Democrats totaled 3,661, Republicans totaled 3,655, a difference of only 6 legislators throughout the entire country at that particular time. They not only had their political affiliations with parties, they also had their political orientations. About half described their political views as conservative, a quarter as liberal, and the other quarter as middle of the road.[9]

How They Adapt

Once they take their seats in the senate or house, those who are elected begin to adapt to what is by no means a normal existence. Being a legislator takes time, usually a good deal of time. Just how many hours a week legislators devote to their job depends on many factors. First, the more days a legislature is in session, the more time legislators are required to be at work. Most legislatures meet for limited periods, beginning early in January, every year. A few, however, still meet biennially, or only every other year. The length of a legislative session is usually limited by the state constitution.

At one extreme are California, Illinois, Michigan, New York, North Carolina, Ohio, Oregon, Pennsylvania, and Wisconsin, which spend the most time in session—usually 130 days or more throughout the year. At the other extreme, Alabama, Arkansas, Florida, Georgia, Hawaii, Indiana, Kentucky, Louisiana, Montana, Nevada, New Hampshire, New Mexico, North Dakota, Rhode Island, South Dakota, Utah, Virginia, and West Virginia spend 60 or fewer days. But even during the interim period, the time when the legislature is officially not in session, legislative work is being done. Standing committees and special commissions hold periodic sessions during the interim, and legislators themselves continue year round to meet with and provide service to their constituents.

In all but a dozen or so states, legislators are considered "citizen legislators" and are expected to earn a living on the outside. That is because legislative compensation in four-fifths of the states is less than $50,000 a year, and in half of these it is less than $25,000. In New Mexico, legislators receive no salary at all, in New Hampshire they receive $100 a year, and in Vermont about $11,000. Only in a handful of states—California, New York, Ohio, and Pennsylvania are among them—do legislators receive substantial pay for their efforts.

Legislators who are wealthy or retired or whose spouses' incomes provide the necessary financial support can afford to devote full time to their legislative duties without having to worry about another job. But 61.4 percent of state legislators work for pay outside of politics.[10] In ten states, about three out of four legislators are essentially full time; in another ten, fewer than one of three is full time. In the thirty remaining states, anywhere from one-third to three-quarters of the members have no other occupation than that of legislator.

It is not at all easy for legislators to meet their responsibilities as public officials on the one hand and private careerists or employees on the other. Frank Smallwood, who served in the part-time, citizen legislature of Vermont, did not think it could be done, because political life is an all-consuming business.[11] He could manage, he believed, only because he had a sabbatical leave for one of the two years he served. Yet, because compensation tends to be low, most legislators have to divide their time between two almost-full-time jobs. During the legislative session, nearly all of them spend fifty or more hours a week at the job. During the interim, most get by with twenty to twenty-five hours a week, including two or three nights at district events.[12]

When asked in a national survey what proportion of a full-time job their legislative work was, almost half said that it was 70 percent or more of a full-time job and another quarter thought that it was more than 50 percent of a full-time job. Only about 5 percent of the legislators indicated that it was a third or less of a full-time job.[13] If the respondents assumed that a full-time job took thirty-five hours a week, then half spend on average twenty-five hours a week, while another quarter spend on average twenty hours a week. And for most of these people, this time is in addition to the time they spend on their careers or occupations outside the legislature.

Usually one's income suffers as a result of being in the legislature. Attorneys, for example, have to cut down substantially on their practice or, for the few who are able to remain in larger law firms, billable hours. Real estate and insurance agents are less available to show houses or sell policies. People in business of one kind or another have to leave things in the hands of partners while they are at the capital. Legislative compensation, in the overwhelming majority of instances, does not make up for income lost from one's private career or occupation. Despite what many members of the public may think, only a few legislators benefit financially.

The families of legislators bear the brunt of their public service. People in legislative office simply have to spend a good deal of time away from spouses and children. During a legislative session, except in states like Delaware, New Jersey, and Rhode Island, where everyone commutes to the capital, or except for members who live in or near the capital, legislators spend three or four nights a week away from home. And even when they are at home, legislators spend at least a few nights a week out at district events. Many a legislator has missed a spouse's birthday, a son's or daughter's Little League game or school play, or other family event.[14]

In adapting, individuals encounter other stresses. They cannot expect the same degree of privacy that ordinary people take for granted. Instead, their private as well as public lives are subject to media scrutiny and can be exploited by an opponent in a political campaign. Public officials are required to make public disclosure of their own and their spouse's financial assets and income. As politicians, they are suspect. They have to concern themselves not only with a possible conflict between their interests as legislators and their interests as private citizens but also with any appearance of a conflict of interests. Their ethics are subject to challenge and, given the cynicism of the media and the public, their reputations are always at risk. Public cynicism toward politicians, political groups, and political processes is something with which today's legislators have to live. They do not feel that they deserve the low esteem in which they are held by the public (but not by their own constituents who are positive toward them and normally vote to reelect them to office).

Even in the most positive environment, the job of legislator is stressful. There is never enough time to do what has to be done. At times things move at too fast a pace, at other times they move too slowly. Stretches of boredom are not unusual, as when members listen to repetitious and seemingly endless testimony at a committee hearing on a bill or when debate at a floor session runs on and on. Then there are periods like the final days of a legislative session, when time is short, when everything seems to be happening at once, and when members find it almost impossible to keep abreast of just which bills and amendments are up for decision. Under such circumstances, it is easy to feel overwhelmed.

The legislature is nothing if not frustrating. In a competitive state, minority party members feel frustrated because they have so little control over the agenda, over what gets done. Still, majority party members, whether they be leaders or rank and file, also suffer from frustration. It can be difficult to get a bill passed, especially a significant and controversial one. Legislators who want to enact a law—leaders and members alike—have to put together majorities in their own chamber, then in the other chamber. This requires strategizing, deliberating, negotiating, and compromising for days, weeks, or even longer. And after all the hard work, a measure can be derailed. Seldom, moreover, do legislators get all or three-quarters, or perhaps even half, of what they want. No matter how worthy they believe their cause or how much they strive, they have to settle for less—and usually much less—than they deem desirable.

Despite the frustration and the other strains, most of the men and women who run for the legislature wind up liking it once they are there. At any given election, some legislators will leave. In the sixteen states that have limited the number of terms legislators can serve, the percentage leaving after each election is higher. Turnover rates vary greatly from state to state, with low rates in places like New Jersey, New York, and Pennsylvania, on the one hand, and higher rates in places like Alaska, Mississippi, New Hampshire, and South Dakota on the other.

Why do legislators leave? Some are defeated in a primary or general election; some, particularly after the decennial redistricting, when district lines are changed, think that they cannot be reelected and prefer to retire than to risk defeat. A few die while in office and others depart because of ill health. Those in term-limited legislatures are permitted to serve no longer than six, eight, or twelve years, depending on the state and chamber; they have no choice, they have to move on. Willie Brown of California left the assembly because his term was limited by law and he had a chance to run for mayor of San Francisco. Roughly one in three or four legislators who voluntarily leave do so to run for another position—statewide office, such as attorney general, lieutenant governor, or perhaps governor, or for the U.S. House.

Only a few legislators give it up quickly, after a term or two. Smallwood was one. He could not reconcile two careers he thought were full time, so he decided after one two-year term in the Vermont Senate to return to full-time teaching at Dartmouth. A few lose their enthusiasm after serving awhile.

Harriet Keyserling of South Carolina was one of them. She left after sixteen years; her close colleagues had already exited, the Republicans had gained control of the house, and partisanship had become intense. She simply did not like it any more. Some feel that it is time for them to go. Tom Loftus thought fourteen years was enough, and he knew that his Democratic colleagues in the assembly were waiting for him to leave so that they could move up the leadership ladder. Some go because they can no longer endure being in the minority. A number leave because they cannot get by on legislative salaries and have to increase their income in order to send children to college.

The fact is that, outside of running for higher office, very few legislators leave voluntarily. At any election, depending on the state, no more than 5, 10, or 15 percent give up their legislative positions. This is obviously because the large majority of legislators like being legislators. With all the stresses, strains, and hardships of legislative life, they adapt. Indeed, adaptation comes easily to people who choose politics.

Whatever an individual's goals, the legislature is a place to work to achieve them. If one aspires to higher office, the legislature is a good launching pad. For instance, almost half the members of the U.S. House once served in their state legislature. If one wants to advance in the ranks of legislative leadership, provided one is in the majority party, it is not difficult to get appointed to chair a committee or to be selected for the leadership team. If one wants to see immediate results, it is possible to assist constituents with all sorts of problems and make a real difference in their lives. If one wants to play the role of maverick, the legislature is a good place to do it. Although colleagues may not appreciate such behavior, the media and the public may reward it.

If one is disposed to work at building consensus to get agreement on legislation—the real challenge of lawmaking—there is probably no more welcoming arena than the legislature. This is where Willie Brown excelled. For him the public interest was the sum total of the interests of all the players sitting around the negotiating table. His most enjoyable and best work was in negotiating legislative deals and picking up one vote at a time. Brown referred to himself as the "ultimate negotiator" and wanted to be remembered as California's premier deal maker.[15]

If one's goal is to exercise power or to shape policy, the legislature is the place to be—as long as one is patient and not overly demanding of particular results. It is not only possible actually to make a difference, but it is also probable that one will feel that he or she did make a difference on issues that matter to a constituency and to the state. Harriet Keyserling backed into the legislature. She had little self-confidence, no wish to exercise power, and was hardly an assertive person. However, she adapted to the contentiousness of legislative politics. She learned how to use power, even to relish it. "When I finally found myself in a position of knowing I could make a difference," she writes, "the passion came building up, like adrenalin during stress."[16]

Staying in Office

On balance, members like being legislators. They want to remain at least until they have a good shot at higher office. That means they have to get reelected. Adapting to legislative life, therefore, includes being concerned about the next election. They do not want to lose; rejection by one's constituents is especially hurtful.

Incumbents normally have an advantage when it comes to reelection. In most cases they represent districts that are relatively safe for their party. Depending on the state, anywhere from two to four out of five legislative districts can be considered fairly safe for either a Democratic incumbent or a Republican incumbent. These districts generally are won with 55 percent or more of the vote. The high percentage of such districts is attributable to the fact that Democrats tend to live in certain kinds of places, cities, for example, and Republicans tend to live in other kinds of places, many suburbs, for example. Added to this, redistricting processes in many states nowadays tend to make legislative seats (and congressional seats as well) safer for incumbents of each party.

Nevertheless, incumbents feel unsafe, whatever the district's party registration or whatever the incumbent's previous margins of victory. They all have seen examples of legislative colleagues who lost, even though they seemed to be politically secure and should have been reelected. A few instances of incumbents who are struck by electoral lightning are taken much more seriously by legislators than simple statistics and probabilities of reelection. An opponent with a huge war chest, an unanticipated event, a scandal—anything can happen, and on occasion it does.

Because they feel threatened, legislators run scared. This means that they take good care of their constituents and constituencies; raise funds to buy television, radio, and direct mail ads; and try to discourage serious challenges from opposition party candidates or even primary opponents. Generally speaking, the more competitive the district, the more money will be raised. Yet, in most states and in the large majority of districts, the amount of money spent on legislative campaigns is not staggering. However much a campaign costs, the impending election is usually at the back, if not the front, of a legislator's mind.

Legislative Organization

Individual legislators bring to the legislature their own values, partisan affiliations, interest-group alliances, constituencies, and personalities. All these characteristics help shape, and in turn are shaped by, a complex organization, the legislature. Among the major organizational dimensions of the legislature are its professionalization, basic structure, division of labor, partisan groupings, and leadership.

Professionalization

Political scientists offer varying definitions of *professionalization* as the concept relates to state legislatures. As employed here, *professionalization* refers to the legislature's capacity to do its several jobs.[17] The work of the legislature requires time and effort. Therefore, the length of the legislative session and the size of the professional staff can be used as the principal indicators of professionalization. Some legislatures, such as in California and New York, have heavy schedules and large staffs. These are the most professionalized legislatures. Others, like Idaho and Wyoming, have light schedules and small staffs. These are the least professionalized legislatures. In between are legislatures with heavy schedules but smaller staffs, like Colorado, Delaware, Maine, and Rhode Island. They are not fully professionalized, but are work intensive. A few legislatures, such as those in Florida and New Jersey, have comparatively light schedules but large staffs. They can be thought of as support-intensive legislatures.

Professionalized legislatures have greater capacity than more amateur ones. But there is no evidence that greater capacity results in the legislature doing a better job. There are other factors at play.

Basic Structure

Except in Nebraska where the legislature is unicameral, all state legislatures are bicameral. Just about everywhere, the differences between the senate and house are substantial. The length of the terms members serve usually differs, four years for senators and two years for representatives. (In twelve states senators serve two-year terms and in five states representatives serve four-year terms.) The two chambers are also different in size. In every case, the house has more members than the senate. The ratio may be two to one (as in Alaska, California, Indiana, and Iowa) or three to one (as in Ohio), or as much as almost seventeen to one (as in New Hampshire).

The two houses may both be controlled by the same party, or control may be divided between the parties. Right after the 2004 elections, for instance, the Democrats had a majority in both chambers of eighteen legislatures, the Republicans had a majority in both chambers of nineteen legislatures, and control was divided in twelve other legislatures (five of which had ties in one chamber or the other).

Whether control is divided or not, the senate and house are dissimilar bodies. They have contrasting cultures and norms. Senators tend to be more experienced than their counterparts in the house, in large part because many of them have served in the house prior to running for the senate. Leadership in a house tends to be more centralized in the presiding officer, party leaders, and leadership teams. Leadership in a senate, by contrast, tends to be more individualistic, with each senator having somewhat greater autonomy in relation to the chamber and party leaders. Ordinarily, within any particular state the senate, because of its smaller size and individualistic norms, is more collegial and less partisan than the house.

House and senate committee systems also operate somewhat differently. There are more house members to divide up the labor. House members have fewer committee assignments and, thus, are apt to be more specialized in their knowledge of public policy. Senators hare somewhat broader purviews. A proposal may be reviewed very differently in the senate from the way it is in the house. So it is not unusual for bills to be passed in different form by each house, thus requiring that the two bodies resolve their differences if a law is to be enacted. Nor is it unusual for bills to pass in one chamber but not the other.

Each chamber has its own institutional pride, especially when it comes to dealing with the other chamber. Each feels that the legislation it endorses is to be preferred. Each feels a sense of competition and wants to prevail over the other. State senates and houses balance each other, just as the separate branches of government balance one another. They are both partners and rivals, and they bring different perspectives to the lawmaking process.

Standing Committees

Much of the lawmaking job of a legislature is done through its standing committees.[18] Committees perform the following functions. First, they process bills that are referred to them, deciding whether to report them favorably or not and whether and how to change or amend them. Second, they provide for a division of labor, whereby the workload of legislation is distributed by policy domain among members. Third, committee service enables members to specialize in one or several domains, become relatively expert, and furnish noncommittee colleagues with advice and cues. Fourth, committee members who report a bill favorably form the basic bloc of a voting coalition when the bill is decided on the floor.

The number of committees varies greatly from chamber to chamber. The New York and Texas houses, at one end of the continuum, operate with about forty standing committees. By contrast, Maryland operates with only six senate committees and seven house committees. Connecticut, Maine, and Massachusetts rely on joint committees. Some legislative committee systems make use of subcommittees; committees with responsibility for enacting the state budget are most likely to divide up the job among a number of subcommittees. The size of committees also varies. Committees can be as small as those in New Jersey, where committees other than appropriations and judiciary have only five members. Or they can be as large as Maryland's house committees, which have over twenty members.

The larger the number of committees and subcommittees, the more positions of chair for legislators to fill and, thus, the more opportunities for them to take on leadership responsibilities. Ordinarily, the chair runs the committee, or at least controls the agenda. A chair cannot get his or her way without the support of a majority of committee members, but whoever controls the agenda and staff can be very persuasive with members who want one of their bills to advance. Furthermore, a chair's opposition to a bill can be decisive.

Committee chairs can be characterized as one of three general styles: advocates, mediators, and facilitators. Whether they pursue one or another style depends on the case and the circumstances. Advocates generally promote a program, policy, or point of view. They place their objectives first and try to lead committee members in their direction. Advocates are apt to believe in and represent the interests of the principal groups under their committee's jurisdiction, such as education, banking, or insurance. Mediators in contrast, try to bring various parties to the table, along with committee members, so that disagreements can be worked out and the committee can agree on a product. The chair as mediator works to reduce the issues to the critical ones and then get things worked out by disputants before the committee even meets. Facilitators make few independent judgments, seeing their role as that of moving legislators' bills through the committee to the floor for passage. That way committee members can be assured that their own bills will receive favorable treatment in committees where they are lodged.

Unless legislative party leaders bypass committees and design a legislative product, as they occasionally do on some major issues, standing committees have the most important role in the lawmaking process. If a committee that is fairly representative of the chamber membership reports a bill favorably, and with few negative votes, chances are that it will pass in that chamber. Of course, it must also pass in the other, and that is another matter.

Legislative Parties

The structural significance of the party is demonstrated by how the legislature is organized. Normally the majority party controls the organization of each body.[19] Except in occasional instances of bipartisan coalitions, the majority party selects the Speaker of the house and the president or president pro tem of the senate. With few exceptions, members of the majority are appointed to chair standing committees on which the majority party also has the majority of members.

The caucus is a key party mechanism in three out of four legislative chambers. In some legislatures majority and minority caucuses meet every day the legislature is in session, in others they meet once a week, and in still others they meet at the beginning of the legislative session and only occasionally thereafter. Members of both majority and minority caucuses select party leaders: majority and minority leaders, assistant leaders, whips, and so forth.

Both caucuses discuss issues facing the chamber and, in particular, bills scheduled for floor action that day or week. The caucus offers the opportunity for members to question bill sponsors and party leaders. It enables leaders to get an idea of how their members, and their members' constituents, feel about issues before the legislature. Members, themselves, can see where their colleagues stand. Leaders inform members of the strategies and tactics they plan to employ in dealing with the other party, other house, or governor. Discussion builds intraparty consensus. Majority party leaders figure out if they have enough votes to pass a bill or amendment on the floor, whereas minority party leaders and members decide whether to take a party position on an issue and how to put the majority on the political defensive.

The legislative parties are competitors for the electorate's votes. The majority party wants to maintain its control of the senate or house, whereas the minority wants to win control. The two parties have somewhat different types of constituencies, somewhat different interest-group alliances, somewhat different policy positions, and somewhat different agendas when they are in power. Therefore, it matters who has control, and thus the stakes associated with winning elections are high.

Previously campaigns had been run by the state and local parties and by the candidates themselves. During the past twenty-five years, however, the legislative parties, and particularly legislative party leaders, have taken responsibility for campaigns for legislative office. They raise and allocate funds to their incumbents who face serious challenges from opposition party candidates. They help recruit and fund candidates who have a chance of unseating opposition party incumbents. They run coordinated campaigns for the legislature, hire consultants, commission and interpret polls, and otherwise work to strengthen their hold on the legislature.

The legislative parties also try to improve the prospects of individual members who have been targeted by the opposition. A targeted majority party member is more likely to receive choice committee assignments, have his or her bills passed, get projects for the constituency, and be allowed to deviate on tough party-line votes.

The legislative parties are constantly looking toward the next election. They try to avoid mistakes, make a record, and blame the opposition for anything that goes wrong or can be made to appear to go wrong. All the while, they scan the environment in an effort to anticipate how the electorate will react to actions they might take. Voters are never far from the legislative party's mind, just as they are not far from the individual legislator's mind.

Leadership

For Willie Brown, the essence of leadership in the California Assembly was serving the interests of his members. Despite the power he exercised, Brown was aptly known as the member's Speaker.[20] Any top leader, in order to remain leader, is responsible to the chamber membership and especially to the majority party caucus. There are no authoritarian leaders in legislative bodies, although some leaders are more forceful than others. Exercising leadership in a democratic body, where members have their own constituencies and own votes, is a delicate balancing act, especially since leaders are faced with quite a number of difficult tasks.

First, as described above, leaders work to get their members reelected and to win, or strengthen, their control of the chamber.

Second, leaders appoint members to standing committees and designate committee chairs. These committees, and particularly the chairs, usually have considerable say in which bills get enacted and which do not.

Third, leaders help their members with a wide range of problems. The doors to their offices are always open to members who want to drop by. Ralph Wright, a former Speaker in Vermont, described his role in this respect: "As long as it wasn't against the law, didn't require that I go to confession, or wouldn't break up my marriage, I did it."[21]

Fourth, leaders take the heat and catch flack for members, protecting them whenever they can. They try to shield members from having to cast unpopular votes. Leaders, themselves, will take responsibility for legislative pay raises that have little public support. Tom Murphy, who served twenty-eight years as Speaker in Georgia, expressed it succinctly: "It's not hard; I give them all the credit and I take all the blame."

Fifth, leaders devote their greatest efforts to building consensus. They work to locate the will of the body as a whole or of the caucus specifically and then work to enact that will, which requires considerable skill at each step along the way.

Sixth, leaders act as the principal strategists on major issues before the legislature. They strategize with respect to how to construct majorities within their own chamber and how to put the other party in a difficult position. When differences exist between the senate and house or between the legislature and the governor, the job of designing strategies to work things out falls to legislative leadership.

Seventh, on major matters leaders are the principal negotiators. Leaders will negotiate with majority party legislators or with minority party legislators to get the votes needed to pass a measure. They will negotiate with their leadership counterparts in the other party or other chamber, and also with the governor.

Eighth, leaders represent the senate or house to the media and to the public. If anyone at all speaks for the chamber, it is the leader of the majority party—the Speaker of the house or the president or president pro tem of the senate.

Legislative Performance

The aggregation of individual members, who are organized by chamber, by standing committee, and by party caucus and who have elected and designated leaders, constitutes the legislature at work. The questions are, what is the work of the legislature and how does the legislature do its work? Essentially, the legislature has three major jobs (as well as a host of less important ones): the first is representing constituents and constituencies; the second, lawmaking; and the third, balancing the power of the executive. These jobs overlap, but for analytical convenience can be considered separately.[22]

Representing Constituents and Constituencies

Representation is one of the jobs of every legislator, and the primary job of many of them. It is also one of the principal jobs of the legislature as a whole. For the individual legislator, just how representation is accomplished depends greatly on the nature of his or her district. Representing an inner-city district is not at all the same as representing a rural district, or a suburban one. The larger the territory of a district, the more difficult it is for legislators to get around and meet face to face with constituents. Compare representing a district in Colorado that spans the Rocky Mountains or one in Maine that consists of a number of coastal islands with representing a district in New York City or Chicago. But the most significant variation in districts across the nation (although not within states) is population size. Contrast representing a senate district in California with 846,791 people to representing a senate district in North Dakota with 13,106 people or a house district in California with 423,396 to a house district in New Hampshire with 3,089.

The first element of representation is that of serving the constituency's interests. This is not difficult for legislators to do; it comes naturally to just about all of them, and they find much of the work along these lines quite fulfilling. They identify with their districts and consider themselves very much a part of the constituency they represent. Moreover, on average, about one-quarter of the nation's legislators have lived in their district for their entire lives. Tom Loftus, for example, was one of them. He describes his upbringing in Sun Prairie, Wisconsin, and what that meant in regard to identifying with people there: "Like many of those represented, I was raised a Lutheran and married a Catholic, can eat lutefish with a smile, speak some Norwegian and some German, know how to play euchre, and with the help of beer, can dance the polka. Like most of those I represent, I understand everything Garrison Keillor has to say."[23] Frank Smallwood, by contrast, was a relatively late arrival to Norwich, Vermont. He moved there just eight years before he ran.[24]

Legislators spend as much time as they can attending events and meetings with constituents and constituency groups. Most of these functions take place in the district, but some constituents visit their representatives in the capitol. When legislators throughout the nation were asked to indicate how much time they spent on keeping in touch with constituents, on a five-point scale (with 1 indicating "hardly any" and 5 meaning "a great deal") they averaged 4.1.[25] They do not treat constituency communication lightly.

Beyond talk, legislators are eager to give people whatever help they can. Constituents have a problem with the renewal of their driver's license, their health plan, local telephone service, or the maintenance of a road, almost anything. If they ask for assistance, their representatives try to intervene on their behalf or direct their request to the right place. When legislators help constituents with their problem involving state government, what they are doing is known as "case work." In the national survey, legislators were asked how much time they actually spent on helping constituents with problems with government. On a scale of 1 to 5 (with 1, "hardly any," and 5, "a great deal"), legislators averaged 4.0, indicating a major commitment of time to these tasks as well.

In addition to serving individual constituents, legislators also provide for the district as a whole. This entails "bringing home the bacon," that is, getting funds for local projects (such as a museum, highway, senior citizens bus) and making sure that state formulas for funding schools and other services benefit their districts as much as possible.

Serving the interests of the constituency is straightforward compared with expressing the views of the constituents. Legislators hear from their constituents by mail, e-mail, fax, and phone and also engage in face-to-face encounters in the district or at the capitol. They want to know how their constituents feel about various issues, and on some issues constituents make their feelings known.

But the issues constituents care about are a small proportion of the entirety of issues with which the legislature deals during any session. Smallwood describes the views of people in his Vermont district as follows: "Most of the people I talked to outside the legislature didn't have the faintest clue regarding 90% of the bills we were considering. . . . As far as John Q. Public was concerned, he couldn't have cared less about the bulk of the more routine bills."[26]

A study of the legislature in five states (Maryland, Minnesota, Ohio, Vermont, and Washington) supports Smallwood's experience. It found that in about half the districts constituents had an opinion on 5 percent or fewer of the issues before the legislature and a clear constituency position on no more than five bills that came up during the year.[27]

The classic question, which actually pertains to only a handful of cases, is that of whether a legislator acts as "delegate," following instructions from the constituency, or as "trustee," following his or her own conscience. Political scientists have devoted great attention to an examination of where legislators position themselves on the delegate-trustee continuum. Generally, legislators come closer to the conscience end than to the delegate end. That is largely because most frequently they cannot act as delegates because there is no clear district view on the matter.

In those instances where constituents do care, for the most part the views of legislators and the predominant views in their district are essentially the same. When it comes to questions of public policy, representatives rely mainly on what their political supporters in the district think. They and their supporters are usually aligned on issues, anyway. In a few instances, and on hot-button issues like abortion, gun control, gay rights, capital punishment, taxes, and gambling, differences between the representative and the constituency may exist. On issues involving questions of morality, representatives usually follow their conscience, whereas on issues such as taxes and gambling they are divided—about half go with conscience, and about half with constituency.

Elected representatives constitute an important channel through which constituents' views come into play, but it is not the only one. Political parties and groups also serve a representational function, channeling people's views.

With hardly any exceptions, legislators are either Democrats or Republicans. The two parties represent different constituencies, at least to some degree. They disagree on some major issues, such as the role and size of government, regulation, and tax and spending policy. For the most part, Americans affiliate with or lean toward one party or the other; and most people vote for their party's candidates. So even members of the minority party living in a particular district have their views expressed by their party's legislators from other districts.

Interest groups also represent people, although this representation is more on specific issues. People's interests are both organized and expressed (or lobbied) by groups, a large number of which align with one political party or the other and many of which provide support for individual members of the legislature.[28] About seven out of ten Americans belong to some interest group, and four out of ten belong to more than one. The views of members of these groups are represented, as are the views of people who share the same ideas and orientations but do not hold membership in the group.

Given the overlapping channels of representation afforded by individual legislators, political parties, and interest groups, just about every view with some backing can get a hearing. Not every view, however, can prevail and be enacted into law. Enactment depends on the lawmaking process in the legislature and the specific circumstances surrounding an issue's disposition.

Lawmaking

"How a bill becomes a law" defines the legislative process for most of us. We recall that a bill is introduced, referred to committee, reported out of committee, and considered on the floor of one house, and that a similar process takes place in the other house. If a bill clears all the hurdles it encounters and if the two houses agree on exactly the same text, the bill goes to the governor for signature or veto. This mapping of stages of the process is accurate as far as it goes, but it gives us only a superficial idea of what is involved in lawmaking by legislatures.

The workload of bills introduced is heavy in any legislature. Everyone seems to need to have a new law enacted or an old law modified. Bills come from all directions. Some, such as the budget, are constitutionally required. Others arise as a result of judicial decision. Bills emanate from the governor and his or her administration. Constituents persuade their legislators to introduce bills on their behalf. Legislators come up with their own ideas. Interest groups and their lobbyists are probably behind the largest number of bills introduced at any legislative session. Some bills fall by the wayside, others go all the way to become law. The percentage of bill enactments to bill introductions ranges greatly among the states, but nationally, depending on the state, roughly one out of three bills that are introduced is enacted.

Of the hundreds or thousands of bills considered, many are noncontroversial, engender no opposition, require no funds, and pass by consent. But some of the measures provoke controversy, engender opposition, and are contested. The latter measures are ones on which legislators disagree, in part because members of the public also disagree. The differences among legislators mainly reflect different values, interests, and priorities held not only by them but also by state and district populations. Conflict also results from the fact that people have different ideas on how to allocate scarce resources and whether to increase taxes in order to fund government programs. Even in healthy economic times, there is not enough money to meet all the demands on the political system. Finally, people have differing ideas on how to solve problems that they agree exist.

The structure and process of the legislature practically ensures conflict where substantial disagreement exists. For a bill to pass and a law to be enacted, a succession of majority votes is required—in committee, perhaps in caucus, on the floors of both houses, and on concurrence between the houses on the same bill. Majority building in the legislature is a complex business, one in which the opponents of a measure have something of an advantage. Proponents have to put together majority votes at successive stages, whereas opponents need only prevent a majority from forming at a single stage in order to defeat a measure.

The process includes the study of an issue in which proponents and opponents present their cases at a committee hearing (and elsewhere) and other information is solicited and analyzed by staff. A major part of the process is deliberation, which can be defined generally "as reasoning on the merits." In this activity, representatives engage in discussion of the merits and demerits, both substantive and political, of a measure and its components, using their skills, experience, and the information available to them. In the process of deliberation, participants are open to learning and persuasion. They are willing to change their positions, at least to some extent, in response not to pressures, bargains, or blandishments, but rather to reasoned argument.

Information used in legislative study and deliberation is acquired from various sources—legislative staff, interest groups and their lobbyists, constituents, commissions and task forces, the executive branch, and elsewhere. Just about everyone has access to and is able to provide input during this part of the process. On substantial issues the legislature and its committee are awash in information, analysis, and argument brought forth by proponents and opponents. Until an issue is decided, study and deliberation proceed—behind the scenes as well as in public places.

Many members are generally on one side or another as an issue emerges. Others make up their minds as it develops. Decisions are made on the substantive and political merits: the former include how a measure promises to address a problem in light of all that is known; the latter include who favors and who opposes it and where the constituency stands.

One or, more likely, several factors influence the position a legislator takes on an issue. Among the predominant ones are his or her record; his or her beliefs; the views of his or her constituency, the legislative leadership, legislative party, the standing committee, interest groups, legislative colleagues, political supporters, and family and friends. On many issues, where the vote may be close, some legislators have to be persuaded. They need some inducement. Their support may be needed in committee, in a party caucus, or on the floor. Usually, it is the job of legislative leaders, along with lobbyists on one side or the other, to try to win the undecided legislators over. They approach this task by negotiating, which often entails a compromise on the legislation in question, the endorsement of a legislator's bill, a project for the legislator's district, or something else of value in return for a vote.

When, as is frequently the case, the house and senate pass different versions of a bill (especially of the budget bill) or when the governor and legislature cannot agree, negotiations are in order to reach common ground. Negotiating involves, among other things, efforts to persuade, offers to trade one bill for another, and a willingness to hold out as long as possible before making a final deal.

In the lawmaking process, it usually takes time, even years, for a measure to garner the support required. When a settlement has finally been reached and a law is enacted, the issue is not necessarily put to rest. Proponents may want to return in the next legislative session to strengthen the law, whereas opponents may want to weaken it; in any case, its implementation and unanticipated events may suggest change in the law after a while.

Balancing the Power of the Executive

Implicit, if not explicit, in state constitutions is that the legislature is a coequal branch of government sharing power with and checking the power of the other two branches. It is not unusual for legislatures and state courts to come into disagreement about their respective roles, but the more customary job of the legislature is both to collaborate with the executive on lawmaking and to counteract the power of the governor.

"It is no trick to invent a government and devise a strong executive," writes Loftus. "The trick of democracy is to devise a strong legislature that can survive transfers of power and shifts of party control."[29] In the colonial period and in the early years of the Republic, the legislature was the dominant branch of state government. This is no longer the case, although in a few places and from time to time the legislature achieves ascendancy.

Ordinarily, the contemporary governor has the upper hand relative to the legislature. This is because of powers that governors, and not legislatures, possess.

First, the power of unity. This, the greatest advantage, stems from the fact that the governor is one, whereas the legislature is many (senate and house, Democrats and Republicans, and many individual members). The governor does consult, but the final decision is his or hers to make. The legislature, unlike the executive, has to work through conflict and a succession of votes to reach agreement. Because the governor speaks with one voice and the legislature speaks with many, the governor and not the legislature has the bully pulpit. The governor receives the attention of the media, and the governor has the opportunity to communicate to the public statewide. Insofar as public opinion matters, and on major issues it does, the governor, not the legislature, has the chance of molding it.

Second, the power of agenda setting. Governors have the advantage of being able to focus on an agenda. They can pick and choose, whereas legislatures have to deal with much that comes their way. If governors focus on a limited number of initiatives, as most do, chances are that these items will be given top billing by their legislatures as well. Governors may not get everything they want, but they generally achieve much of what is on their agenda in one form or another.

Third, the power of budget formulation. The state budget is undoubtedly the most important bill of the legislative session. The budget is where priorities are set, not only by the decisions of how much in state revenues is raised and from whom and on what they are expended, but also by the introduction of new substantive policies. In most states the governor formulates the budget and the legislature responds, usually at least roughly along the lines the governor has proposed.

Fourth, the power of provision. Governors have what legislators want and need—a bill to be signed, an appointment of a constituent to be made, an item for the district in the budget submission, or just acknowledgment by the state's chief executive. Nearly every governor learns quickly how to use the resources needed to win the support of key legislators.

Fifth, the power of denial. If governors are able to bestow and reward, they are also able to deny and punish. The veto is the principal weapon of denial, but governors have far more subtle ways of indicating their displeasure, including the refusal to do favors for or give recognition to legislators. Out-and-out punishment is rare but still a possibility.

The governor benefits, at least with partisans, by virtue of being leader of the state Democratic or state Republican Party. Members of a political party have a disposition to be loyal to one another, if they possibly can. They share beliefs, interest group supporters, and an incentive to defeat the opposition party in the next state election. If the governor and the majority in the two houses of the legislature belong to the same party, the legislative leadership role of the executive is enhanced.

It is difficult for legislatures to maintain parity with governors who want to exercise leadership and have the ability to do so. Relatively few governors defer to the legislature, and relatively few are lacking in the skills necessary to deal effectively with their legislature. Whether gubernatorial leadership works is largely a function of the governor's approach, but to some extent it is a function of the legislature too.

What counts initially is whether the legislature recognizes its institutional prerogatives in regard to the executive. Many legislative leaders do, Brown and Loftus among them. These leaders believed strongly in the co-equal role of the legislative branch in governing the state. Ralph Wright of Vermont was another leader with the same philosophy.

> I had a clear sense of the Founding Fathers' intent regarding the separation of powers between the three branches of government, and I paid careful attention to any endeavor on a governor's part to weaken or abridge the legislative prerogative to make the law.... I didn't pursue this philosophy for any reason of self-aggrandizement. I believed, in fact, all that went on in the State House was a matter for the legislature, and the legislature only. It was the Executive Branch's job to enforce what we did; it wasn't their job to tell us what to do. The governors were never in agreement with this type of thinking, as 200 years of history had afforded them entrance into the process to exert great pressure on us.[30]

Despite the governor's advantages, the influence of the legislature should not be discounted. In the first place, on the overwhelming number of issues involved in lawmaking the legislature takes the initiative and the governor's role is secondary. Lobbyists and interest groups, for example, turn to the legislature to have their agendas enacted. In the second place, on those matters—relatively few in number—initiated by the governor, the legislature plays an important role in several respects. It works out the details, which can be extremely complicated. It modifies to its liking what the governor has proposed. And from time to time it turns down the governor's priority items.

Most important, the legislature rarely allows the governor a free hand on the budget. It may be the "governor's budget," but nearly always, the legislature contests key items and other important parts of it. The governor gets, but the governor also has to give, as is wonderfully illustrated by New York's intense budget negotiations year after year among Republican governor George Pataki, the Republican senate, and the Democratic assembly. It may be an uphill battle, but nearly everywhere the legislature struggles to balance an inherently stronger executive.

Conclusion

Legislatures do extraordinarily well in performing their representational functions. Their performance of the lawmaking function varies from state to state, but legislatures overall do a creditable job of handling divisive issues and dealing with serious problems. Where their performance may fall somewhat short is in balancing the power of the executive.

Legislatures, however, are given little credit for their generally effective performance. Indeed, one of the major challenges legislatures face today is the lack of public understanding and support. They are confronted instead by public cynicism and distrust. Except in a few states, people are negative toward their legislative institutions and processes, which are at the very foundation of representative democracy. This negativism is evidenced by the adoption of term limits by referendum in the overwhelming number of states where it went on the ballot.

Like their members, legislatures are imperfect—but the system has been working remarkably well. The question is, how long can legislatures continue to work as well without public understanding and support?

Notes

1. Frank Smallwood, *Free and Independent* (Brattleboro, Vt.: Stephen Greene Press, 1976); Tom Loftus, *The Art of Legislative Politics* (Washington, D.C.: CQ Press, 1994); Harriet Keyserling, *Against the Tide* (Columbia: University of South Carolina Press, 1998); James Richardson, *Willie Brown* (Berkeley: University of California Press, 1996).
2. Harold Lasswell, *Psychopathology and Politics* (New York: Viking Press, 1960).
3. James David Barber, *The Lawmakers* (New Haven: Yale University Press, 1965).
4. Karl T. Kurtz, Alan Rosenthal, and Cliff Zukin, *Citizenship: A Challenge for All Generations* (Denver: National Conference of State Legislatures, 2003), 9.
5. See Alan Rosenthal, "The Effects of Legislative Ethics Law: An Institutional Perspective," in *Ethical Governance*, ed. Denis St. Martin and Fred Thompson (New York: Oxford/Elsevier, forthcoming).
6. Loftus, *Art of Legislative Politics*, 8.
7. These and other data used here are from a nationwide survey undertaken as part of a term-limits study in which the author participated (hereafter referred to as "Term Limits Survey"). The survey was conducted in 2002 by the National Conference of State Legislatures, the Council of State Governments, and the State Legislative Leaders Foundation, along with fourteen political scientists. The survey findings are based on replies from 2,982 legislators (40.1 percent of those to whom questionnaires were mailed).
8. Alan Rosenthal, *Heavy Lifting: The Job of the American Legislature* (Washington, D.C.: CQ Press, 2004), 20.
9. Data from Term Limits Survey.
10. Data from Term Limits Survey.
11. Smallwood, *Free and Independent*, 221.
12. See Rosenthal, *Heavy Lifting*, 20–23.
13. Data from Term Limits Survey.
14. Alan Rosenthal, Burdett A. Loomis, John R. Hibbing, and Karl T. Kurtz, *Republic on Trial: The Case for Representative Democracy* (Washington, D.C.: CQ Press, 2003), 68–94.
15. Richardson, *Willie Brown*, 351, 365.
16. Keyserling, *Against the Tide*, 374.
17. This section is based on Alan Rosenthal, *The Decline of Representative Democracy* (Washington, D.C.: CQ Press, 1998), 54–71.
18. This section is drawn from Rosenthal, *Decline of Representative Democracy*, 133–145.
19. This section is drawn from Alan Rosenthal, "Is the Party Over? Trends in State Leg-

islative Parties," *Spectrum: The Journal of State Government* 75 (Fall 2002): 5–9.
20. See Richardson, *Willie Brown.*
21. Ralph Wright, *All Politics Is Personal* (Manchester Center, Vt.: Marshall Jones Company, 1996), 24–25; see also Wright's recent revision, *Inside the Statehouse* (Washington, D.C.: CQ Press, 2005).
22. This section is based on Rosenthal, *Heavy Lifting,* 57–164.
23. Loftus, *Art of Legislative Politics,* 7.
24. Smallwood, *Free and Independent.*
25. Data from Term Limits Survey.
26. Smallwood, *Free and Independent.*
27. Rosenthal, *Heavy Lifting,* 38–41.
28. The Term Limits Survey asked legislators which groups were among their strongest supporters. Of the respondents, 65 percent mentioned business; 58 percent, teachers; 48 percent, gun owners; 43 percent, labor; and 38 percent, pro-life groups.
29. Loftus, *Art of Legislative Politics,* 63.
30. Wright, *All Politics Is Personal,* 117–118.

4

Being Governor

Thad L. Beyle

Since the 1960s, state government and politics have been in a state of change. Reform has been most apparent in the governorships of the fifty states. Individually, governors have been strengthened and have become the key political and governmental leaders in their states. As a group, they have worked to solidify their position within the federal system but now find their roles within their states so compelling and difficult, especially with a federal government on retreat from domestic matters and an economy in trouble, that they have little time to spend on national concerns.

This change in the governorships has had ramifications in other areas of states' political and governmental policy systems. Conflicts have grown between the governors and certain other actors in the executive branches, as well as between governors and stronger state legislatures. The state supreme courts have become players in the political process, serving as umpire in some situations and as part of the conflict in others.

A strengthened governorship facing greater challenges has made the position more attractive. The type of politician that used to seek the office and the kind of person interested in running for it have changed. Dollar and consultant politics have replaced party leader and factional politics in many states.

With the political changes in the governorship came a change in the presidential recruitment process. In each of the eight presidential elections from 1976 to 2004, at least one of the major party candidates had served as a governor and four of them were elected president.

Two basic cycles have had a considerable effect on the states in the federal system and on the governors within the states and in the federal system. The first is the cycle of values undergirding the development of American government—representation, neutral competence, and executive leadership. The second is the cycle of leadership, which oscillates between the state and national levels—the shifting locus of activism within the federal system to provide government services.

Tensions between the values of representation, neutral competence, and executive leadership affect governors within their own state governmental systems. Shifting policy activism affects the governors within the federal system as responsibilities for various government services are transferred, in subtle and not so subtle ways, from states to the national government and, more recently, back to the states. These two cycles provide the setting in which states and governors function.

Governors as Chief Executive Officers

The office of governor has developed significantly since the establishment of colonial governments in America. After an initial period of imposed colonial executive dominance, the new state constitutions promoted the value of representation. Legislatures reigned supreme, with governors often serving as mere figureheads. By 1800 the situation began to change as the power and prestige of governors gradually increased. However, the direct election of some of the other state administrative officers was an important legacy of the pursuit of representation.

Following the Civil War, and in reaction to the excesses of achieving representation, the value of neutral competence gained in stature. The goal was to remove favoritism and patronage from government, substituting neutrality, or the concept of "not who you know, but what you know." This movement fostered the establishment of independent boards and commissions that diluted gubernatorial power. During this period, the drive for a civil service or merit system was launched. Thus, the goal of attaining neutral competence in government was added to the goal of representation. Thousands of state merit service employees were not only insulated from the winds of politics but also from management by the governor.

In the twentieth century, the need for strong executive leadership emerged. Woodrow Wilson, Democratic governor of New Jersey from 1911 to 1913, championed the cause, along with several other strong governors—Republican Charles Evans Hughes in New York (1907–1910), Republican Robert La Follette in Wisconsin (1901–1906), Republican and Progressive Hiram Johnson in California (1911–1917), and Republican Frank Lowden in Illinois (1917–1921).

The stature of governors has increased greatly across the states and in the federal system over the past few decades because of historic reforms, the type of individuals holding office, the actions taken under their direction, and an increased capacity in the office. Governors are now compared with private sector corporate leaders; they are public sector, state-level chief executive officers (CEOs). Expectations for gubernatorial performance have increased, perhaps beyond realistic levels.

Enhanced Capacity

Governors are responsible for running large enterprises that are similar in scope to Fortune 500 companies. For example, in 2003 the total expenditures of two states ranked with the sales in the top 50 corporations, and nine states had expenditures equal to or greater than the top 100 companies.[1]

The magnitude of the dollar decisions made by California administrators and legislators is comparable to those made by executives at American International Group and Hewlett-Packard, the tenth and eleventh largest companies; and those by New York State leaders to those by executives of Valero

Energy Co. and Marathon Oil Co., the thirty-fourth and thirty-fifth largest companies. Other states in range of the top 100 corporations are Texas, between fifty-second and fifty-third; New Jersey, between seventy-four and seventy-five; Ohio, between seventy-nine and eighty; Massachusetts, between eighty-three and eighty-four; Illinois, between eighty-four and eighty-five; and Florida and Pennsylvania, both between ninety-two and ninety-three.

Do the governors have adequate executive tools to manage such large enterprises? Are they as prepared to be the CEOs of their states as their private sector counterparts are to run businesses? Do the offices of the governors have the necessary capacity to assist the governors in managing their enterprises in state government?[2] Certainly, progress has been made. Since the early 1960s, no shortage of reforms has taken place throughout the states. The agenda for these reforms was drawn from changes at the national level initiated by the president and from a series of reports calling for reform in state governments.[3]

The general goals of government reforms have been to enhance gubernatorial and legislative abilities to lead the states in more progressive directions. In 1967 former North Carolina Democratic governor Terry Sanford called upon the states "to make the chief executive of the state the chief executive in fact"; a decade later political scientist Larry Sabato declared that executive branch reforms had made the governors "truly the masters" of state government.[4]

One common reform has been to lengthen the term of office. Since 1955, the number of governors eligible for four-year terms instead of two-year terms has increased from twenty-nine to forty-eight. This change allows governors to spend more time on policy and administrative concerns and less on reelection campaigns.[5] By 2005 only New Hampshire and Vermont still restricted their governors to a two-year term.

Another reform has increased opportunities for succession. Since 1955, the number of states precluding their governors from serving successive terms has declined from seventeen to just one—Virginia. The number of states allowing a governor to serve two consecutive terms has increased from six to thirty-five in 2005. Fourteen states in 2005 had no restrictions on the number of terms a governor could serve, despite a movement to impose term limits on many state-level officials in the last decade and a half. Changes in succession ability allow a governor to spend more time on policy and administrative concerns, that is, if the voters return the governor to office. Lifting term limitations also allows voters to retain a governor who is doing a good job.[6]

Yet another reform shortens the ballot, but the numbers indicate that more modifications are needed to reduce the still large number of separately elected executive branch officials. In 1955, 514 separately elected state-level officials, besides the governor, headed state agencies. In 1994, 511 separately elected officials, other than the governor, headed 260 state agencies in the fifty states.[7] In 12 major state offices, not too much change occurred: 308 officials, other than the governor, were separately elected in 2004 compared with 306 in

1972.[8] Fewer elective offices, and thus more appointed offices, would give the governor a broader policy and administrative reach and the citizens a governor with greater control of the executive branch of state government.

The final reform is the veto. Between 1955 and 1995 the number of governors who could veto all legislation rose only from forty-seven to forty-nine. The governor of North Carolina was the only one who lacked veto power. Finally, in 1995, toward the end of the third term of Gov. James B. Hunt Jr., the North Carolina legislature gave the voters the opportunity to amend the state constitution, which they did by a 3-to-1 ratio. As of 1995 the number of governors with an item veto had risen to forty-four. And ten governors had the power to cut specific spending items; twenty-six others had the power to veto substantive language in appropriations bills.[9]

Governors' offices have expanded rapidly over the past decades. In 1956 political scientist Coleman B. Ransone Jr. reported that governors' offices averaged 11 staff members, with a range from 3 to 43 among the states.[10] In 1976 the National Governors Association (NGA) found an average of 29 staff members, with a much broader range of 7 to 245.[11] In 2004 there were nearly 59 staff members per governor's office, with a range of 8 in Wyoming to 310 in Florida.[12] Thus, in nearly five decades, the average number of gubernatorial staff members grew slightly over fivefold. Increased staff means more flexibility and greater support for the governor in his or her many roles. Growth also creates more patronage positions—and more opportunity for confusion.

The configurations of gubernatorial staffs can be classified from the very personal to the very institutional. Their makeup correlates closely with the size of the state. Larger states have larger and more institutionalized offices and processes, with adequate and specialized staff resources to assist the governor. Smaller states have smaller and more personalized offices that often lack the breadth and depth possessed by those in larger states. In these offices, the governor must rely on a small pool of individuals to cover all the various responsibilities. In between are the growing mid-sized states. Here, a governor may feel the need for an institutionalized office but actually have only a small, personalized staffing structure and process at his or her disposal.[13]

A critical expression of gubernatorial authority is the budget process. A chief executive must be able to control the development and execution of the state's budget. Governors have consolidated their power over the budget process by placing state budget offices under their direct control. As of 2004, thirty-six governors had full responsibility for the budget, whereas fourteen others shared that responsibility with someone.[14] In so doing, they have refocused the budgetary process from an earlier preoccupation "with the custodial functions of auditing and accounting" to emphasizing "new and conceptually rich systems of management decision making."[15] The budget and the budgetary process remain mechanisms by which a governor controls a state's finances, but as the budget process has been opened to include planning and policy analysis approaches, the management capability of governors has been greatly enhanced. The budget can now more nearly be "the ultimate statement of any government's (and governor's) policy choices."[16]

The policy planning process is also critical. Initially seen as part of the economic development function of state government, and thus located in those departments, state planning agencies have been migrating closer to the governor. In 1960 only three of the thirty-seven state planning agencies were located in the governor's office; two others were housed in departments of administration and finance. A decade later all fifty states had state planning agencies. Twenty-nine were in the governor's office, and seven were in the departments of administration or finance.[17]

Many of these agencies became policy planning offices, taking on a broad set of activities and responsibilities. By 1988 all but five states had policy planning offices to assist the governor. These offices are usually located in the governor's office, within the budget office, or in the department of administration or finance. Policy planning agencies that stand free of the budget agency and process generally reflect strong governorships. Their close ties to the state's chief executive are indicative of their importance within the state's governmental system.[18]

What do these offices accomplish? A 1985 survey by the Council of State Planning Agencies indicated that they have two major responsibilities, varying in emphasis from state to state: policy development and administration.[19] The goal of policy planning offices is to see to it that factors other than narrow agency perspectives and purely budgetary or political concerns be brought to bear in the policy process.

The ability to reorganize government is a powerful tool. In 1956 only two governors had the power to initiate state government reorganization by executive order, subject to legislative confirmation; by 2004 twenty-three governors had this power.[20] During the 1960s many reformers argued that the residue of past trends and decisions had left state governments unmanageable and unresponsive to gubernatorial direction. Such criticism spurred the executive branches of nearly two dozen state governments to undertake comprehensive reorganization, and nearly all states engaged in partial reorganizations. In comprehensive reorganizations the executive branch is consolidated to various degrees under the control of the governor. Most partial reorganizations bring many programs and agencies working in the same functional area under one departmental roof. These reforms have been most prevalent in economic development, environmental protection, transportation, and human services.[21]

Reorganization enables a governor to reshape the executive branch for a variety of reasons. These include providing a clearer focus on particular problems and delivering government services efficiently. Additional steps that can be taken to allow governors to make state governments more focused and responsive include, for example, a decrease in the numbers of separately elected officials. Several states today would benefit from giving their governors the ability to initiate reorganization, subject to confirmation by the legislature.

Appointing and Removing Personnel

Chief executive officers, whether in the private or public sector, must be free to choose those who will serve in their administration. The power of appointment is a dual power, for it also includes the power to remove.

Many governors are constrained by the number and types of positions to which they can make appointments. First, governors cannot appoint any of the separately elected boards and commissions in a state. These boards are charged with responsibilities in public education, public utilities, higher education, and various regulatory activities, and in 1994 there were thirty-three separately elected boards and commissions in twenty-three states.[22]

Second, governors cannot appoint separately elected officials to office, except to fill a vacancy created by death or resignation. These officials have their own constitutional base of authority and their own constituency of supporters. In effect, most states operate under a plural executive model rather than the presidential model we see at the national level, in which the president and vice president are the only elected executive branch officials, and they are elected as a team. The number of statewide elected officials ranges from only the governor in Maine and New Jersey to twelve in North Dakota.[23]

Third, governors cannot appoint officials who by constitutional authority are to be appointed by some other officer or by the legislature. Some argue that this constraint is less than it seems, as those making some of these appointments are the governor's own appointees. Although this may be true in some states, in Texas, for example, boards and commissions in effect run much of state government. Because of the staggered terms of the officials appointed to these boards and commissions, a Texas governor may be well into a second term before gaining some control, and then only indirectly through the newly appointed members.[24] However, in her first year in office former governor Ann Richards (1991–1995) was able to get the legislature to provide her with more executive power by adding some important appointments to the governorship and giving it effective control over several others.[25]

Practical political concerns affect a governor's appointment choices.[26]

- The sheer number of appointments to be made can so overwhelm a governor that he or she may fail to focus sufficiently on key appointments. Replacing too many people can draw a governor too deeply into the bureaucracy, obviating any policy or administrative benefits.
- Patronage appointments serve as rewards, but many individuals and groups feel they should be rewarded. Appointments are evaluated with a jealous eye, and jealousy is not a positive basis on which to build a working relationship.
- Conflicting expectations over how an appointive office should be conducted can lead to struggles within the governor's coalition.

Coupled with the power of appointment is the power of removal. If changes in policy are needed, incumbent officeholders often must be replaced with those who will carry out the proposed reforms. In most situations key officeholders resign as a new administration comes in. But conflicts arise when resignations are not forthcoming or when a change in priorities elevates previously minor positions to importance, creating the need to appoint new officials to them.

Only twenty-three state constitutions provide governors with the power to remove individuals from positions in the state executive branch, and all but six put varying degrees of restrictions on this power. The power of removal is constrained in the original constitutions of just five states. However, as more constitutions are being revised, the power of removal is being built in. Eleven of the states that revised their constitutions after 1945 included this power for the governor. Other states provide statutory removal powers for their governors.

Governors can still experience problems exercising their right to remove personnel. Joseph Schlesinger noted that "even when a governor can remove an official, he is constrained by the wrangle which would result."[27] It is a power, therefore, that tends to be used only as a last resort. Moreover, a series of federal court decisions placed potentially severe restrictions on the removal power. In a 1976 case, *Elrod v. Burns,* the U.S. Supreme Court decided (5–4) that a patronage firing violates an individual's political liberties under the First Amendment. The ruling said that "political belief and association constitute the core of those activities protected by the First Amendment to the U.S. Constitution."[28]

This strict standard was relaxed in two subsequent decisions. In a 1980 case, *Branti v. Finkel,* the Court reaffirmed (6–3) its 1976 decision but also ruled that "if the employee's private political beliefs would interfere with the discharge of his public duties, the First Amendment rights may be required to yield to the state's vital interest in maintaining governmental effectiveness and efficiency." The burden of proof would be on the employer.[29] In a 1983 case, *Connick v. Myers,* the Court decided (5–4) to add another restriction on the employee's right by holding "that the First Amendment does not protect from dismissal public employees who complain about their working conditions or their supervisor."[30] In these cases, the Court indicated that a balance was needed between an individual's rights and the administration's needs, and it was the Court's role to weigh those conflicts.

Although none of these cases involved them, governors were aware of the problems the decisions could cause. At the 1982 "New Governors' Seminar," sponsored by the National Governors Association, the newly elected governors were cautioned:

> Know the *Elrod v. Burns* case, the 1976 five-to-four Supreme Court decision regarding the firing of personnel. You cannot fire for political reason, and you are personally liable. It even destroys the privacy privilege of counsel.
> The *Elrod v. Burns* decision requires an indemnification statute, and be sure that it covers the unpaid boards and commissions as well as full-time state officials.[31]

In 1990 the Court handed down a 5 to 4 ruling in *Rutan et al. v. Republican Party of Illinois* that directly affected the removal powers of governors. The decision, which focused on the patronage process of the Illinois governor's office in the administration of James R. Thompson (R, 1977–1991), said that state and local governments violate an individual's "First Amendment rights when they refuse to hire, promote or transfer . . . [an employee] on the basis of their political affiliation or party activity."[32]

The decision on how Thompson handled so-called blue-collar patronage—"the conventional doling out of state jobs to the party faithful"—struck down "the hiring freezes Thompson imposed, more or less continuously throughout his tenure . . . [as] merely patronage tools used to ensure that worthy Republicans got available state jobs." Thompson found the decision ironic as he had been chided by Republican Party leaders in the state for not being "grateful enough to those who labored in the GOP vineyards." Thompson, at the end of his tenure in office, said, "the Supreme Court of the United States certifies what these Republican chairmen refused to believe all along—that I had the best patronage machine in the nation, that it was a Republican machine."[33]

Gubernatorial Powers

Political scientists and other researchers have often attempted to compare the powers of the fifty state governors—both qualitatively and more recently quantitatively. In 1965 political scientist Joseph Schlesinger published the first comparative quantitative gubernatorial power index, and it has served as the foundation of subsequent indexes and updates. At its base are the governor's appointment power, budget-making power, tenure potential, and veto power. It has been updated and expanded over the decades, including in this author's five chapters on governors in later editions of the book in which Schlesinger's original analysis appeared.[34]

In 1987 the NGA Office of State Services issued a State Management Note in which the same questions pertaining to the comparative institutional powers of the governors were addressed. The NGA concluded that "the framework in which a governor performs his or her job can be an important factor in a successful governorship." It noted that the indexes were used only as a suggestion of the framework and that some "governors have proven to be vital and strong leaders in many areas despite institutional shortcomings that may hamper their success," whereas others "have failed to provide strong leadership to their states even where formal provisions indicate an authoritative office."[35]

The NGA analysis included the four main items in the Schlesinger index—appointment powers, budget-making power, tenure potential, veto power—and two additional measures: the governor's political strength in the legislature and the legislature's ability to change gubernatorial budgets. The first three indices primarily concern the governor's power within the executive

Table 4-1 Governors' Institutional Powers

Institutional Power (range)	National Governors Association		
	1965	1985	Change (%)
Appointments (0–7)	3.8	4.0	+ 5.3
Budget making (1–5)	4.5	4.8	+ 6.7
Tenure potential (1–5)	3.3	4.1	+24.4
Veto power (1–5)	4.2	3.6	−14.3
Party control (1–5)	3.8	3.4	−10.5
Legislative budget-changing power (1–5)	1.3	1.2	−7.7
Average score	20.9	21.1	+ 1.0
Possible range	5–32	5–32	—
Actual range	14–29	16–27	—

Formal Power (range)	Schlesinger/Beyle		
	1960	2005	Change (%)
Separately elected officials (1–5)	2.3	2.9	+28
Tenure potential (1–5)	3.2	4.1	+28
Appointment power (1–5)	2.9	3.1	+7
Budget power (1–5)	3.6	3.1	−14
Veto power (1–5)	2.8	4.5	+61
Gubernatorial party control (1–5)	3.6	3.0	−17
Totals (6–30)	18.4	20.7	+12.5

Sources: NGA index: Office of State Services, "The Institutionalized Powers of the Governorship, 1965–1985," in *Management Note* (Washington, D.C.: National Governors Association, June 1987), 12–13; Schlesinger/Beyle index: www.unc.edu/~beyle.

Note: Scores = total divided by six to keep 5-point scale; dashes = not applicable; total = sum of the scores on the six individual indexes.

branch; the second three concern the governor's power vis-à-vis the legislature (Table 4-1).[36]

According to the NGA indexes, governorships experienced minimal growth in strength. Between 1965 and 1985, out of a total of 32 possible points, the average score rose from 20.9 to just 21.1—slightly less than a 1 percent increase overall. Appointment and budget-making power indicators held at about the same level, whereas tenure potential increased, and the control of the legislature by the governor's party and veto power decreased. This latter decline was due primarily to the effects of an increasing number of states with a "powersplit"—a situation in which the governor faces a legislature controlled either totally or in part by the opposition party.[37]

Since World War II, the power of the political parties in the states has declined.[38] Nowhere is this more apparent than in the increasing number of states faced with a powersplit. In 1954 nine of the then forty-eight states (19 percent) had a politically divided state government, mainly in states outside the South. By the mid-1960s only thirteen of the fifty states (26 percent) were divided politically, again mainly outside the South.

Now, in 2005, twenty-nine of the fifty state governors (58 percent) face a legislature controlled by the opposition either totally or partially. Montana's situation is unique in that one member of the state house lost his position in a December 2004 state supreme court case, leaving the parties with fifty members each. But because the newly elected governor of 2004 was a Democrat, the Democrats received the ability to organize the state house and were placed in the leadership position—and the Democrats hold a four-seat margin in the state senate.

In Table 4-1 we can see greater change in the governors' formal powers between 1960 and 2005 than between 1965 and 1985. Governors gained the most power in their veto power ability, especially when the North Carolina governor was granted this power in the mid-1990s, as noted earlier. Also as noted earlier, governors gained some powers in regard to other statewide elected executive officials and in their tenure potential. They did not gain much in their appointment power and actually lost some power in the budgetary area owing to reforms to the legislative budgetary power.

The governorships with the most formal power in 2005 on the five-point scale were Alaska, New Jersey, and West Virginia at 4.1 and Utah at 4.0. One quick observation on these states with the most powerful offices: in 2004 the Democratic governor of New Jersey, James McGreevey, resigned because of a developing sex scandal; the governor of West Virginia, Democrat Bob Wise, decided not to seek reelection owing to his low job approval ratings in state polls and some bad publicity; and the governor of Utah, Republican Olene Walker, was denied a spot on her own party's primary ballot to seek another term. So, being in a powerful office does not guarantee a successful reign or a second term. The states with the weakest ranking were Rhode Island at 2.6; Alabama, New Hampshire, and Oklahoma at 2.8; and Mississippi at 2.9.

These findings demonstrate what many have suggested: reforms have been made on both sides of the separation-of-powers relationship, and although governors may now have more formal, institutionalized powers at their disposal (budget-making, tenure potential, veto), state legislatures possess powers that are often used at the expense of the executive (budget-changing authority, party control).

The irony of a powersplit is that as reformers successfully change or enhance institutions at the state level, a growing malaise in the political world undermines the abilities of certain key, state-level actors to follow through on those reforms. Some decry this situation as detrimental to effective government, but at least one observer suggests that it may actually lead to better policy through forcing necessary compromises that take in many points of view.[39]

Gubernatorial Conflict with Other State Government Actors

Political reforms do not always achieve their intended purposes. Some create unanticipated consequences that then generate additional reforms; others create conflict with previous reforms. And politics may render some reforms unworkable.

Conflicts within the Executive Branch

Governors often face their greatest conflicts within the executive branch itself. Several governors have had serious problems with the lieutenant governor's power while the governor was out of state. For example, conflict has arisen over calling special legislative sessions, appointments to administrative and judicial positions, pardons, the governor's salary, and control of the state's National Guard. Other problems have come about when the governor and the lieutenant governor were of different parties or different factions within the same party. Also, difficulties have emerged when the lieutenant governor had constitutional leadership responsibilities in the legislature that provided a separate power base.

Governors have at times found themselves at odds with the state's attorney general when legal issues took on a political cast. An attorney general may challenge a gubernatorial action in court on constitutional grounds. Who is to serve as the governor's legal adviser in such a case? Alternatively, who is to lead the prosecution of a governor when he or she has been accused of wrongdoing? This problem arose during the impeachment of Arizona governor Evan Mecham (R, 1987–1988).

Finally, governors must face other statewide elected officials intent on seeking the governorship. In the 371 gubernatorial elections between 1977 and 2004, lieutenant governors were candidates in 100 of the races (27 percent) and won 28 of them (28 percent). In the same period, attorneys general were candidates in 83 of the races (22 percent) and won 21 of them (25 percent). Over these twenty-seven years state treasurers were candidates in 22 of the races (6 percent), winning 6 of them (27 percent).[40] Two recent situations indicate how potentially lethal this can be. In 2002 Republican governor Scott McCallum of Wisconsin was defeated in his bid for another term by the Democratic attorney general, and in 2004 Missouri governor Bob Holden's bid for a second term was derailed in the Democratic primary by Democratic state auditor Claire McCaskill. Obviously, under such circumstances, conflict instead of cooperation is often the rule.

Conflicts with Other Branches of Government

With the concept of separation of powers built into state constitutions and the American constitutional system, conflict between the executive and the legislative branches is inevitable. Conflicts may occur over setting state government policy, raising and spending money, administering policy, appointing officials to executive and judicial positions, controlling the legislative process, and calling special sessions.

When the governor and the legislature are of opposite parties, conflict can take on a divisive partisan tone. If gubernatorial and legislative leaders have conflicting ambitions, strife may result between the branches. In the 371 gubernatorial races between 1977 and 2004, state house Speakers were candidates in 27 of the races (7 percent) and won 9 of them (33 percent).[41]

Gubernatorial-legislative tensions are greatest in most states at budget time, when the money and policy decisions must be made. It is the "governor's budget," but it must be passed by the legislature—and it also must be balanced. Dollar decisions become particularly difficult to make in the harsh economic times we have experienced in the early 1990s and early 2000s. Budget makers face declining resources coupled with increasing demands for services and assistance. Skeptics aside, however, some states are able to rise to the challenge of getting a workable budget passed and signed into law by elevating the level of cooperation between the two branches.

The execution of the budget by the governor leads to a second area of potential conflict—the legislature's interest in how the budget items are administered. Legislatures have tried several ways to make sure legislative intent is followed. Governors often read these efforts as legislative intrusion into executive branch responsibilities. For example, some executive branch positions are appointments that must be confirmed by the legislature. However, some state legislatures have either constitutional or statutory authority to make appointments. In certain cases, they can appoint legislators to boards, commissions, or councils in the executive branch. If these bodies maintain an advisory role, problems may not arise. However, if they exercise management responsibilities, as twenty states allowed in the mid-1980s, charges of legislative intrusion may be lodged and challenged in state courts as a violation of separation of powers.[42]

Another area of conflict concerns vetoes, both gubernatorial and legislative. In 1947 governors vetoed about 5 percent of the bills presented to them. These vetoes were overridden by a legislative vote in only 1.8 percent of the cases.[43] In the 1992–1993 legislative years, 5.6 percent of the bills presented to the governor were vetoed; 3.2 percent of these vetoes were overridden. However, in these averages there were some interesting extremes: Gov. Ned McWherter, D-Tenn., did not veto a single bill presented to him, whereas Gov. Pete Wilson, R-Calif., vetoed 21 percent of the bills presented to him, none of which was overridden.[44] In the four years of his fourth and last term in office, Gov. Jim Hunt, D-N.C., did not veto a single bill presented to him even though he was the first governor in North Carolina to have the veto power—clearly, he knew how to get what he wanted from the state legislature.

As the ability of governors to use the item and amendatory vetoes grows, conflicts with the legislative branch escalate. A governor can veto special policy provisions in budget bills that have not run the full course of legislative review, thereby forcing the legislature to consider the issues in open debate.[45]

Conflicts between the executive and legislative branches of state government have increasingly gone before state courts for resolution. These courts usually decide in favor of the governor and the executive branch, citing the separation-of-powers clause in the state's constitution.[46] However, they sometimes rule against the executive when separation of powers is not in question, as in policy and civil rights issues.

Governors and judges are often at odds over specific decisions, such as the death penalty or the selection of judges. In 1986 three states—California, North Carolina, and Ohio—had highly contested, negative, policy-related contests for the chief judgeship of the state's supreme court. In all these races the incumbent governors were actively involved in judicial politics.

A new area of contention has been brewing between governors and legislatures on one side and the courts on the other. As governors propose and legislatures adopt state budgets with severe cuts in appropriations, the courts, like all parts of state government, find themselves unable to fulfill their responsibilities with the reduced amounts of available funds. Can the courts force the other two branches to take the necessary monetary actions, including raising taxes, to ensure that the courts receive enough money to operate? According to experiences in fourteen states, yes, they can. In September 1991 the chief judge of New York's State Court of Appeals, that state's highest appellate court, filed suit charging that the governor and the legislature failed to provide the courts with adequate funds—a violation of the state constitution.

Another area of conflict with governors and legislatures on one side and the courts on the other side concerns funding of K-12 education across a state. State constitutions often call for equal education opportunities for certain students in elementary and secondary schools, but since many states rely on local property taxes to support primary and secondary education there are great discrepancies in how these levels of education are financed—and hence great discrepancies in the type of education students receive in a state. Law suits in state courts have challenged this situation, and the courts have generally sided with those filing the suits. Hence, the court decisions demand that the governor and the state legislatures rectify this situation. This means major shifts in money in the state budget, even to the point of raising taxes, especially from those who can afford such increases. These are tough decisions for legislators and governors to make.

Measuring Gubernatorial Performance

Gubernatorial performance can be rated in several ways. The first and most obvious way is by the voters when they decide whether or not to reelect an incumbent governor. Table 4-2 provides a picture of gubernatorial elections from 1970 to 2004 and indicates just how well incumbent governors have fared in their reelection bids.

Table 4–2 Gubernatorial Elections, 1970–2004

Year	Number of races	Number of Democratic winners	Number of incumbent governors			
			Eligible to run	Ran	Won	Lost in primary	Lost in general election
1970	35	22 (63)	29 (83)	24 (83)	16 (64)	1	7
1971	3	3 (100)	0	—	—	—	—
1972	18	11 (61)	15 (83)	11 (73)	7 (64)	2	2
1973	2	1 (50)	1 (50)	1 (100)	—	1	—
1974	35	28 (80)[a]	29 (83)	22 (76)	17 (77)	1	4
1975	3	3 (100)	2 (66)	2 (100)	2 (100)	—	—
1976	14	9 (64)	12 (86)	8 (67)	5 (63)	1	2
1977	2	1 (50)	1 (50)	1 (100)	1 (100)	—	—
1978	36	21 (58)	29 (81)	23 (79)	16 (73)	2	5
1979	3	2 (67)	0	—	—	—	—
1980	13	6 (46)	12 (92)	12 (100)	7 (58)	2	3
1981	2	1 (50)	0	—	—	—	—
1982	36	27 (75)	33 (92)	25 (76)	19 (76)	1	5
1983	3	3 (100)	1 (33)	1 (100)	—	1	—
1984	13	5 (38)	9 (69)	6 (67)	4 (67)	—	2
1985	2	1 (50)	1 (50)	1 (100)	1 (100)	—	—
1986	36	19 (53)	24 (67)	18 (75)	15 (83)	1	2
1987	3	3 (100)	2 (67)	1 (50)	—	1	—
1988	12	5 (42)	9 (75)	9 (100)	8 (89)	—	1
1989	2	2 (100)	0	—	—	—	—
1990	36	19 (53)[b]	33 (92)	23 (70)	17 (74)	—	6
1991	3	2 (67)	2 (67)	2 (100)	—	1	1
1992	12	8 (67)	9 (75)	4 (44)	4 (100)	—	—
1993	2	0	1 (50)	1 (100)	—	—	1
1994	36	11 (31)[a]	30 (83)	23 (77)	17 (74)	2	4
1995	3	1 (33)	2 (67)	1 (50)	1 (100)	—	—
1996	11	7 (36)	9 (82)	7 (100)	7 (100)	—	—
1997	2	0	1 (50)	1 (100)	1 (100)	—	—
1998	36	11 (31)[b]	27 (75)	25 (93)	23 (92)	—	2
1999	3	2 (67)	2 (67)	2 (100)	2 (100)	—	—
2000	11	8 (73)	7 (88)	6 (86)	5 (83)	—	1

Table 4–2 *(continued)*

Year	Number of races	Number of Democratic winners	Number of incumbent governors				
			Eligible to run	Ran	Won	Lost in primary	Lost in general election
2001	2	2 (100)	0	—	—	—	—
2002	36	14 (39)	22 (61)	16 (73)	12 (75)	—	4
2003	4[c]	0	2 (50)	2 (100)	0	—	2
2004	11	6 (55)	11 (100)	8 (73)	4 (50)	2	2
Totals	481	264 (55)	367 (76)	286 (78)	211 (74)	19 (25)	56 (75)

Sources: Council of State Governments, *The Book of the States, 2005* (Lexington, Ky.: Council of State Governments, 2005), 192; and selected issues of *Congressional Quarterly Weekly Report.*

Note: Percentages are given in parentheses; dashes indicate none in that category.

a. One Independent candidate won.

b. Two Independent candidates won.

c. The California recall election and replacement vote of 2003 is included in the 2003 election numbers, and as a general election in the last column.

During the period 1970–2004, there were 481 separate gubernatorial elections in the fifty states. In 114 of these contests (24 percent), the incumbent governor was term limited and could not seek reelection; 81 others (17 percent) decided against seeking another term. Reasons for not seeking reelection could include a decision to retire from public life, a desire to return to the more lucrative private sector, a bid to seek a higher office—usually a U.S. Senate seat-or simply an acceptance of the futility of attempting reelection in the face of negative media and dissatisfied voters.

Of the 286 incumbent governors who did seek reelection, 211 of them (74 percent) won another term in office. Thus nearly three-quarters of the incumbent governors facing the electorate passed the "gubernatorial performance test."

Of the 75 incumbent governors defeated in their bids for reelection, 56 of them (75 percent) lost in the general election, whereas 19 (25 percent) failed to receive their own party's renomination in the primary. These defeated incumbents came from all parts of the country, although there was a greater tendency for them to be from the South (26) and Midwest (22) than from the Northeast (15) or West (12). The hardest state on incumbents is Texas, where five incumbents have been defeated for reelection since 1970, followed by Alabama and New Hampshire, where four incumbents in each state met the same fate.

The unsuccessful incumbents were almost evenly split between Democrats (38) and Republicans (37), with primary losers more likely to be Democrats (13) than Republicans (6) and general election losers slightly more likely to be Republicans (31) than Democrats (25). Republican incumbent losses were more pronounced in the 1970s; Democratic losses have been spread fairly equally over the three decades, but with an uptick in the 2000 races.

A second way to measure gubernatorial performance is through use of the rapidly growing number of statewide opinion polls that ask respondents how well they feel their governor is performing his or her job. These statewide polls are conducted by an array of individuals and organizations, ranging from university institutes, to the media, to political parties, to political candidates, to professional pollsters. Questions are asked of samples of adults, of registered voters, and of likely voters. The results of these polls are disseminated through the media and become a political fact of some importance to those serving as governors.

For example, three incumbent governors decided not to seek reelection in 2004, in part because of low job approval ratings. Judy Martz, R-Mont., with only a 20 percent positive job approval rating; Gary Locke, D-Wash., with only a 33 percent positive job approval rating; and Bob Wise, D-W. Va., with only a 39 percent positive job approval rating saw themselves facing an electorate that was more negative than positive on their job performance-not a good way to start out on a campaign for reelection.

Table 4–3 presents gubernatorial performance ratings taking the 2005 incumbent governors by "class"—that is, the year the governor was first elected or succeeded to office for his or her current tenure. Overall, these forty-one governors for which such ratings are available had an average positive job approval rating of 54 percent as of August 2005. This average masks a considerable range of approval ratings—from 83 percent for Mike Rounds, R-S.D., and 79 percent for Jodi Rell, R-Conn., to 19 percent for Bob Taft, R-Ohio. Twenty-nine of the governors are currently holding positive ratings in excess of 50 percent. On average, Democratic governors had slightly higher job approval ratings: 55.4 percent versus the Republicans' 52.4 percent.

One comment on Rell's high ratings: As lieutenant governor she succeeded to the governor's chair in July 2004 upon the resignation of third-term governor John Rowland, a Republican, who was facing a criminal indictment over corruption charges and a possible impeachment effort by the state legislature. In December 2004 he pled guilty to one count of corruption and is now serving a federal prison sentence. Rell obviously was a positive relief as the new governor after that previous governor's scandalous situation.

One striking aspect of these ratings is their diversity within classes. For example, in the Class of 2002 there is a fifty-eight-point difference between the highest rating of 83 percent (for Governor Rounds of South Dakota) and the lowest rating of 25 percent (for Governor Riley of Alabama). In the Class of 2004 there is a forty-three-point difference between the top rating of 79 percent (for Governor Rell of Connecticut) and the lowest rating of 36 percent (for Governor Christine Gregoire of Washington).

One comment on New Jersey governor Richard Codey's rating. As pres-

Table 4–3 Job Approval Ratings of Current Governors, Mid-2005

Class, governor, party, state	Highest/lowest rating (%)	Most recent rating (%)
Class of 2004		
M. Jodi Rell, R-Conn.	83/73	79 (7/05)
Jon Huntsman, R-Utah	62	62 (1/05)
John Lynch, D-N.H.	61/43	61 (7/05)
Brian Schweitzer, D-Mont.	57	57 (5/05)
Mitch Daniels, R-Ind.	55	55 (3/05)
Richard J. Codey, D-N.J.	76/41	44 (4/05)
Christine Gregoire, D-Wash.	43/36	36 (8/05)
Class of 2003		
Kathleen Babineaux Blanco, D-La.	69/60	69 (12/04)
Ernie Fletcher, R-Ky.	53/52	52 (2/05)
Arnold Schwarzenegger, R-Calif.	69/34	34 (8/05)
Class of 2002		
Mike Rounds, R-S.D.	83/69	83 (5/04)
Brad Henry, D-Okla.	72	72 (6/05)
Phil Bredesen, D-Tenn.	72/56	72 (2/04)
James E. Doyle, D-Wis.	68/34	62 (5/05)
Donald L. Carcieri, R-R.I.	72/57	57 (6/05)
Linda Lingle, R-Hawaii	71/56	56 (8/04)
Tim Pawlenty, R-Minn.	60/49	56 (5/05)
Jennifer M. Granholm, D-Mich.	77/51	54 (8/05)
Janet Napolitano, D-Ariz.	79/46	53 (7/05)
Sonny Perdue, R-Ga.	62/45	53 (8/05)
Robert L. Ehrlich, Jr., R-Md.	59/51	51 (4/05)
John Baldacci, D-Maine	72/43	50 (7/05)
Mitt Romney, R-Mass.	60/44	50 (8/05)
Jim Douglas, R-Vt.	48/43	48 (4/04)
Edward G. Rendell, D-Pa.	54/37	46 (7/05)
Theodore R. Kulongoski, D-Ore.	46/41	46 (6/05)
Frank H. Murkowski, R-Alaska	36	36 (3/03)
Rod R. Blagojevich, D-Ill.	58/35	35 (5/05)
Bob Riley, R-Ala.	69/25	25 (11/03)
Class of 2001		
Mark Warner, D-Va.	74/56	74 (7/05)
Rick Perry, R-Texas	67/37	51 (2/05)
Class of 2000		
John Hoeven, R-N.D.	75	75 (2/03)
Michael F. Easley, D-N.C.	62/40	55 (6/05)
Class of 1998		
Bill Owens, R-Colo.	70/48	65 (10/02)
Tom Vilsack, D-Iowa	73/48	56 (5/05)
Jeb Bush, R-Fla.	62/49	55 (8/05)

(continued)

Table 4-3 *(continued)*

Class, governor, party, state	Highest/lowest rating (%)	Most recent rating (%)
Kenny Guinn, R-Nev.	53/43	53 (9/99)
Dirk Kempthorne, R-Idaho	43	43 (6/02)
Bob Taft, R-Ohio	69/19	19 (6/05)
Class of 1996		
Mike Huckabee, R-Ark.	70/50	50 (10/02)
Class of 1994		
George E. Pataki, R-N.Y.	81/34	49 (8/05)
Averages: All Govs, 53.6; Dem. Govs, 55.4; Rep Govs, 52.4		

Source: Author, www.unc.edu/~beyle.

Note: Dates of most recent ratings are given in parentheses.

ident of the New Jersey State Senate he became acting governor upon the resignation of Gov. Jim McGreevey in November 2004 over a building scandal tied to his homosexuality. Codey had to stay in his position as president of the Senate because that is why he was named acting governor. Should he resign the Senate presidency, he would cease being acting governor. Hence, he holds two major state-level elected positions until the 2005 elections determine who the next governor will be.

A third way to measure gubernatorial performance is to ask a sample of interested observers to rate the governors. In the summer of 1994 I asked some 388 political scientists, members of the media, and other knowledgeable individuals how they felt their governors were doing.[47] This reading of the incumbent governors by these interested observers found considerable consistency with how the public sized up their governor's performance.

Where there were differences, the public was more volatile in their views on governmental performance. Interested observers were neither as negative nor as positive as the public was in their ratings.

One interesting finding of this survey was the correlation between how well governors interacted with the media, the executive branch, and the state legislature and how highly they were rated.[48] Governors who maintained solid relationships with the media generally received higher ratings. This should come as no surprise as public knowledge and feelings toward a governor are most readily shaped by the nature of media coverage, be it negative or positive.

Some Changes Afoot in the Governorships

Several changes have occurred in the governorship in recent years that are of interest. They range from the increasing costs of gubernatorial races, to the changes in just who governors are, to a rising number of governors who are forced to leave office for a variety of reasons.

Increasing Cost of Gubernatorial Elections

Over the past three decades the cost of gubernatorial elections has risen considerably. By the mid-1970s, after the Watergate and some other political campaign scandals in the states, state governments began adopting campaign finance regulations and reporting requirements. So beginning in 1977 we have a continuing picture of just how much money is spent on the gubernatorial campaigns in all the states (Table 4–4).[49]

In the 1977 to 1980 cycle of gubernatorial elections, the 428 candidates in the 54 races spent nearly $508 million in 2004 dollars for an average of $9.4 million per race.[50] In the most recent cycle of gubernatorial elections, 2001 to 2004, the more than 475 candidates in 53 races spent over $1.161 billion for an average of $21.9 million per race. That is an increase of 129 percent over the nearly three decades. Over the entire period 1977 to 2004, candidates spent nearly $5.055 billion in the 371 separate gubernatorial races for an average of just over $13.6 million per race.

Table 4–4 Gubernatorial Election Expenditures, 1977–2004 (in 2004 dollars)

Years	Races	Expenditures in 2004 dollars[a]	Average per race	% + last 4-year total
1977–1980	54	507,809,366	9,403,877	—
1981–1984	54	575,236,643	10,652,530	+13.3
1985–1988	53	656,859,546	12,393,576	+14.1
1989–1992	53	709,404,283	13,384,986	+ 8.0
1993–1996	52	716,055,943	13,770,307	+ 0.9
1997–2000	52	727,522,632	13,990,820	+ 1.6
2001–2004	53[b]	1,161,314,683[c]	21,911,598	+59.7
Totals	371	5,054,203,096	13,623,189	+128.7[d]

Source: Author, www.unc.edu/~beyle.

Note: Dash = not applicable.

a. 2004 dollars—Using the 2004 CPI Index, which was 1.889 of the 1982–1984 Index = 1.000. Converted the actual expenses for each of the years by dividing the CPI Index figure for the year involved by the 2004 CPI figure, then divided the total expenditures for that year by the result. For example, the 1977 CPI Index figure was .606 and that divided by the 2004 CPI Index figure = .321. The 1977 actual expenditures of $12,312,383 divided by .321 = $38,356,333 in 2004 dollars.

b. Includes the 2003 California recall and replacement election.

c. Includes the expenditures by the California candidates for the replacement election.

d. The percentage increase between the 1977–1980 cycle of elections and the 2001–2004 cycle of elections.

The greatest changes occurred in the 2001–2004 cycle, when the costs jumped by more than 59 percent over the 1997–2000 cycle. Four states had races that cost over $110 million each, with the 2002 New York race costing just over $154 million, followed by the 1998 California race costing over $143 million, the 2002 California race costing just over $115 million, and the 2002 Texas race costing just under $111 million.

Why this upward surge in the costs of gubernatorial elections? The first and major reason has been the changes that have been going on in how these campaigns are waged. Very few, if any, candidates let the party or a faction of a party run their campaigns. The candidates now develop their own personal party by using outside consultants, opinion polls, creating media ads and buying time on the media to run them, and making extensive fund-raising efforts to pay for this new approach. And the old "ground war" campaigns, when candidates worked the streets and factory gates, have been replaced by "air war" campaigns that rely on television ads as the basic way to contact potential voters. The cost of these television ad campaigns is growing, as it costs a lot to get the right consultants to develop and then place the ads—and with greater use of them also come higher costs. Few states would be surprised by a high-price, high-tech campaign now.

Another factor is the increasing number of candidates who are either wealthy or have access to wealth and are willing to tap those resources to achieve their goal of becoming a governor. Raising and spending a lot of money can win elections. For example, California governor Gray Davis spent over $67.5 million in his successful reelection bid in 2002, and New York governor George Pataki spent over $46.4 million in his successful bid for a third term in 2002. But spending a lot of money doesn't always guarantee a win. For example, in the 2002 New York election, Independent candidate Thomas Golisano spent over $80.1 million and came in third with only 14 percent of the vote. In the 2002 Texas race, Democratic candidate Tony Sanchez also spent over $80.1 million but lost when he received only 40 percent of the vote. Both lost to a successful incumbent seeking reelection to another term. Although money does count, so does a successful incumbency.

More Diversity in the Governor's Chair

In the last few decades the diversity in who becomes a governor has grown. Obviously, as the old Solid Democratic South became more competitive, considerable growth was seen in the number of Republican governors in these previously one-party, Democratic states.[51] In 1960 thirteen of the fourteen southern governors were Democrats, and all twenty-eight state legislative chambers were controlled by Democrats. Forty-five years later, in 2005, a Republican sat in eight of these gubernatorial chairs to only six Democrats, and the control of the twenty-eight legislative chambers was almost equal, with Democrats holding a 15-to-13 edge.

There have also been some surprises in particular states in regard to who won a gubernatorial race. In the 1989 Virginia election, Douglas Wilder, a Democrat, won and became the first black American elected to the office, and in the Washington state elections in 1996 and 2000, Democrat Gary Locke became the first governor of Chinese descent ever elected to the governor's chair.[52] We have also seen a few Independents elected to become governor in the states of Alaska, Connecticut, Maine, and Minnesota as they defeated rival candidates of the two major parties.[53]

Finally, women have risen to the governorship in greater numbers.[54] This trend has three distinct phases. In the first phase, prior to the passage of the Nineteenth Amendment to the U.S. Constitution in 1920 granting women the right to vote, no woman had ever served as governor. Then over the next five decades, three women were elected governor—but they were all women married to a governor or former governor who was not eligible for reelection.[55] In this second phase, women's political strength was their marriage to former and well-known governors, who helped get them elected and wanted to keep their hands on what was happening in the governor's office.

The most recent phase began in the 1970s and continues to this day. Now the women who become governor are politicians who are moving up the state's political ladder and win the governor's chair in their own right. Ella Grasso, D-Conn., was the first to succeed in this fashion in 1974, followed by Dixie Lee Ray, D-Wash., in 1976. Several other women became governor in these recent decades when, while serving as lieutenant governor, they succeeded a governor who had died or left office.

Now, in the first years of the twenty-first century, twelve women have become governor, nine elected in their own right[56] and three as lieutenant governors succeeding a departing governor.[57] In the last half of 2004, nine women were serving as governor, and in 2005, eight. More will be expected in the future as the diversity of who wins or succeeds to the governors' chairs increases. As of 2005 seventy-two women had been elected to statewide elective offices other than the governorship. They included sixteen lieutenant governors, twelve secretaries of state, seven state treasurers, and five state attorneys general, and more than a few of them are now waiting in the wings for their turn to seek the governorship in a future election.[58]

Gubernatorial Removals and Exits

There are ways for governors to leave office other than by being defeated in a primary or general election, by accepting an appointment to another office, or by retiring.[59] In the last three decades we have seen nine governors leave office because of problems they faced over their actions either prior to or while serving as governor. One governor was impeached, convicted, and removed from office by the state legislature, and another governor resigned from the office as the state legislature began to threaten an impeachment over some of his actions while serving in the office for nearly three terms.[60] Two others were removed from office following a criminal conviction in a federal or state court, and two others resigned after a criminal conviction in federal court.[61]

In a unique removal in 1979, Governor Ray Blanton, D-Tenn., found his term in office shortened by several days and the locks on his gubernatorial office changed so neither he nor his staff could enter the office to remove or destroy potentially incriminating evidence. Governor-elect Lamar Alexander was thus sworn into office three days early. This was tied to a bipartisan agreement with FBI investigators looking into allegations that Blanton and his staff were selling pardons to state prisoners in the last days of his tenure.[62] He later was tried and found guilty of charges of accepting bribes while governor and served time in federal prison.

In 2003 we witnessed a startling political event—a grassroots initiative to recall Gov. Gray Davis, D-Calif, from office less than a year after he had won reelection to his second term as governor in 2002 with 3,469,025 votes (47.4 percent of the vote). The initiative effort was certified in July 2003, and two questions were placed on the early October ballot for the California voters: "Should Gray Davis be recalled from the office of governor?" and "If Davis is recalled, who should replace him?" The nearly 9 million voters decided 55.4 percent to 44.6 percent that he should be recalled. Davis thus became only the second state governor ever to be recalled from office.[63]

The replacement question was complicated by the filings of more than 140 individuals to be candidates, and in August 2003, 135 of them were certified to run on the early October ballot. They included 49 Democrats, 42 Republicans, 33 Independents, and 11 candidates from six minor parties, so there were no official party candidates on this ballot. Although most candidates were not well known to the voters, attention did focus on the former Los Angeles mayor Bill Simon, a Republican, whom Davis had defeated in the 2002 gubernatorial election; Lt. Gov. Cruz Bustamante, a Democrat; state senator Tom McClintock, a Republican; and actor, bodybuilder, and businessman Arnold Schwarzenegger, a Republican. The well-known Schwarzenegger won with 48.6 percent of the vote, followed by Bustamante with 31.5 percent and McClintock with 13.5 percent. They were the only candidates to receive more than 1 million votes of the 8.348 million votes cast on this question.

Then, in 2004, two governors resigned from office. As already noted, John Rowland, R- Conn., resigned on June 30 over a threatened impeachment possibility. Then Gov. Jim McGreevey, D-N.J., announced that in November he would resign because of his homosexuality and his relationship with a male appointee while in office. So in two years three incumbent governors left office in some sort of trouble—a message that other governors surely have heard clearly.

Governors in Association

Governors have taken significant steps to revitalize and redirect multistate organizations during the last few decades. Foremost among these organizations is the National Governors Association. The NGA's precursor emerged in 1908 after a call by President Theodore Roosevelt to the governors to meet with him to discuss conservation issues.

Getting Organized

For many years, the governors met regularly as the Governors' Conference to discuss a broad agenda, with the Council of State Governments (CSG) serving as secretary. During the mid-1960s, as federal grant-in-aid programs proliferated and the federal government intruded further into the states in the form of Lyndon Johnson's Great Society programs, the governors felt the need for a more permanent organization. They set up an office in Washington, D.C., to press their views, interests, and needs upon the federal government. State legislative and local government leaders were taking similar steps.

The strong showing of state executive and legislative organizations in the nation's capital was significant. Distrusting the efficacy of their U.S. congressional members, state leaders felt that a strong and independent state presence in Washington was one of several steps that had to be taken for adequate representation in the national policy process.[64]

Growth of the National Governors Association

Under the leadership of a series of strong governors, the Governors' Conference began to broaden its agenda and approach.[65] In 1966 it changed its name to the National Governors' Conference (NGC) "to distinguish it clearly from the regional conferences which had sprung up."[66] In 1967 the NGC switched from an ad hoc committee structure to a system of eleven standing committees. The NGC began advocating a body of policy positions that were agreed to in annual meetings.[67] In 1977 the NGC became the National Governors Association "to signify the broad scope and ongoing nature of the organization."[68]

During the 1970s the NGA began a series of activities to enhance the performance of governors within their own states. "The New Governors' Seminar," held within two weeks after general elections in even-numbered years, used incumbent governors as faculty. Subjects included organizing the governor's office, press and public relations, management of the executive branch, executive-legislative relations, intergovernmental relations, the governorship as a partnership involving one's spouse, and the transition period from campaigning to governing.[69] In addition, printed materials and guidebooks were prepared for governors to take back to their home states, and transition assistance was made available.[70]

A growing emphasis on the states and governors as innovators appeared in series of surveys and publications. These surveys and reports helped disseminate ideas across the states on how to solve problems through innovative programs. What had been known as a governor's "show and tell" now became more systematic and analytical. Two organizations of gubernatorial staff—the Council of State Planning Agencies and the National Association of State Budget Officers—became NGA affiliates, providing it with needed policy and budget-planning capabilities.[71]

In 1983 Carol Weissert concluded that the NGA "has gone from serving primarily as a social event to providing information, technical assistance and research needed for responsible state leadership; from shying away from taking issue stands to assuming leadership in charting a national policy course; and from having no Washington presence to spearheading a strong Washington lobbying effort."[72]

Larry Sabato argued that the governors used the NGA as a vehicle to assert themselves at the "national level in an unprecedented and surprisingly effective manner . . . revolutionized from the hollow shell of yore to a bustling, professional lobby that can achieve results (and overcome serious handicaps to effectiveness inherent in a high-powered constituency such as the governors)."[73]

Regional governors' associations also became more active in policy concerns. Some of this interest flowed naturally from the region itself, for example, energy and natural resources in the West, agriculture in the Midwest, and race and economic development in the South. Some stemmed from the allocation of federal grant-in-aid funds or other federal decisions. In some instances states in a particular region banded together to provide improved higher education or to seek a "pork barrel" project.

Although the results of these activities varied, the governors of the fifty states, by joining together, became more a part of the national policymaking process. They took new and innovative steps to provide their states with enhanced representation at the national level.

Conclusion

Over the last four decades of the twentieth century, many of the states were involved in reforming their state governments to better meet the challenges of the day. In this process, the governors gained a great deal of strength and tools to help them fulfill their responsibilities. So too did the state legislatures and state courts.

Now as we are moving through the first decade of the twenty-first century, we are seeing some changes occurring in the states. Some of these are tied to the governors—the cost of running for the office has escalated greatly, there is more diversity in who is elected and serving across the states, and most governors are still in their first terms. We have also seen some governors forced to resign from office for some negative or questionable steps they have taken. And for only the second time in the history of the states, a governor was impeached and removed from office. And, with the changes in the political parties, more of the governors are facing state legislatures in which at least one house if not both houses are controlled by members of the opposition party. So change is afoot and we must continue to watch the various developments in the states.

Notes

1. "List of the Fortune 5000," www.usatoday.com/com/money/companies/3-22-04, and NASBO, *The Fiscal Survey of the States: December 2004* (Washington, D.C.: National Association of State Budget Officers, 2004), table A-1, 17.
2. Regina Brough, "Powers of the Gubernatorial CEOs: Variations among the States," *Journal of State Government* 59 (1986): 58–63.
3. Among these were the Advisory Commission on Intergovernmental Relations (ACIR), various reports; Committee for Economic Development, *Modernizing State Government* (New York: Committee for Economic Development, 1967); Terry Sanford, *Storm over the States* (New York: McGraw-Hill, 1967); National Municipal League, *Model State Constitution*, rev. ed. (New York: National Municipal League, 1968); and Citizens Conference on State Legislatures, various publications between 1967 and 1971.
4. Sanford, *Storm over the States*, 188; and Larry Sabato, *Goodbye to Good-time Charlie: The American Governor Transformed, 1950–1975* (Lexington, Mass: Lexington Books, 1978), 63.
5. Advisory Commission on Intergovernmental Relations, *The Question of State Government Capability* (Washington, D.C.: ACIR, 1985), 129.
6. Thad L. Beyle, "Term Limits in the State Executive Branch," in *Limiting Legislative Terms*, ed. Gerald Benjamin and Michael J. Malbin (Washington, D.C.: CQ Press, 1992), 159–180.
7. Keon S. Chi, "State Executive Branch Reorganization; Options for the Future," *State Trends and Forecasts* 1, no. 1 (December 1992): 8.
8. Kendra A. Hovey and Harold A. Hovey, eds., "Number of Satewide Elected Officials, 2004," *CQ's State Fact Finder 2005* (Washington, D.C.: CQ Press, 2005), table D-12, p. 113.
9. Advisory Commission on Intergovernmental Relations, *The Question of State Government Capability*, 129; and Ronald C. Moe, *Prospects for the Item Veto at the Federal Level: Lessons from the States* (Washington, D.C.: National Academy of Public Administration, 1988), 3–50.
10. Coleman B. Ransone Jr., *The Office of Governor in the United States* (University: University of Alabama Press, 1956), 44.
11. Center for Policy Research, National Governors Association, data from a 1976 survey of thirty-eight governors' offices. The average was adjusted to exclude the two largest states, as their size would skew the overall averages.
12. Council of State Governments, *The Book of the States, 2004* (Lexington, Ky.: Council of State Governments, 2004), 160–161.
13. Thad L. Beyle, "Governors' Views on Being Governor," *State Government* 52 (Summer 1979): 108–110.
14. Council of State Governments, *The Book of the States, 2004*, 162–163.
15. Lynn Muchmore, "Planning and Budgeting Offices: On Their Relevance to Gubernatorial Decisions," in *Being Governor: The View from the Office*, ed. Thad L. Beyle and Lynn Muchmore (Durham, N.C: Duke University Press, 1983), 174.
16. Carl W. Stenberg, "States under the Spotlight: An Intergovernmental View," *Public Administration Review* 45 (March/April 1985): 321.
17. Thad L. Beyle and Deil S. Wright, "The Governor, Planning, and Governmental Activity," in *The American Governor in Behavioral Perspective*, ed. Thad L. Beyle and J. Oliver Williams (New York: Harper and Row, 1973), 194–195.

18. Thad L. Beyle, "The Governor as Innovator in the Federal System," *Publius* 18 (Summer 1988): 133–154.
19. Under policy development were policy analysis and new initiatives (thirty-four states), briefing the governor on policy concerns (twenty-eight states), assisting on major gubernatorial initiatives (fifteen states), and impact analysis (seven states). Under administration were coordinating and providing service to the governor's cabinet and subcabinet councils (seventeen states); to interagency commissions, task forces, and working groups (sixteen states); and in the regulatory areas of state government (ten states).
20. Council of State Governments, *The Book of the States, 2004*, 162–163.
21. James K. Conant, "In the Shadow of Wilson and Brownlow: Executive Branch Reorganization in the States, 1965 to 1987," *Public Administration Review* 48 (September/October 1988): 892–902.
22. Council of State Governments, *The Book of the States, 1994–1995* (Lexington, Ky.: CSG, 1994), 70–71 and 483.
23. Hovey and Hovey, "Number of Statewide Elected Officials, 2004," *CQ's State Fact Finder 2005*, table D-12, p. 113.
24. Jack Brizius, of Brizius and Foster, Management Consultants, telephone conversation with author, September 27, 1987.
25. Richard Murray and Gregory R. Weiher, "Texas: Ann Richards, Taking on the Challenge," in *Governors and Hard Times*, ed. Thad L. Beyle (Washington, D.C.: CQ Press, 1992), 179–188.
26. Dianne Kincaid Blair, "The Gubernatorial Power: Too Much of a Good Thing?" in Beyle and Muchmore, *Being Governor*, 118–121.
27. Joseph A. Schlesinger, "The Politics of the Executive," in *Politics in the American States*, ed. Herbert Jacob and Kenneth N. Vines (Boston: Little, Brown, 1965), 225.
28. Elder Witt, "Patronage Firings," *Congressional Quarterly Weekly Report*, July 3, 1976, 1726.
29. Elder Witt, "Supreme Court Deals Blow to Public Employee Firings for Solely Political Reasons," *Congressional Quarterly Weekly Report*, April 6, 1980, 889–890.
30. Elder Witt, "Employee Rights," *Congressional Quarterly Weekly Report*, April 6, 1983, 791–792.
31. Thad L. Beyle and Robert Huefner, *Evaluation of the 1982 Seminar for New Governors*, report submitted to the National Governors Association, February 23, 1983.
32. Cheri Collis, "Cleaning Up the Spoils System," *State Government News* 33, no. 9 (September 1990): 6.
33. Charles N. Wheeler III, "Gov. James R. Thompson, 1977–1991: The Complete Campaigner, the Pragmatic Centrist," *Illinois Issues* 16, no. 12 (December 1990), 16.
34. Schlesinger, "The Politics of the Executive" ; Joseph A. Schlesinger, "The Politics of the Executive," in *Politics in the American States*, 2nd ed., ed. Herbert Jacob and Kenneth N. Vines (Boston: Little, Brown, 1971), 210–237; Thad L. Beyle, "Governors," in *Politics in the American States*, 4th ed., ed. Virginia Gray, Herbert Jacob, and Kenneth N. Vines (Boston: Little, Brown, 1983), 180–221; Beyle "Governors," in *Politics in the American States*, 5th ed., ed. Virginia Gray, Herbert Jacob, and Robert Albritton (Glenview, Ill.: Scott, Foresman, 1990), 574; Beyle, "Governors," in *Politics in the American States*, 6th ed., ed. Virginia Gray and Herbert Jacob (Washington, D.C: CQ Press, 1996), 237; Beyle, "Governors," in *Politics in the American States*, 7th ed., ed. Virginia Gray and Russell Hanson (Washington, D.C.: CQ Press, 1999), 191–231; Beyle, "Governors," in *Politics in the American States*, 8th ed., ed. Virginia Gray and Russell Hanson (Washington, D.C.: CQ Press, 2003), 194–231.
35. Office of State Services, *The Institutionalized Powers of the Governorship, 1965–1985* (Washington, D.C.: National Governors Association, 1987).
36. Some differences exist between the NGA index and those based on Schlesinger's study: (1) The NGA indexes were called institutional and not formal, which allowed a broader

interpretation of what could be brought into the presentation and analysis. (2) The added measures—the legislative budget-changing ability and the governor's political strength in the legislature—probably reflected a real-world view of the constraints on governors not captured in previous efforts. Including the governor's political strength in the legislature could lead to more varied results, as each election could change this score, especially because so many states are experiencing a political party powersplit between the governor and the legislature. (3) Only six offices were used to develop the appointment power index. The range of potential appointment power was greater (up to seven) than for the indicators (up to five), reflecting the importance of this indicator, where a large effect can be felt. (4) A twenty-year comparison of these indexes showed just how far the American governorship had come during that recent era of state government reform.

37. Sharon Sherman, "Powersplit: When Legislatures and Governors Are of Opposing Parties," *State Legislatures* 10, no. 5 (May-June 1984): 9–12.
38. Morris P. Fiorina, "Divided Government in the States," *PS: Political Science and Politics* 24, no. 4 (December 1991): 646.
39. Alan Ehrenhalt, "The Political Virtue of Partisan Deadlock," *Governing* 8, no. 4 (January 1995): 7–8.
40. Information updated from Thad Beyle, "The Speaker's Office as a Political Stepping Stone?" *North Carolina Insight* 15, no. 1 (January 1994): 30–31.
41. Ibid.
42. National Conference of State Legislatures, "Legislators Serving on Boards and Commissions," in *State Legislative Report* (Denver: National Conference of State Legislatures, 1983), 4–5; and North Carolina Center for Public Policy Research, *Boards, Commissions, and Councils in the Executive Branch of North Carolina State Government* (Raleigh: North Carolina Center for Public Policy Research, 1984).
43. Charles W. Wiggins, "Executive Vetoes and Legislative Overrides in the American States," *Journal of Politics* 42 (1980): 1112–1113.
44. Council of State Governments, *The Book of the States, 1994–1995*, 148–150.
45. Ran Coble, *Special Provisions in Budget Bills: A Pandora's Box for North Carolina Citizens: A Special Report* (Raleigh: North Carolina Center for Public Policy Research, 1986), 9–12.
46. Walter J. Oleszek, *Congressional Procedures and the Policy Process*, 4th ed. (Washington, D.C.: CQ Press, 1995), 340.
47. Thad L. Beyle, "Enhancing Executive Leadership in the States," *State and Local Government Review* 27, no. 1 (Spring 1995): 26–28.
48. Beyle, "Enhancing Executive Leadership in the States," 32–33.
49. North Dakota is an exception to this in that it only requires candidates to report the amounts of money that they raise for the campaign—and who the donors are. There is no requirement to report how those funds were spent in the campaigns.
50. All dollar amounts in this section are 2004 dollars, unless otherwise noted.
51. The states included in the definition of the South are: Alabama, Arkansas, Florida, Georgia, Kentucky, Louisiana, Mississippi, North Carolina, Oklahoma, South Carolina, Tennessee, Texas, Virginia, and West Virginia.
52. Michael Barone, *Almanac of American Politics, 2002* (Washington, D.C.: National Journal, 2001), 1554, 1594–1595.
53. These Independent winners were James Longley of Maine in 1974, Walter Hickel of Alaska and Lowell Weiker of Connecticut in 1990, Angus King of Maine in 1994, and Jesse Ventura of Minnesota and King of Maine, reelected in 1998.
54. For more details, see Beyle, "Governors: Elections, Campaign Costs and Powers," *The Book of the States, 2005* (Lexington, Ky.: Council of State Governments, 2005), table D, p. 151.
55. These women governors were Nellie Tayloe Ross of Wyoming and Miriam Amanda ("Ma") Ferguson of Texas in 1924, and Lurleen Wallace of Alabama in 1966.
56. They are Ruth Ann Minner (D-Del.), Judy Martz (R-Mont.), and Sila Calderon

(Popular D-Puerto Rico) in 2000; Janet Napolitano (D-Ariz.), Linda Lingle (R-Hawaii), Kathleen Sebelius (D-Kan.), and Jennifer Granholm (D-Mich.) in 2002; Kathleen Blanco (D-La.) in 2003; and Christine Gregoire (D-Wash.) in 2004.

57. They are Jane Swift (R-Mass.) and Olene Walker (R-Utah) in 2003; and M. Jodi Rell (R-Conn.) in 2004.
58. "Women Officeholders: Current," Center for American Women and Politics Web site (http://www.cawp.rutgers.edu), Eagleton Institute of Politics, Rutgers, State University of New Jersey, March 10, 2005.
59. For more detail see Beyle, "Governors: Elections, Campaign Costs and Powers," *The Book of the States, 2005* (Lexington, Ky.: Council of State Governments, 2005), table E, p. 152.
60. Evan Mecham (R-Ariz.) was removed by the legislature in 1988. John Rowland (R-Conn.) resigned in June 2004; in December of that year he pled guilty to one federal criminal charge of corruption and is now serving time in a federal prison.
61. Marvin Mandel (D-Md.) was removed in 1977 as a result of a federal court conviction, and H. Guy Hunt (R-Ala.) was removed in 1993 because of a state court conviction. Jim Guy Tucker Jr. (D-Ark.) resigned in 1996, and J. Fife Symington (R-Ariz.) resigned in 1997.
62. See Lamar Alexander, *Steps Along the Way: A Governor's Scrapbook* (Nashville, Tenn.: Thomas Nelson, 1986), 21–29, for a discussion of this unique transition between governors.
63. The other recalled governor was Lynn Frazier, R-N.D., in 1921.
64. Jacqueline Calmes, "444 North Capitol Street: Where State Lobbyists Are Learning Coalition Politics," *Governing* 2 (February 1988): 17–18, 20–21.
65. Among these governors were John Volpe, R-Mass., 1965–1969; Daniel Evans, R-Wash., 1965–1977; Calvin Rampton, D-Utah, 1965–1977; Marvin Mandel, D-Md., 1969–1977; Robert Ray, R-Iowa, 1969–1983; Scott Matheson, D-Utah, 1977–1985; and Lamar Alexander, R-Tenn., 1979–1987.
66. Carol Weissert, "The National Governors Association," *State Government* 56 (Spring 1983): 49.
67. Ibid., 60.
68. Ibid., 49.
69. Thad L. Beyle, "Gubernatorial Transitions: Lessons from the 1982–1983 Experience," *Publius* 14 (Summer 1984): 13.
70. Publications on the transition by the National Governors Association, Washington, D.C., include *The Critical Hundred Days: A Handbook for New Governors* (1975), *The Governor's Office* (1976), *Governing the American States: A Handbook for New Governors* (1978), *Transition and New Governors: A Critical Overview* (1982), *The Transition: A View from Academia* (1986), *The Departing Governor: Transition Out of Office* (1986), *Gubernatorial Perspectives on Transition* (1988), *The Governor's Final Year: Challenges and Strategies* (1990), and *Organizing the Transition Team* (1990).
71. Scott Matheson, *Out of Balance* (Salt Lake City, Utah: Peregrine Smith, 1986), 240.
72. Weissert, "The National Governors Association," 52.
73. Larry Sabato, *Goodbye to Goodtime Charlie: The American Governorship Transformed*, 2nd ed. (Washington, D.C: CQ Press, 1983), 180.

5

State Courts in Their Political Environment
Lawrence Baum

Courts occupy an ambiguous place in the political system. They are political institutions by any definition, yet they possess a degree of insulation from politics. That insulation stems from several characteristics of courts. Much of their work lies outside the mainstream of public policymaking, a condition that limits their involvement in political conflicts. Courts are also protected by a widespread belief that judges should be free to interpret legal questions according to their best understanding of the law. Finally, judges on the major federal courts and those who serve in a few states hold life terms that free them from concern about their tenure in office.

Yet even judges with life terms are subject to influence from their political environment. That influence is all the greater for judges who must win re-election or reappointment to maintain their positions. Primarily for this reason, state courts as a whole enjoy less insulation from politics than do their federal counterparts.

The relationship between courts and their political environment evolved over time. Today, state courts and their judges are under considerable pressure than usual. The extent of this pressure is difficult to ascertain and easy to exaggerate. But it is clear that in the early twenty-first century there is more conflict than usual between state courts and their political environments.

That change is significant in itself, and it illuminates the roles of the courts and their place in state politics. Thus it provides a useful focus for the examination of state courts in this chapter. I give primary attention to supreme courts, which are the most prominent state courts and which are affected the most by changes in the political environment.[1]

State Courts in Policy and Politics

Like the other branches of government, the courts vary in their structure from state to state. However, most states have a three-level structure: a set of courts to conduct trials and related proceedings, intermediate appellate courts to hear appeals from trial-court decisions, and supreme courts that hear cases after decisions of intermediate courts. Since trial courts hear far more cases than the courts above them, they directly affect the largest number of people. But supreme courts have the broadest impact, because they are the final arbiters of state law on the issues they address. Their position in the judicial system also attracts the greatest attention from people who are interested in state public policy.

Areas of Activity

State supreme courts and lower courts take action of three general types. The first and most straightforward is interpretation of state statutes—legislative enactments—in such fields as criminal law, labor relations, and environmental protection. Through their decisions state courts shape the law established by legislatures. In recent years, for instance, their decisions have applied statutory rules to a variety of new issues in family law.

Second, courts develop and interpret what is called the common law. In certain areas, the rules of state law were originally established through court decisions rather than statutes enacted by legislatures. The most important areas of the common law are property law, which governs the ownership and transfer of property; contract law, which concerns the enforcement of contracts; and tort law, which deals with liability for wrongful acts that cause property damage, personal injuries, or death. Legislatures can enact statutes to override court-made rules in these areas. But in the property and tort fields, most of the law continues to be made by the courts.

Finally, state courts interpret the federal and state constitutions. Their interpretations of the federal Constitution are subject to review by the U.S. Supreme Court. In contrast, state supreme courts are the ultimate interpreters of their own state constitutions. A state decision that ascribes a particular meaning to a provision of a state constitution cannot be reversed by the Supreme Court. As interpreters of constitutions, state courts rule on such issues as the division of power between governors and legislatures, the balance between free speech and other values, and the obligation of state governments to fund public schools.

Relationships with Other Policymakers

State courts have strong connections with other courts and with the other branches of government. Within the judicial branch, one important connection is between state supreme courts and the U.S. Supreme Court. As noted earlier, the Supreme Court can review state decisions that interpret provisions of federal law. More broadly, state courts are obliged to follow the Supreme Court's interpretations of federal law. In this way, the Supreme Court influences the content of state court decisions. At the same time, state courts have some leeway in how they apply Supreme Court decisions, and their use of this leeway shapes the ultimate impact of those rulings. All state judges are obliged to apply the *Miranda* rules for police questioning of suspects, but the way they interpret those rules in individual cases helps to determine actual police practices. At the extreme, state courts sometimes refuse to follow Supreme Court rulings or implicitly evade those rulings, most often on issues of criminal procedure.

In addition to this "vertical" relationship, state supreme courts have "horizontal" relationships with their counterparts in other states. Courts in different states have no obligation to pay attention to each other's rulings. Even if Illinois and Pennsylvania, for example, have statutes with exactly the same wording, the Illinois Supreme Court need not follow a Pennsylvania decision that interprets the Pennsylvania statute. Judges do, however, give credence to decisions in other states, and courts in different states provide ideas and cues to each other in their opinions.

The courts have multifaceted relationships with the other branches of state government. Their interpretations of statutes and constitutional provisions help to determine the impact of policies adopted by the legislature and executive branch. For their part, the other branches can adopt statutes to modify or overturn state court decisions on statutory or common-law issues, and they can initiate constitutional amendments to overturn decisions interpreting the state constitution.

The legislature and executive branch hold significant powers over courts and judges themselves. They control judicial budgets. Within the limits of their constitutions they can change a court's jurisdiction (the kinds of cases it has power to hear), consolidate two courts, or even abolish a court. They can also initiate constitutional amendments when needed to accomplish the same ends. In several states governors, legislatures, or the two together decide whether to grant new terms to sitting judges.[2] Nearly all state legislatures have the power to remove judges through impeachment.

Voters play a part in the constitutional amendment process. In nearly all states they hold the power to accept or reject constitutional amendments proposed by the legislature, and in about one-third of the states they can adopt amendments on their own through the initiative process. More important, the great majority of state judges—87 percent by one count—come before the voters when they seek new terms.[3] Many states select judges through partisan or nonpartisan elections. Many others employ retention elections in which sitting judges face a yes-no vote rather than an opposing candidate, typically requiring approval by a majority of voters to retain office.

Thus, institutions in the courts' political environment have the power to exert strong control over judges and their policies. Legislators might overturn court decisions on a regular basis, limit courts' power to hear cases, punish courts with budget cuts, and remove judges who arouse their wrath. Voters might defeat judges who have joined in unpopular decisions or lines of legal policy. The question is the extent to which policymakers and the public actually use these means of control.

The broad answer is that they generally do relatively little with their powers. The great majority of court decisions are left standing. Courts seldom have their jurisdiction narrowed for punitive reasons. Far more judges win new terms than lose bids for reelection or reappointment. Yet even a limited use of such powers can have considerable impact on judges and their policies, and any increase in their use enhances these effects. In recent years, several developments have combined to reduce the insulation of courts from their political environment.

Sources of Increased Conflict

These developments are not specific to the states. Rather, they are broad trends that have affected federal courts as well. However, they have greater impact on courts and judges in the states. The most important developments take two forms. First, perceptions of liberal and activist courts have increased the level of unhappiness with courts and judges among people in and out of government. Second, changes in the political process have eaten away at the insulation of courts from their environment.

Perceptions of Liberal Activism

Of all the terms used in American politics, *judicial activism* is among the most ambiguous. One scholar has cataloged a wide range of meanings for *judicial activism*, and that term is often used with considerable imprecision.[4] Frequently, people employ the word *activist* simply as an epithet to describe judges and decisions that they dislike. According to Supreme Court justice Stephen Breyer, "By judicial activism, what you mean, in part, is a judge who doesn't decide the way I'd like it decided."[5]

Still, activism is a useful way to describe an important aspect of judicial behavior. Perhaps the most important type of activism is decisions that make significant changes in public policy, especially in policies that the other branches have established. This type of activism can differ considerably in its extent across courts and over time.

Many people in politics believe that this is an era of heightened judicial activism, activism whose content is overwhelmingly liberal. This perception initially arose from the innovative Supreme Court decisions that expanded constitutional protections of civil liberties in the 1950s and 1960s. As the Court continued to hand down decisions establishing new rights, this perception hardened. Meanwhile, judges on lower federal courts drew attention for their own civil liberties decisions.

The perception of liberal activism in state courts developed more slowly. Indeed, the most prominent policies of state courts in the 1950s and 1960s were ideologically conservative. Some southern judges strongly resisted the legal claims brought by the civil rights movement. Throughout the country, some judges resisted the Supreme Court's expansions of defendants' rights. Gradually, however, observers of the courts became aware of several strands of state court policy that could be characterized as liberal and activist.

These strands have provided an impetus for efforts by people in and out of state governments to secure greater control over state courts. They are also significant developments in themselves. On both counts they merit consideration in some detail.

One strand is in tort policy. As noted earlier, state courts play the primary role in shaping legal rules for compensation of personal injuries. Most issues in tort law involve conflict between two types of parties. People who appear as plaintiffs in tort cases, those who make claims for personal injuries, benefit from rules that make it easier to sue and to establish liability for injuries and that allow larger damage awards for plaintiffs who win cases. On the other side are defendants, most often businesses and professionals, such as doctors, along with the insurance companies that typically would pay any damages awarded against defendants. For their part, political liberals tend to favor plaintiffs, conservatives defendants.

At any given time the courts' policies in tort law are ideologically diverse, so they can be summarized only with caution. Still, the legal rules established by state courts in the nineteenth century can be characterized as more conservative than liberal.[6] This direction of tort policy was largely reversed in a process that began in the first half of the twentieth century and accelerated in the 1950s and 1960s. On issue after issue, supreme courts eliminated traditional legal doctrines that limited tort liability, replacing them with doctrines that favored plaintiffs over defendants. Every state participated in this shift to some degree, and most changed their traditional doctrines quite substantially.[7]

The reversal of traditional doctrines involved an impressively large range of issues. And in undertaking these changes, courts frequently had to overturn well-established legal principles. When the South Carolina Supreme Court in 1985 abolished the immunity of state and local governments from lawsuits, it overruled at least 118 of its past decisions, handed down from 1820 through 1984.[8]

It took a long time for this trend to gain wide notice. But by the 1980s business groups were calling attention to what they called a "liability crisis," arguing that businesses were losing enormous sums of money and that the economy was damaged by frivolous lawsuits and unjustified court verdicts against defendants. As these groups saw it, the liberalizing changes in tort law were one important source of the crisis. Talk about a liability crisis has grown since that time, even though state courts in the 1980s began to draw back from the liberal trend in torts.[9]

A second strand of perceived liberal activism is in criminal procedure. As noted earlier, state supreme courts in the 1960s often expressed skepticism about the Supreme Court's expansions of defendants' rights and sometimes limited the application of those expansions in cases in their states.[10] But in the 1970s, as the Supreme Court began to narrow defendants' rights, some state courts were equally skeptical of that narrowing. They had a legitimate means to act on their skepticism: if the Supreme Court holds that a right is not protected under the U.S. Constitution, a state court can hold that the right is protected under *its* constitution, thereby making the Supreme Court's ruling irrelevant to that state.

State supreme courts have used this power frequently to protect defendants' rights. One study found 232 decisions of this type in forty-four states between the late 1960s and the late 1980s.[11] Most supreme courts participated in this development only to a limited degree: more often than not, courts that were asked to find new defendants' rights in their constitutions held that such rights did not exist. Still, the cumulative effect was to expand rights significantly. For instance, in 1984 the Supreme Court held that the evidence from some illegal police searches could be introduced in court because officers had acted in good faith. Since that time, at least thirteen state supreme courts have made this decision irrelevant in their states by holding that there is no good faith exception in their own constitutions.[12]

In 1972 the Supreme Court held that existing capital punishment laws were unconstitutional. State legislatures immediately began to adopt new laws to meet the Court's objections to the old ones, and ultimately three-quarters of the states reestablished the death penalty. Since 1973, more than 7,000 defendants have been sentenced to death.[13] Most states with capital punishment provide for automatic appeals of death sentences to their supreme courts, so supreme courts in many states have heard a steady stream of such appeals. In some states, such as California, death penalty cases account for a substantial proportion of the supreme court's decisions. One study across the states found that in about 40 percent of the appeals, the supreme court overturned the death sentence.[14] Many supreme courts, including those of New York and Kansas in 2004, have ruled that provisions of death penalty statutes violated the state or federal constitutions.[15] These decisions overturned multiple death sentences and required further legislative action to restore capital punishment.

Decisions that favor criminal defendants tend to be unpopular among people who are aware of them. Indeed, there is probably no other area of state policy on which public opinion is so intense and so one-sided. Thus liberal rulings in criminal justice potentially create problems for the courts and judges who make them.

A third strand of perceived liberal activism involves a specific issue, the funding of public schools. Traditionally, most funds for public schools in the United States have come from local property taxes. As a result, the property values in a school district strongly influence the level of financial support for its schools. State contributions to school funding usually reduce financial disparities among school districts but fall well short of eliminating them.

In 1973 the Supreme Court held that these disparities did not violate the equal protection clause of the Constitution.[16] After this decision, groups challenging the disparities focused on state courts and state constitutions. In the 1970s and 1980s, when challenges generally were based on inequalities across districts, most were unsuccessful. Since then, these groups have shifted ground, attacking state funding systems primarily on the basis of constitutional provisions that require adequate support for public schools. These challenges have been more successful. By now, twenty supreme courts have ruled that their states' systems were invalid, the most recent being Kansas in 2005.[17]

The politics of school funding is more complex than that of criminal justice, since the views of the public are divided (largely on the basis of which school districts would benefit from changes in funding systems). But implementation of these court rulings is typically quite expensive, in that states are required to provide additional funding for districts with limited capacity to raise money through property taxes. Legislators and governors often resent the burdens they bear in raising taxes to obtain the required money. Further, many of them believe the courts are intruding on a matter of basic state policy that should remain the domain of the other branches. For these reasons, decisions that mandate changes in school-funding systems are a potential source of friction between courts and the other branches.

State courts have adopted other noteworthy strands of policy involving interpretations of state constitutions. For instance, courts in fifteen states have held that prohibitions on state funding of abortion under the Medicaid program are unconstitutional.[18] Some state supreme courts ruled that criminal laws against sodomy violated state constitutions. In both instances these rulings found rights in state constitutions that the Supreme Court had not found in the U.S. Constitution, although the Court overturned its earlier ruling and struck down laws against homosexual sodomy in 2003.[19]

Of all the strands of state court policy in the current era, one stands out for the level of attention it has attracted. Two supreme courts interpreted state constitutions to require that same-sex couples be allowed to marry (Massachusetts) or to join in civil unions similar to marriage (Vermont). The Hawaii Supreme Court did not rule definitively on the issue but gave the state a heavy burden of proof in its efforts to justify prohibition of same-sex marriage.[20]

These strands of policy have given state courts reputations for liberal activism. In doing so, they have created conditions for conflict with some political interest groups and policymakers in the legislature and executive branch. In turn, that conflict has spurred efforts by these groups and policymakers to exert greater control over courts and their policies.

Changes in the Political Process

Perceptions of judicial activism are one source of increased friction between courts and their political environment. Another source is two developments in the political process. The first was a major change in politics during the late twentieth century: a burgeoning of political interest groups and of group campaigns to influence public policy. With this change government is now under greater scrutiny, and it is confronted with more demands for action. This development has been most visible in national politics, but it extends to the states as well.[21] Increasingly, leaders of groups that had focused their efforts on shaping national policy realized that state policy affected them in important ways and that they needed to have an active presence in state politics.

This certainly is true of state courts. Interest groups came to recognize the importance of state law and sought to shape it by participating in litigation. Since the 1970s, for instance, civil liberties groups have brought more cases in state courts, seeking an alternative to an increasingly conservative federal judiciary. One measurable aspect of interest group involvement in state litigation is the submission of amicus curiae briefs by interest groups that want to add their arguments to those made by the litigants. Traditionally, state supreme courts received few amicus briefs, but their number has grown considerably.[22]

Interest groups can also stimulate efforts to control the courts. Among other things, groups help to put court policies on the agendas of the other branches and the general public. Thus the growing involvement of groups in state politics as a whole and specifically in state courts increases the potential for conflicts between courts and other institutions.

The second political development, a decline in what may be called comity, should be put in broader context. Since the presidential election of 2000, journalists have written an enormous amount about what they see as the polarization of the American electorate. That theme is captured in the frequent references to "red" (Republican) and "blue" (Democratic) states, whose residents are depicted as holding different views of the world and strong partisan attitudes.

It is debatable whether this image captures the reality of public attitudes. Indeed, considerable evidence suggests that Americans are not especially polarized in their attitudes toward politics and policy.[23] But at the elite level, among people in government and those who are active in politics, the image of polarization has considerable accuracy. Accompanying that polarization has been a decline in comity, or harmony and cooperation in politics and government.[24]

Perhaps the key source of the decline in comity is ideological changes in the political parties in government. Half a century ago, Congress included many Republican liberals and even more Democratic conservatives. Today, these mavericks have nearly disappeared, and even moderates have become more scarce. As a result the parties face each other across a bigger divide, and the stakes in their victories and defeats have become considerably larger. In turn, self-restraint in political battles has declined. Indeed, there is something of a downward cycle in self-restraint, as Democrats and Republicans seek to match each other's initiatives. To take one example, this downward cycle is one reason for the growth of contention over Senate confirmation of federal judges.

Talk about declining comity in politics has focused on the national level, especially Congress. However, this trend inevitably has extended to the states, and we would expect it to affect reactions to the courts by participants in state government and politics. If perceptions of liberal activism arouse disapproval of judges and courts, those who disapprove have become more likely to act on their feelings. To the extent that state courts have enjoyed some protection from political attack, that protection is weakened by the decline in political comity.

Forms of Action against the Courts

When institutions in the political environment of state courts disapprove of what the courts are doing, they can take several kinds of action. The most direct involves efforts to change the policies in question. Alternatively, the public or the other branches of government can remove from office the judges who have made unpopular decisions. Finally, policymakers can attack the courts as institutions.

Altering Court-Made Policy

It is the exception to the rule for legislatures and governors to override judicial policies through new statutes or constitutional amendments, but such action is hardly rare. These overrides do not necessarily involve serious animosity toward the courts. However, animosity has been present in responses by the other branches to some strands of activist court policy.

When state supreme courts changed the tort law in ways that made it more favorable to plaintiffs, they were modifying and overturning rules they had made themselves. Thus there was no direct conflict between the courts and the other branches. But legislatures intervened to override some of the new rules in areas of tort law such as liability for defective products and medical malpractice. Across the states, legislatures negated a good many liberal doctrines in tort law, replacing court-made rules with their own.

The new legislative rules were frequently challenged on the basis of provisions in state constitutions. Responding to these challenges, the courts ruled that many of the new rules were unconstitutional. Between 1983 and 2000, according to one count, courts in twenty-six states struck down provisions of eighty-one new statutes.[25] By doing so, they aroused considerable wrath from interest groups that represent defendants in tort cases and from policymakers in the other branches.

In Ohio, for instance, the supreme court and the legislature were embroiled in conflict during the 1990s. Between 1991 and 1995 the supreme court handed down a series of decisions holding that provisions of recent tort statutes were unconstitutional. In 1996 the legislature enacted a broad tort statute, changing a large number of substantive and procedural rules. Several provisions in the new statute were intended to overturn earlier decisions of the state supreme court. In 1999 the court struck down the whole statute by a 4–3 vote, ruling that it infringed on powers of the courts and that it violated a constitutional rule against inclusion of multiple subjects in one statute.[26] At least for the time being, the supreme court had blocked legislative change in the tort law, and legislators who supported change were understandably unhappy with that outcome. That unhappiness led to considerable anger at the offending supreme court justices.

As suggested earlier, court decisions that overturn school-funding systems create the potential for even greater conflict between the branches.

These decisions present governors and legislatures with the task of establishing new funding systems. This task is usually difficult and unpleasant, because substantial increases in state spending on education are required and because the interests of different regions of the state are pitted against each other.

In at least a few states, the other branches reacted positively to the judicial mandate and sought to carry it out effectively. Some legislators in these states seized on their supreme court's decision as an impetus for educational changes they supported. In New Jersey, in contrast, the supreme court and the other branches battled over changes in the funding system for twenty-five years before reaching agreement. At one point the supreme court issued an order that prohibited the state's public schools from operating unless the legislature provided money for a new funding system.[27] Although New Jersey was an extreme case, across the states interbranch conflict over school-funding decisions has been more common than cooperation. And to the extent that judges insisted on compliance with their rulings, they aroused considerable resentment from legislators and governors.[28]

Decisions that expand the rights of criminal defendants often require implementation by police and prosecutors, and this implementation may be highly imperfect. Legislators sometimes act to overturn these rulings altogether by proposing amendments to state constitutions, and interest groups sponsor initiative measures to achieve the same end. In both instances, the proposals must go before the electorate to win adoption. Because criminal defendants and their rights are not especially popular, voters usually approve these proposals. By doing so, they reestablished the death penalty in Massachusetts and nullified decisions limiting the use of certain evidence against defendants in Florida and Pennsylvania. In California they did both.

Legislatures and voters have enacted an array of other laws that are unfavorable to defendants. Most of these laws are not aimed at specific court decisions, but they are often impelled by a perception that the courts are unduly lenient. This was one of the motivations for the "three-strikes" laws, which mandate long sentences for certain repeat offenders. About half the states enacted three-strikes laws in the 1990s, although these laws have had little impact on the severity of sentences in most of those states.[29] Like some other measures adopted in response to the courts, these laws have served largely as symbols of unhappiness with the courts.

An episode in Massachusetts provides another example of the frictions that can arise over policy. The legislature refused to provide money for a voter-approved system of public funding for state election campaigns. After this refusal was challenged, the supreme court in 2002 required that the legislature provide the funding or repeal the law. The legislature balked, and in response the supreme court forced the sale of some state property. Legislators reluctantly provided some funding for campaigns in 2002, but in 2003 they repealed the law.[30]

Challenging Judges at the Polls

Because the great majority of state judges must win new terms from the voters, elections are a powerful mechanism with which to influence what the courts do. Indeed, judges as a group seem to be increasingly fearful of electoral challenges based on the content of their decisions.

This fear can be understood in relation to the character of judicial elections. In contrast with contests for president, governor, and U.S. senator, most contests for judgeships are not very visible to the public. Voters typically go to the polls with only limited information about the candidates from whom they are asked to choose.

For sitting judges, this is mostly a favorable situation. Service in a judgeship allows them to develop a degree of name recognition, and incumbents have advantages in garnering endorsements and campaign contributions. Still, even sitting judges may not be very well known, a condition that makes them vulnerable to strong campaigns by opponents.

The perils that face sitting judges depend largely on the election system in place. Judges at all levels do best in states with retention elections: asked simply to vote yes or no on a sitting judge, most voters who know little about the judge's performance are inclined to cast positive votes. Between 1964 and 1994, judges who faced retention elections had a 99 percent success rate.[31]

Judges do less well in partisan and nonpartisan elections that give the voters a direct alternative to the incumbent. This is especially true of partisan elections, in which people may vote for a challenger on the basis of party affiliation. In the 1990–2000 period, state supreme court justices were defeated 2 percent of the time in retention elections, 5 percent in nonpartisan elections, and 31 percent in partisan elections.[32] Lower-court judges are less vulnerable to electoral defeat, but almost surely they too lose most often in states that elect judges on a partisan basis.

The 31 percent rate of defeat for supreme court justices in partisan elections, far higher than the rate for members of Congress, is noteworthy. The impact of partisan elections is reflected in Alabama and Texas. In both states growing Republican strength has benefited Republican candidates for judgeships, who often defeat incumbent Democrats.[33] In self-defense, some Democratic judges have switched parties.[34]

Beyond partisanship, judges can suffer defeats for a variety of other reasons. One, of course, is unhappiness with their choices in deciding cases—either single decisions or a broader line of policy. There have always been judges who lose their positions or barely escape defeat because voters disapprove of their decisions. What has changed in recent years is the frequency with which judges face strong challenges based on the content of their decisions.

The harbinger of this development was the elections of 1986. In California, three supreme court justices lost retention elections after a well-funded campaign highlighted their numerous votes to overturn death sentences.[35] In Ohio, the chief justice lost a nonpartisan election. His opponent emphasized allegations of misconduct by the incumbent, but those who supported the challenger cared primarily about reversing the supreme court's liberal policies in tort law.[36]

These kinds of challenges gradually became more common, and this trend has accelerated since the late 1990s. One source of this change is the growing use of independent campaigns by interest groups to support candidates in supreme court contests, usually by criticizing their opponents. Challengers and independent campaigns attack some judges for decisions that favor criminal defendants, attacks whose effectiveness is enhanced by the public's conservatism on criminal justice issues. Other judges face opposition based on their positions on economic issues, especially tort law. Groups on both sides of these issues have sought to defeat incumbents. A major source of growth in campaign spending has been business groups, groups that oppose supreme court justices who take liberal positions in tort law. Since 2000, for instance, the U.S. Chamber of Commerce has spent millions of dollars in independent campaigns to remove such justices.[37]

Because economic issues divide voters far more than criminal law, campaigns motivated by economic issues are often couched in other terms. In 2004, for instance, a large-scale independent campaign was launched against a West Virginia Supreme Court justice, a campaign funded primarily by the chief executive of a coal company. That campaign emphasized the justice's vote in a criminal case rather than the economic matters that motivated the campaign. The justice was defeated.[38]

It is uncertain whether the growing frequency of issue-based campaigns against judges actually has produced higher overall rates of defeat for incumbents.[39] But this trend has had two clear effects. The more direct effect is on the membership of supreme courts. In some states, including Alabama, Ohio, and Texas, the electoral successes of conservative groups and the Republican Party produced court majorities with conservative views on tort law and other economic issues. As a result, court policies on these issues have shifted.

The less direct effect is on the perceptions of incumbent judges, especially those who serve on supreme courts. When judges lose their positions because of their votes and opinions in cases, when other judges have to battle hard to win new terms, a feeling of vulnerability spreads through the judiciary. Thus, to take one example, the 1996 defeat of a Tennessee judge in a retention election on the basis of a single death penalty decision attracted widespread attention and concern.[40] That defeat exemplifies the special vulnerability of judges who cast votes or write opinions that favor criminal defendants. Judges with liberal positions on criminal justice issues may feel that they must choose between adherence to the policies they favor and security in their positions.

The size of campaigns for judgeships is growing at an accelerated rate, and the 2004 supreme court contests across the country stood out for the level of spending. In an Illinois contest for an open seat, the two sides spent more than $9 million.[41] Meanwhile, the Supreme Court in 2002 loosened limits on the freedom of judicial candidates to raise policy issues in their campaigns, and the content of campaigns has begun to change in response to that decision.[42] One result will be to increase judges' fears that their decisions can make them vulnerable to defeat.

Judicial Tenure and the Other Branches

Judges who do not have to face the voters are not necessarily secure in their positions. In the eight states in which the other branches of government decide whether to retain judges in office, mostly on the East Coast, judges who displease the governor or legislature can be denied new terms.

It appears that such denials are uncommon, but judges in these states increasingly face scrutiny because of their decisions. In Virginia, where the legislature chooses judges, members of the Republican majority have questioned several judges about specific decisions before reelecting them.[43] In states with gubernatorial appointment of judges, some judges have lost their positions as a result of governors' unhappiness with their decisions. This apparently was the fate of two judges who were not reappointed by governors in the 1990s. One was a Delaware judge who had favored stockholders over corporate management in some cases; the other was a New York judge charged with excessive liberalism in criminal cases.[44]

Judges who hold their positions for life still may be threatened with impeachment. Republicans in Congress have made such threats against some federal judges in recent years. In the states, the most consequential threat was against the chief justice of New Hampshire in 2000. David Brock was charged with misdeeds involving court procedures, but he had aroused legislators' wrath with decisions holding that the state's system for school funding was unconstitutional and disapproving some proposed changes in the system.[45] Chief Justice Brock was impeached by the lower house of the legislature, but he was acquitted by the state senate.[46] The Illinois legislature considered impeachment of Chief Justice James Heiple in 1997, citing his alleged misconduct on and off the court, but his unpopular set of rulings in a well-publicized child custody case helped spur this effort.[47] In other states, such as Massachusetts, individual legislators have talked about impeaching judges whose decisions they disliked but have not achieved serious consideration of impeachment.

These incidents have not received as much attention as the issue-driven defeats of judges in elections. Still, they affect the thinking of judges whose careers depend on the other branches of government. Judges' concern is enhanced by the fact that governors and legislators are more attentive to court decisions than the electorate.

In a few states legislators have discussed changes in rules of judicial selection and tenure as a means of retaliation or control. In Colorado, for instance, the president of the state senate in 2004 introduced a constitutional amendment that would have changed these rules in several ways, including a requirement that the senate confirm the governor's choices for judgeships and the creation of term limits for the state's judges.[48] Officials in the other branches can also encourage the voters to remove judges, and governors have been successful in some removal efforts. For instance, the 1986 defeats of three California Supreme Court justices that served as a harbinger of the current era were strongly encouraged by Republican governor George Deukmejian.

Attacking Courts as Institutions

The other branches can put heat on judges in another way: through their powers over courts as institutions. Especially important are judicial budgets and jurisdiction to hear cases. The significance of these powers is suggested by two extreme examples of their use. Early in the nineteenth century, one state legislature apparently reduced the salaries of its supreme court justices to twenty-five cents per year.[49] In the 1820s the Kentucky legislature abolished the supreme court and replaced it with a new court. When the old court continued to operate in defiance of the legislative action, a two-year conflict ensued. Ultimately, the legislature retreated by eliminating the new court.[50]

Nothing even vaguely resembling these actions has occurred in recent years. On the whole, relationships between the judiciary and the other branches in the states seem reasonably placid. But friction between the branches over institutional issues has increased.

Some of the friction relates to judicial budgets. Like officials of administrative agencies, judges and court administrators tend to believe that their organizations are underfunded. To the extent that courts receive less money than they need, it appears that the primary reason is the constraints on spending that apply to state programs as a whole. However, legislators sometimes express pique with court policies through their budgeting decisions. In a survey of chief court administrators in forty-one states in 1999 and 2000, fifteen administrators reported that legislatures had threatened to reduce the judicial budget "to influence or protest court rulings or policies," and in eleven states legislatures had actually reduced the budget for that reason.[51]

Occasionally the threat of retaliation for unpopular policies is quite direct. In 1991 the California Supreme Court upheld a provision adopted by the voters that reduced the state legislature's budget by 38 percent. One house of the legislature reacted by cutting the court's own budget by 38 percent, and the other house came close to agreeing on the cut.[52]

Legislators sometimes threaten even more extreme action. In 2005 a Montana legislator who was unhappy with decisions of the state supreme court introduced a set of retaliatory bills. Among other things, the bills would have opened the court's deliberations to the public, allowed the legislature and governor to overturn decisions that struck down state laws, and cut the justices' salaries by 80 percent.[53] Even when such bills go nowhere, they may raise concern within the judiciary.

Florida provides an especially good example of the growth in attacks on courts as institutions in some states.[54] As the Republican Party gained legislative majorities and then the governorship in the 1990s, liberal decisions by the courts produced a good deal of unhappiness. Governor Jeb Bush was displeased with rulings that overturned some of his initiatives and policies that he favored, including a school voucher program and his use of a line-item veto. Then came the presidential election of 2000, after which Florida courts issued some rulings that supported Al Gore's legal challenges to the election of George W. Bush. Although the Florida courts favored Bush with some of their decisions, the rulings on the other side aroused considerable wrath from state Republicans.

From the late 1980s on, Republicans in the Florida legislature presented an array of proposals to attack or rein in the state courts, especially the supreme court. Among other things, these proposals would have taken from the supreme court the power to issue procedural rules for the courts, allowed Governor Bush to add two justices to the supreme court, limited the supreme court's jurisdiction, and established term limits for judges. The only significant proposal to win adoption was a 2001 statute allowing the governor to choose all nine members of the commissions that nominate the slate of candidates from which the governor appoints judges. But some other proposals received considerable support in the legislature, and the state's judges undoubtedly recognized the displeasure of policymakers in the other branches.

The Impact of External Pressures on the Courts

If state judges are feeling greater pressure from the other branches of government and the voters, how does this pressure affect their choices on the bench? This is a difficult question to answer. Judges might be highly averse to the risk of negative responses in their political environment. If so, they would carefully avoid decisions that could provoke those responses. Alternatively, they might resolve to reach the judgments they see as the most appropriate and disregard the possibility of retaliation for those judgments.

It is clear that at least some judges worry a good deal about negative responses to their decisions. These worries are most pronounced when judges perceive a threat to their tenure in office. A series of studies indicates that some supreme court justices who feel vulnerable to electoral defeat minimize their votes to overturn death sentences.[55] Another study found that Pennsylvania trial judges become more severe in their sentencing as they approach reelection.[56] It is understandable that elected judges would respond to pressure in criminal justice, where public opinion is one-sided and strong. But one scholar concluded that judges take their political environment into account even in some fields that are less visible and controversial, such as unemployment compensation.[57]

Still, the pressures of recent years have not deterred some judges from taking positions that could be expected to provoke strong opposition. The supreme court justices who questioned or struck down laws prohibiting same-sex marriage are a good example. It may not be coincidence that those justices all sat in states where they do not face the voters, but even so they were risking conflict with the other branches. And judges continue to overturn state systems to fund education and death penalty laws despite the likely political price.

In this respect as well, Florida provides an interesting case. Despite pressure from the governor and legislators, the state's judges have continued to reach decisions that make these policymakers unhappy. For example, in 2003 the supreme court struck down a state law requiring that the parents of a young girl be notified before she obtained an abortion. (The decision was overturned by the voters in 2004.) In 2004 an intermediate appellate court struck down part of the state's program assisting parents in paying tuition for private schools, an important initiative for Governor Bush.[58]

The Florida courts also withstood considerable pressure in the long-running battle over the continuation of life-sustaining treatment for Terri Schiavo. With no dissent, courts at each level of the court system struck down a 2003 law that allowed the governor to issue a stay "to prevent the withholding of nutrition and hydration" from Schiavo.[59] When this battle turned into a national issue in 2005, the Florida courts were pressed by legislators, Governor Bush, and even Congress to rule in favor of Schiavo's parents. But in a series of rulings, the courts refused to intervene on the parents' behalf.

Perhaps the Florida courts in recent years would have been even bolder in the absence of external pressure. In this instance, as in others, it is difficult to ascertain the impact of the political environment on judges' choices. Still, it is clear that at least some judges are willing to accept political conflict as the price for adopting positions that they see as appropriate.

Conclusion

State courts have always stood in an ambiguous place in the states, partly but not completely insulated from politics. However, their place has shifted in recent years, with the other branches of government and the voters playing a more active role in overseeing the courts. As a result, the courts are less autonomous than in some earlier eras.

This development is understandable. In the current era state courts are important and highly visible participants in the making of public policy, and the content of their policies is often at odds with the views of other policymakers and of voters. Moreover, changes in the character of state politics make courts and judges more vulnerable to scrutiny and criticism.

Although the autonomy of the courts has been reduced, it remains substantial. Serious attacks on the courts as institutions are threatened far more than they are carried out. With the major exception of supreme court justices in states with partisan elections, judges do rather well in winning new terms. Most grievances against the judiciary have no concrete effects on courts and judges.

One key question is the extent to which concern with the political environment affects judges' choices as decision makers. Those effects are very difficult to measure. Even so, there is strong evidence that at least some judges take more pro-prosecution positions in criminal cases than they would in the absence of concern about voters and the other branches. To a lesser extent, the same may be true in some other areas of legal policy. But state judges continue to engage in policymaking that can be characterized as activist, often taking positions that they could expect to be unpopular.

It is important to keep in mind that the preponderance of what state courts do occurs out of sight of the voters and the other branches. Courts at all levels routinely make decisions that affect public policy without attracting much attention. Whatever the relationship between the courts and other institutions may be at a given time, this routine activity ensures that courts help to determine the state of government and politics in the states.

Notes

1. Throughout this chapter the term *supreme court* is used to refer to the highest court of each state. Most of these courts are called supreme courts, but there are some exceptions. For instance, in New York the court called the supreme court is a lower court and the highest court is called the court of appeals. The supreme courts of Texas and Oklahoma hear only civil cases; each state has a court of criminal appeals that acts as the supreme court for criminal cases. Where *Supreme Court* is capitalized, without any state designation, it refers to the U.S. Supreme Court.
2. Altogether, eight states require sitting judges to win new terms through action by the governor, the legislature, or both. Thirty-nine states require judges to win new terms from the voters. (New York is counted in both figures, because some judges face the voters and others the governor and legislature.) Judges in three states—Massachusetts, New Hampshire, and Rhode Island—hold terms for life or until age seventy. In Hawaii, a commission determines whether to retain judges. This information is from *Judicial Selection in the States: Appellate and General Jurisdiction Courts* (Des Moines, Iowa: American Judicature Society, 2004).
3. Roy Schotland, "Judicial Campaign Finance Could Work," *National Law Journal*, November 23, 1998, A21.
4. Bradley C. Canon, "A Framework for the Analysis of Judicial Activism," in *Supreme Court Activism and Restraint*, ed. Stephen C. Halpern and Charles M. Lamb (Lexington, Mass.: Lexington Books, 1982), 385–419.
5. Janine DeFao, "Judicial Activism on the Docket at Stanford Event," *San Francisco Chronicle*, October 24, 2004, A7.
6. There is some disagreement about the extent of this conservatism. See Peter Karsten, *Heart versus Head: Judge-Made Law in Nineteenth Century America* (Chapel Hill: University of North Carolina Press, 1997).
7. Lawrence Baum and Bradley C. Canon, "State Supreme Courts as Activists: New Doctrines in the Law of Torts," in *State Supreme Courts: Policymakers in the Federal System*, ed. Mary Cornelia Porter and G. Alan Tarr (Westport, Conn.: Greenwood Press, 1982), 83–108.
8. *McCall v. Batson*, 329 S.E.2d 741 (S.C. 1985).
9. That reversal is discussed in James A. Henderson Jr. and Theodore Eisenberg, "The Quiet Revolution in Products Liability: An Empirical Study of Legal Change," *UCLA Law Review* 37 (February 1990): 483–488.
10. Bradley C. Canon, "Organizational Contumacy in the Transmission of Judicial Policies: The *Mapp, Escobedo, Miranda*, and *Gault* Cases," *Villanova Law Review* 20 (November 1974): 50–79.

11. Barry Latzer, "The Hidden Conservatism of the State Court 'Revolution,'" "*Judicature* 74 (December–January 1991): 190–197.
12. Matthew A. Nelson, "An Appeal in Good Faith: Does the *Leon* Good Faith Exception to the Exclusionary Rule Apply in West Virginia?" *West Virginia Law Review* 105 (Spring 2003): 748–750.
13. Thomas P. Bonczar and Tracy L. Snell, *Capital Punishment, 2003* (Washington, D.C.: U.S. Bureau of Justice Statistics, 2004), 10.
14. James S. Liebman, Jeffrey Fagan, Valerie West, and Jonathan Lloyd, "Capital Attrition: Error Rates in Capital Cases, 1973–1995," *Texas Law Review* 78 (2000): 1847.
15. The 2004 decisions were *People v. LaValle*, 817 N.E.2d 341 (N.Y. 2004); and *State v. Marsh*, 102 P.3d 445 (Kan. 2004). As discussed in an earlier note, the highest New York court is called the court of appeals, and it is this court that ruled against the death penalty.
16. *San Antonio Independent School District v. Rodriguez,* 411 U.S. 1 (1973).
17. See Karen Swenson, "School Finance Reform Litigation: Why Are Some State Supreme Courts Activist and Others Restrained?" *Albany Law Review* 63 (2000): 1147–82; and Douglas S. Reed, *On Equal Terms: The Constitutional Politics of Educational Opportunity* (Princeton: Princeton University Press, 2001). The count of state supreme courts was based on lists in those two sources, updated with more recent decisions. In a few other states, lower courts have held that funding systems are unconstitutional but the supreme court has not yet ruled. The Kansas decision was *Montoy v. State,* 102 P.3d 1160 (Kan. 2005).
18. *Simat Corp. v. Arizona Health Care Cost Containment System,* 56 P.3d 28, 35–36 (Ariz. 2002).
19. *Lawrence v. Texas,* 539 U.S. 558 (2003).
20. The decisions were *Goodridge v. Department of Public Health,* 798 N.E. 2d 941 (Mass. 2003); *Baker v. State,* 744 A.2d 864 (Vt. 1999); and *Baehr v. Lewin,* 852 P.2d 44 (Hawaii 1993). Based on the Hawaii Supreme Court's ruling, a trial court in the state held that Hawaii's prohibition of same-sex marriage violated the state constitution. That decision was effectively overturned by a state constitutional amendment; the state supreme court confirmed that this was the effect of the amendment in *Baehr v. Miike,* 994 P.2d 566 (Hawaii 1999).
21. Virginia Gray and David Lowery, "The Institutionalization of State Communities of Organized Interests," *Political Research Quarterly* 54 (June 2002): 265–284.
22. Lee Epstein, "Exploring the Participation of Organized Interests in State Court Litigation," *Political Research Quarterly* 47 (June 1994): 335–351.
23. Morris P. Fiorina, with Samuel J. Abrams and Jeremy C. Pope, *Culture War? The Myth of a Polarized America* (New York: Pearson Longman 2005).
24. Jon R. Bond and Richard Fleisher, eds., *Polarized Politics: Congress and the President in a Partisan Era* (Washington, D.C.: CQ Press, 2000).
25. Victor E. Schwartz and Leah Lorber, "Judicial Nullification of Civil Justice Reform Violates the Fundamental Federal Constitutional Principle of Separation of Powers: How to Restore the Right Balance," *Rutgers Law Journal* 32 (2000–2001): 939–951.
26. The decision was *State ex rel. Ohio Academy of Trial Lawyers v. Sheward,* 715 N.E.2d 1062 (Ohio 1999). This history is discussed in the court's opinion and in Stephen J. Werber, "Ohio: A Microcosm of Tort Reform versus State Constitutional Mandates," *Rutgers Law Journal* 32 (Summer 2001): 1045–1070.
27. Russell S. Harrison and G. Alan Tarr, "School Finance and Inequality in New Jersey," in *Constitutional Politics in the States: Contemporary Controversies and Historical Patterns,* ed. G. Alan Tarr (Westport, Conn.: Greenwood Press, 1996), 178–201.
28. The final decision in New Jersey was *Abbott v. Burke,* 710 A.2d 480 (N.J. 1998). Responses to school-funding decisions are discussed more generally in Matthew H. Bosworth, *Courts as Catalysts: State Supreme Courts and Public School Finance Equity* (Albany: State University of New York Press, 2001); and Reed, *On Equal Terms.*

29. See David Schichor and Dale K. Sechrest, eds., *Three Strikes and You're Out: Vengeance as Public Policy* (Thousand Oaks, Calif.: Sage Publications, 1996); and Franklin E. Zimring, Gordon Hawkins, and Sam Kamin, *Punishment and Democracy: Three Strikes and You're Out in California* (New York: Oxford University Press, 2001).
30. This episode is discussed in Mark C. Miller, "Court-Legislative Conflict in Massachusetts," *Judicature* 88 (September–October 2004): 97.
31. Larry Aspin, William K. Hall, Jean Bax, and Celeste Montoya, "Thirty Years of Judicial Retention Elections: An Update," *Social Science Journal* 37 (2000): 9–10.
32. Chris W. Bonneau, "Electoral Verdicts: Incumbent Defeats in State Supreme Court Elections," *American Politics Research* 33 (November 2005): 818–841.
33. See L. Douglas Kiel, Carole Funk, and Anthony Champagne, "Two-Party Competition and Trial Court Elections in Texas," *Judicature* 77 (May–June 1994): 290–299.
34. Kevin Sack, "GOP Drive Spreads as 10 Alabama Judges Switch Parties," *New York Times,* January 4, 1996, A14.
35. John T. Wold and John H. Culver, "The Defeat of the California Justices: The Campaign, the Electorate, and the Issue of Judicial Accountability," *Judicature* 70 (April–May 1987): 348–355.
36. The election and its context are discussed in G. Alan Tarr and Mary Cornelia Aldis Porter, *State Supreme Courts in State and Nation* (New Haven, Conn.: Yale University Press, 1988), 124–184.
37. These changes in the character of judicial elections are discussed in Deborah Goldberg, Craig Holman, and Samantha Sanchez, *The New Politics of Judicial Elections* (New York: Justice at Stake Campaign, 2002); Deborah Goldberg, Sarah Samis, Edwin Bender, et. al., *The New Politics of Judicial Elections 2004* (Washington, D.C.: Justice at Stake Campaign, 2005); and Research and Policy Committee of the Committee for Economic Development, *Justice for Hire: Improving Judicial Selection* (New York: Committee for Economic Development, 2002).
38. Carol Morello, "W. Va. Supreme Court Justice Defeated in Rancorous Contest," *Washington Post,* November 4, 2004, A15.
39. Data for state supreme courts are in Bonneau, "Electoral Verdicts," 823–824 (for the years 1990–2000) and Melinda Gann Hall, "State Supreme Courts in American Democracy: Probing the Myths of Judicial Reform," *American Political Science Review* 95 (June 2001): 319 (for the years 1980–1995). The rate of defeat for incumbents seems to be increasing considerably in partisan elections, but that is not true of nonpartisan and retention elections.
40. Traciel V. Reed, "The Politicization of Judicial Retention Elections: The Defeat of Justices Lanphier and White," in *Research on Judicial Selection, 1999* (Chicago: American Judicature Society, 2000), 41–72.
41. Goldberg et al., *New Politics of Judicial Elections 2004*, 14. The same table shows spending totals for the 2004 supreme court elections in other states.
42. The decision was *Republican Party of Minnesota v. White,* 563 U.S. 765 (2002).
43. R. H. Melton, "House Speaker Presses Judge on Case," *Washington Post,* January 25, 2002, B8; "Virginia Judges Under Siege" (editorial), *Washington Post,* February 2, 2003, B8.
44. Karen Donovan, "Shareholders' Advocates Protest Justice's Removal," *National Law Journal,* June 6, 1994, B1; Jan Hoffman, "A Prominent Judge Retires, Objecting to the Governor's Litmus Test," *New York Times,* December 14, 1997, sec. 1, p. 49.
45. *Claremont School District v. Governor,* 703 A.2d 1353 (N.H. 1997), 744 A.2d 1107 (N.H. 1999).
46. Ralph Ranalli, "N.H. Senate Acquits State's Chief Justice," *Boston Globe,* October 11, 2000, A1.
47. See Lawrence Baum, *American Courts: Process and Policy,* 4th ed. (Boston: Houghton Mifflin, 1998), 303.

48. John J. Sanko, "Lawmaker Presses for Changes to Bench," *Rocky Mountain News,* April 22, 2004, 14A.
49. Evan Haynes, *The Selection and Tenure of Judges* (Newark, N.J.: National Conference of Judicial Councils, 1944), 95.
50. Stephen L. Carter, *The Confirmation Mess: Cleaning Up the Federal Appointments Process* (New York: Basic Books, 1994), 105–107.
51. James W. Douglas and Roger E. Hartley, "The Politics of Court Budgeting in the States: Is Judicial Independence Threatened by the Budgetary Process?" *Public Administration Review* 63 (July–August 2003): 449.
52. Leonard Post, "Chief Justices to Huddle on Independence," *National Law Journal,* July 26, 2004, 18.
53. Jennifer McKee, "Bills Seek Huge Change in Top Court," *Billings* (Montana) *Gazette,* January 9, 2005.
54. This discussion is based on newspaper reports and on Rebecca Mae Salokar and Kimberly A. Shaw, "The Impact of National Politics on State Courts: Florida after Election 2000," *Justice System Journal* 23 (2002): 57–74.
55. Melinda Gann Hall, "Constituent Influence in State Supreme Courts: Conceptual Notes and a Case Study," *Journal of Politics* 49 (1987): 1117–1124; Hall, "Justices as Representatives: Elections and Judicial Politics in the American States," *American Politics Quarterly* 23 (October 1995): 485–503.
56. Gregory A. Huber and Sanford C. Gordon, "Accountability and Coercion: Is Justice Blind When It Runs for Office?" *American Journal of Political Science* 48 (April 2004): 247–263.
57. Laura Langer, *Judicial Review in State Supreme Courts: A Comparative Study* (Albany: State University of New York Press, 2002).
58. These decisions were, respectively, *North Florida Women's Health and Counseling Services v. State,* 866 So. 2d 612 (Fla. 2003); and *Bush v. Holmes,* 886 So. 2d 340 (Fla. Dist. Ct. App., 1st Dist., 2004).
59. *Bush v. Schiavo,* 885 So. 2d 321 (Fla. 2004).

6

Accountability Battles in State Administration
William T. Gormley Jr.

State bureaucracies have paid a price for their growing importance, and that price is a loss of discretion. In recent years state bureaucracies have become more permeable, more vulnerable, and more manipulable. They are subject to a growing number of controls, as governors, state legislators, state judges, presidents, members of Congress, federal bureaucrats, interest groups, and citizens all attempt to shape administrative rule making, rate making, and adjudication at the state level.

In other words, state bureaucracies have become more accountable for their actions. In a sense, this is both understandable and desirable. Even state bureaucrats concede the virtues of accountability, at least in theory. Yet accountability is a multidimensional concept. Increasingly, the question is not whether state bureaucracies shall be accountable, but to whom. A related question is how accountability can best be structured to avoid damage to other important values, such as creativity and flexibility.

Controls that limit the discretion of state bureaucracies have proliferated, primarily in the areas of legislative oversight, executive management, due process, and regulatory federalism. A key development at the turn of the century was the introduction of performance measures as a mechanism for achieving greater accountability. In theory, the concept of managing for results offered an opportunity to focus more on outcomes and less on process in holding state administrative agencies accountable. In practice, states embraced the rhetoric of managing for results more enthusiastically than its operational implications. Even in states that took performance measures seriously, managing for results became one of many tools for achieving accountability.

The Proliferation of Controls

During the late twentieth century, as state bureaucracies grew larger and more important, politicians, judges, and citizens strengthened their leverage over state bureaucracies by institutionalizing a wide variety of control techniques. These techniques included legislative oversight, sunset laws, ombudsmen, proxy advocacy, executive orders, conditions of aid, and performance measures, among others. Control techniques differed in their directness, formality, durability, and coerciveness. However, they all shared a common purpose—to make state bureaucracies more accountable to other public officials or to the people.

Legislative Oversight

During the 1970s state legislatures discovered oversight as a form of bureaucratic control. Legislative committees took an active interest in bureaucratic implementation or nonimplementation of state statutes and conducted hearings aimed at identifying and resolving problems. This became easier as the legislator's job became a full-time profession in most states and as legislative staffs became larger and more professional. More than their congressional counterparts, state legislators decided not to leave oversight to chance. Perhaps oversight needed an extra push at the state level. In any event, state legislatures established regular mechanisms for legislative review.

Following the lead of Colorado, approximately two-thirds of the state legislatures adopted sunset laws, which provide for the automatic expiration of agencies unless the state legislature acts affirmatively to renew them. Although the threat of extinction is far-fetched in the case of large agencies, the threat of review must be taken seriously by all agencies. The sunset review process is especially important for obscure agencies that might otherwise escape scrutiny by legislative committees.

In addition to sunset laws, many state legislatures substantially upgraded the quality of their legislative audit bureaus. Gradually, these organizations came to place greater emphasis on program evaluation and policy analysis, less emphasis on auditing and accounting. By 2003 virtually every state legislature housed a nonpartisan policy research organization.[1] Some states, such as Florida, Kentucky, and Wisconsin, boasted staffs of considerable size and sophistication. The information that these organizations supply strengthens state legislatures' capacity for lawmaking and oversight.

The overwhelming majority of state legislatures also provided for legislative review of administrative rules and regulations. In sixteen states, legislative vetoes enable the legislature to invalidate an administrative rule or regulation. Through the legislative veto process, state legislatures have exercised closer scrutiny of administrative rule making. The U.S. Supreme Court declared the legislative veto unconstitutional at the federal level, and state courts have invalidated legislative vetoes in eight states.[2] Nevertheless, the legislative veto continues to be an important mechanism for legislative control in one-third of the states.

Perhaps most important, thirty-one state legislatures adopted "performance-based budgeting" requirements during the 1990s.[3] Although the specifics varied from state to state, common elements included a required strategic planning exercise and meaningful information about program outcomes. In theory, performance-based budgeting should strengthen the capacity of state legislatures to guide and monitor administrative agencies and to allocate resources based on results.

In thinking about legislative controls, a useful distinction can be made between inward-looking and outward-looking legislative changes. As the political scientist Alan Rosenthal has observed, state legislatures have become more fragmented, more decentralized, and less cohesive in recent years. In some sense, this might be characterized as legislative decline. However, a fragmented legislature is not necessarily weaker in its dealings with other units of government, such as state bureaucracies. A highly fragmented legislature may provide more occasions for legislative oversight and more incentives for individual legislators to engage in oversight. Thus, as legislatures become weaker internally, they may become stronger externally. This is especially true of those forms of legislative control that do not require a legislative majority.

Executive Management

For years, governors have complained about the fragmented character of the executive branch. Many executive branch officials are elected or appointed to office for fixed terms that do not coincide with the governor's term. The number of state agencies, boards, and commissions can be overwhelming and disconcerting. Also, agencies have their own traditions and habits and may be reluctant to follow the priorities of a new governor. All these factors have inhibited executive integration, coordination, and leadership.

During the later twentieth century, many governors took steps to deal with these problems. Most governors spearheaded reorganizations of the executive branch, striving for greater rationality and a reduction in the number of boards and commissions. Some proposals were bold and dramatic. Upon taking office, Republican governor Arnold Schwarzenegger of California promised to "blow up the boxes" of state government and proposed the elimination of eighty-eight boards and commissions. Although "the Terminator" later softened his reorganization plans, he did merge California's adult and youth corrections systems.[4]

Governors also used cabinet meetings, subcabinet meetings, or both to secure greater coordination and integration. Some subcabinets proved quite successful. For example, Maine's children's cabinet, established in 1995, resulted in regular information exchanges and collaborative undertakings across agencies that addressed children's problems.[5]

At the same time, governors fought successfully for shorter ballots to bring more top state officials under gubernatorial control. Between 1962 and 1978 the number of elected state executives declined by 10 percent.[6] As a result of these reforms, governors today are more likely to deal with state agencies headed by gubernatorial appointees, in whom they can have confidence.

Governors also relied on new budget techniques, such as zero-based budgeting (popular during the 1970s) and performance-based budgeting (popular during the 1990s). In addition to thirty-one states that adopted performance-based budgeting legislation, sixteen other states required performance-based budgeting through gubernatorial or administrative action.[7]

Finally, executive orders have become more popular in recent years. Many executive orders are aimed at controlling state bureaucracies, and some of them are both significant and controversial. For example, California governor

Pete Wilson issued an executive order in June 1995 eliminating affirmative action for state jobs.[8] State hiring and promotion practices changed significantly as a result.

These gubernatorial control techniques have become even more important as a result of limitations on political patronage imposed by the U.S. Supreme Court in 1990. In *Rutan v. Republican Party of Illinois*, the Court ruled that party affiliation could not be a factor in most state personnel decisions in Illinois.[9] That ruling, which has reverberated throughout the nation, has encouraged governors to control state agencies through other means.

Interest Representation

Unable or unwilling to control state agencies directly in every instance, politicians relied on surrogates to ensure better representation for favored points of view, such as consumers, environmentalists, and the elderly. The political scientists Mathew McCubbins and Thomas Schwartz referred to this phenomenon as "fire-alarm oversight" because politicians in effect depend on citizens or other public officials to spot fires in the bureaucracy and help extinguish them.[10] During the later twentieth century, states took steps to improve representation for broad, diffuse interests or other underrepresented interests, especially before state regulatory agencies; a "representation revolution" occurred.[11]

For example, many states established "proxy advocacy" offices to represent consumer interests in state public utility commission proceedings, such as rate cases. In some instances, attorneys general served this function; in other instances, separate consumer advocacy offices were established. Wisconsin, meanwhile, established a Citizens Utilities Board, funded by citizens through voluntary contributions but authorized by the state legislature to include membership solicitations in utility bills.[12] State legislatures in Illinois, New York, and Oregon subsequently established similar organizations, though without provisions for inserts.[13]

In policy arenas where interest representation through intermediaries is not mandated, interest groups have often emerged to represent underrepresented interests. For example, child advocacy groups in at least forty-four states have intervened in state government proceedings to shape public policy on child health, child care, child welfare, and related issues. Although child advocacy groups converse about twice as often with state legislators and their staffs as with civil servants, groups report on average about forty-six conversations per year with civil servants.[14] These conversations, along with other more formal interventions, have helped to alert state administrators to resource constraints and implementation problems.

Many state legislatures require public hearings on important issues, especially environmental issues. Pursuant to the California Coastal Act of 1972, a coastal zoning commission must call for a public hearing whenever a developer submits a construction permit request for a project that might have an "adverse environmental impact" on coastal resources. The federal government has also promoted citizen participation in environmental policymaking. For example, Congress required states to cooperate with the Environmental Protection Agency (EPA) in providing for public participation under the Federal Water Pollution Control Act, the Resource Conservation and Recovery Act, the Comprehensive Environmental Response, Compensation, and Liability Act, and other statutes.

Regulatory Federalism

The dynamics of regulatory federalism differ significantly from those of interest representation reforms. In both cases, politicians exercise indirect control over state bureaucracies, relying on surrogates to articulate their concerns. However, regulatory federalism is much more intrusive. If a consumer advocacy group recommends a new rule or regulation, a state agency may consider and reject it. If a federal agency instructs a state agency to adopt a rule or face a sharp cutback in federal funds, the state agency does not have much of a choice.

Regulatory federalism is a process whereby the federal government imposes conditions on state governments that accept federal funding.[15] Regulatory federalism arose as an adjunct to the new social regulations of the 1970s and as an antidote to the laissez-faire of general revenue sharing. Regulatory federalism includes a variety of techniques, such as direct orders (unequivocal mandates), crossover sanctions (threats in one program area if actions are not taken in another program), crosscutting requirements (obligations applicable to a wide range of programs), and partial preemptions (the establishment of minimal federal standards if states wish to run their own programs).[16] Some of these techniques apply to state legislatures; some apply to state agencies; many apply to both.

The number of federal statutes imposing significant new regulatory requirements increased dramatically during the 1970s. Given the Reagan administration's public support for federalism and deregulation, many observers expected regulatory federalism to decline during the 1980s. However, as the political scientist Timothy Conlan has shown, the number of federal statutes with significant intergovernmental controls directed at the states increased even further.[17] Moreover, a disproportionate increase came about in the most coercive regulatory control techniques—namely, direct orders and crossover sanctions. In Conlan's words, "the 1980s rivaled the previous decade as a period of unparalleled intergovernmental regulatory activity."[18]

In 1995 regulatory federalism gave way to a concerted effort to devolve power to the states. Led by Republican governors and members of Congress, advocates of state discretion pushed for program consolidation, block grants, and the elimination of unfunded federal mandates. Their most important accomplishment was the adoption of a welfare reform law in 1996, which eliminated welfare as a federal entitlement and authorized states to determine which, if any, poor people would be eligible for welfare payments.[19] Although welfare reform included a fair number of restrictions on the states, it was more devolutionary than regulatory. The creation of a state Children's Health Insurance Program (CHIP) the following year also exemplified a devolutionary impulse. States were free to serve children of the working poor through Medicaid, CHIP, or a hybrid approach. Congress also stipulated a more generous federal funding match under CHIP than under Medicaid. Overall, state agency heads reported a decline in the federal government's fiscal and regulatory influence from 1994 to 1998.[20]

A different era dawned in 2001 with the passage of a federal education bill. The No Child Left Behind Act, enacted with bipartisan support, triggered howls of protest from both Democratic and Republican state officials soon after implementation began. The legislation, which significantly expanded both federal funding and federal control, sought to promote goals that most states shared, including accountability for results and greater parental choice. However, the law also imposed requirements that many states found objectionable. For example, states must give parents the right to switch their child from any public school that fails to make "adequate yearly progress." As the number of failing schools proliferated, it became clear that other public schools would be unable to accommodate children wanting to leave failing schools. Connecticut challenged the law as unconstitutional, and school districts in three other states also filed suits.[21] The argument is that the law was insufficiently clear in specifying what states must do to receive federal funding and that the law effectively promised more aid than the states eventually received.[22] Although the federal courts are unlikely to accept this argument, the U.S. Department of Education made significant concessions to the states in 2005, when it relaxed some of its most important rules.

The USA Patriot Act, enacted in 2001 in the wake of the September 11 terrorist attacks, also signaled a new relationship between the federal government and state and local agencies. Federal funding enabled state and local governments to strengthen their law enforcement and public health infrastructures. At the same time, federal regulations reduced the discretion of state and local agencies and imposed new restrictions on civil liberties. Local libraries, for example, must report information to federal law enforcement officials on who checked out which books and when, if a search warrant is issued. Under the terms of the law, libraries may not disclose to patrons that their records were given to law enforcement officials. The Patriot Act also shifted resources from more traditional law enforcement functions to the war on terrorism. Many states attempted to compensate for the FBI's diminished involvement in the war against drugs and organized crime by shifting their own resources to these areas.[23]

Due Process

In addition to serving as arbiters in intergovernmental disputes, federal judges have been active participants in efforts to control state bureaucracies.

They have intervened vigorously in pursuit of such constitutional rights as "due process of law" and freedom from "cruel and unusual punishment." Dissatisfied with progress at the state level, they have gone so far as to seize, for example, state prisons and homes for the mentally ill or the mentally retarded, substituting their managerial judgment for that of state public administrators.

The 1971 case *Wyatt v. Stickney* was the first in a long line of institutional reform cases in which federal judges decided to play a strong managerial role.[24] Alabama's homes for the mentally ill and the mentally retarded were overcrowded, understaffed, dangerous, and unsanitary. In response to a class action suit, Judge Frank Johnson held that mentally disabled patients have a right to adequate and effective treatment in the least restrictive environment practicable. To secure that right, he issued extremely specific treatment standards and ordered rapid deinstitutionalization.

Shortly after the *Wyatt* decision, Judge Johnson found himself embroiled in an equally bitter controversy over Alabama's prisons. By most accounts, conditions in the state's prisons were deplorable. Rapes and stabbings were widespread, food was unwholesome, and physical facilities were dilapidated. In response to inmate complaints, Judge Johnson issued a decree calling for adequate medical care, regular fire inspections, and regular physical examinations.[25] When conditions barely improved, he issued detailed standards, including cell-space requirements, hiring requirements, and a mandatory classification system.[26]

The Alabama cases set the stage for a large number of similar cases throughout the country. In state after state, federal judges mandated massive changes in physical facilities, staffing ratios, health services, and amenities. They specified the size of prison cells, the credentials of new employees, and plumbing and hygiene standards. They shut down facilities and prohibited new admissions, even where alternative facilities were not available.

The U.S. Supreme Court in 1982 finally applied the brakes on mental health orders in *Youngberg v. Romeo*.[27] In that decision, the Court ruled that mentally retarded clients are constitutionally entitled to minimally adequate treatment and habilitation but that professionals, including state administrators, should be free to decide what constitutes minimally adequate training for staff. Thus, the decision was viewed as a partial victory for state administrators. Subsequently, the Court restricted other federal courts from correcting prison conditions in the absence of "deliberate indifference." In *Wilson v. Seiter,* the Court ruled that federal judges may address "cruel and unusual punishment" by state prison officials only if the plaintiff has demonstrated that prison officials exhibited a "culpable state of mind."[28] This imposes a higher hurdle for prison reform interventions than was previously the case.

Federal district court judges have responded to Supreme Court opinions and other factors by playing a more restrained role in institutional reform litigation. During the 1990s federal district court judges supported defendant school districts in the overwhelming majority of school desegregation cases they heard. Even in cases in which they sided with the plaintiffs, they tried to strike a lower profile. In other cases, the parties resolved disputes on their own. As one legal scholar put it, "The model of the all powerful (federal) judge in school desegregation is outdated."[29]

If the federal courts seem to be relaxing their control of state institutions, state courts appear to be asserting themselves more strongly. That is especially true of elementary and secondary education. Beginning in the 1970s, state courts responded to "equity suits" by ordering state politicians to reallocate school resources to ensure that poor students living in communities with relatively low property tax revenues received a high-quality education. These suits, in Connecticut, Kentucky, New Jersey, and elsewhere, have been effective in reducing education spending disparities within states.[30]

More recently, state courts have responded to "adequacy suits" by insisting that state politicians allocate more resources to elementary and secondary education throughout the state. In Kansas, for example, a local judge ordered the state to spend an additional $1 billion a year on education. Gov. Kathleen Sebelius proposed spending $300 million over three years instead, but the state legislature balked at even that. Approximately two dozen states are now involved in education adequacy suits.[31]

Types of Controls

It is useful when thinking about recent efforts to control state bureaucracies to imagine a spectrum ranging from catalytic controls at one end to coercive controls at the other end, with hortatory controls falling in between. Catalytic controls stimulate change but preserve a great deal of bureaucratic discretion. Coercive controls require change and severely limit bureaucratic discretion. Hortatory controls involve more pressure than catalytic controls but more restraint than coercive controls.[32]

Moreover, different types of controls have different types of effects. In their public policy implications, catalytic controls have been surprisingly effective and coercive controls have been notably counterproductive.

Catalytic Controls

Catalytic controls require state bureaucracies to respond to a petition or plea but do not predetermine the nature of their response. As a result, such controls are action forcing but not solution forcing. Although they alter bureaucratic behavior, they nevertheless permit a good deal of discretion and flexibility. Examples of catalytic controls include public hearings, ombudsmen, proxy advocacy, and lay representation.

Public hearings have enabled environmentalists to win important victories in their dealings with state bureaucracies. For example, citizens have used public hearings on state water quality planning in North Carolina to secure important modifications of state plans concerning waste water disposal, construction, and mining.[33] Similarly, citizens used public hearings before the

California Coastal Commission to block permits for development projects that would have an "adverse environmental impact" on coastal resources.[34]

Ombudsmen have been active in several areas but especially on nursing home issues. According to one report, nursing home ombudsmen have been effective in resolving complaints on a wide variety of subjects, including Medicaid problems, guardianship, the power of attorney, inadequate hygiene, family problems, and the theft of personal possessions.[35] Another study found that nursing home ombudsmen provide useful information to legislators and planners.[36]

Proxy advocates have effectively represented consumers in rate cases and other proceedings held by state public utility commissions. As a result of the interventions, utility companies have received rate hikes substantially lower than those originally requested. Proxy advocates also have been instrumental in securing policies on utility disconnections and payment penalties that help consumers who are struggling to pay their bills.[37] Even in complex telecommunications cases, proxy advocates have successfully promoted competition on behalf of consumers.[38]

Catalytic controls may be too weak in some instances. In several southern states, for example, public hearing requirements in utility regulatory proceedings have been pointless because consumer groups and environmental groups have not materialized to take advantage of such hearings.[39] Lay representation on occupational licensing boards also has been a disappointment. Lacking expertise, lay representatives typically have deferred to professionals on these boards.[40]

Overall, though, catalytic controls have been remarkably successful in making state bureaucracies more responsive to a vast array of formerly underrepresented interests. In effect, they have institutionalized what the political scientist James Q. Wilson refers to as "entrepreneurial politics," or the pursuit of policies that offer widely distributed benefits through widely distributed costs.[41] Moreover, catalytic controls have achieved results without engendering bureaucratic hostility and resentment. Studies show that state administrators welcome citizen participation and interest group interventions.[42] At their best, catalytic controls provide state bureaucrats with ammunition to justify policies that promote the public interest.

Hortatory Controls

Hortatory controls involve political pressure, or "jawboning," usually by someone in a position of authority. They strike a balance between bureaucratic discretion and bureaucratic accountability. Some, such as sunset laws and administrative reorganizations, are relatively mild; others, such as partial preemptions and crossover sanctions, are relatively strong.

The strength of hortatory controls depends primarily on two factors: their specificity (are the goals of the controllers clear?) and the credibility of the threat (how likely is it that penalties will be invoked?). Thus, sunset laws are relatively weak because the threat of termination is remote, except in the case of extremely small agencies.

To argue that some hortatory controls are mild is not to say that they are ineffective. A study of legislative audit bureau reports reveals that they do lead to changes in legislation, administrative practice, or both. Research by legislative audit bureaus is more likely than other types of research to be used by state legislators.[43] Indeed, such research is the second most important source of information for state legislators, just behind constituents.[44] The literature on administrative reorganizations reveals that they do not reduce government spending but that they can promote coordination and integration if they are well crafted and well executed.[45] The key seems to be to put agencies with interrelated missions under the same roof.

Research on sunset laws roughly parallels the findings on administrative reorganizations. As a cost-containment device, sunset legislation has been a failure. However, as a mechanism for focusing legislative attention on agencies and issues low in visibility, sunset legislation has been a success. In several states, such as Connecticut and Florida, sunset laws have resulted in significant changes in statutes and agency rules.[46]

Stronger hortatory controls have been even more effective, although they also have been dysfunctional in some respects. In response to quality control systems in welfare, "errors of liberality" declined, but "errors of stringency" increased.[47] In effect, states have sacrificed accuracy for cost containment. States also have enforced federal regulations that they know to be unreasonable, in response to partial preemptions in environmental policy. For example, the Minnesota Pollution Control Agency enforced a rigid EPA definition of hazardous waste, even though it meant that a lime sludge pile could not be removed from a highway site, could not be used for waste-water treatment, and could not be used to clean an electric utility company's smokestack emissions.[48]

Strong hortatory controls place a premium on uniform standards and universal compliance with such standards. In some instances, such as civil rights, no practical alternative exists to strong controls, because local prejudices are too deeply ingrained to permit cooperation. In others, however, strong hortatory controls may impose premature closure, discouraging the innovation and experimentation that are necessary for the states to serve as "laboratories" for the nation and for other states.

Strong hortatory controls have been particularly prominent in intergovernmental relations. Indeed, conditions attached to federal grants-in-aid epitomize hortatory controls. Such conditions have remained formidable, despite periodic rhetoric in support of a new federalism. In 1995 Congress took steps to soften or eliminate certain restrictions that states found offensive. For example, Congress voted to eliminate federal speed limit requirements for automobiles on federally financed highways except for some rural freeways.[49] However, the No Child Left Behind Act and the USA Patriot Act, both enacted in 2001, strengthened the federal government's hortatory controls over state and local agencies.

Coercive Controls

Coercive controls rob state bureaucracies of their discretion. They compel a specific response, often within a specific time frame. Neither the solution nor the deadline may be reasonable, but the state bureaucracy does not have the luxury of responding reasonably. Immediate compliance becomes more important than rationality, and short-term "outputs" become more important than long-term "outcomes."

Coercive controls often trigger bureaucratic circumvention or resistance. In the former case, bureaucrats comply with the letter, but not the spirit, of a tough requirement. In the latter case, the bureaucracy goes to court. In both cases, an adversarial relationship develops that precludes cooperation, bargaining, and persuasion.

As a response to legislative vetoes, some state agencies have issued emergency rules, which are not subject to the usual legislative review process. In Wisconsin, for example, state agencies issued a total of fifty-four emergency rules during the 1985–1986 legislative session—a sharp increase over earlier years.[50] Reliance on emergency rules is especially unfortunate, because they do not involve public hearings. Thus, in escaping highly threatening legislative vetoes, agencies avoid less threatening public hearings as well.

Court orders have triggered some of the more dysfunctional bureaucratic responses. When Judge Frank Johnson required state prisons to reduce their overcrowding, Alabama prison officials simply released large numbers of prisoners, forcing county jails to take up the slack. Unfortunately, county jails were poorly equipped for the task; they lacked adequate space and personnel. Consequently, many prisoners, shipped to county jails, were forced to endure conditions even worse than those they had experienced in the state prisons.[51] Yet, the state agency was technically in compliance with the court decree.

A key problem with coercive controls is that they place far too much emphasis on formal authority. Many state agencies depend considerably on a series of informal understandings. This is especially true of prisons, where quick-thinking guards and cooperative inmates help to maintain a delicate balance between order and chaos. When that balance is disrupted, tragedy may result. This is precisely what happened in Texas, when Judge William Justice restricted the use of force by prison guards and ordered an end to the state's "building tender" system, in which inmates in effect guarded other inmates. The court's order dissolved the informal networks that enabled the prisons to function on a daily basis. As guards became more timid, direct challenges to authority rose sharply. Disciplinary reports reveal abrupt and dramatic increases in incidents where a guard was threatened or assaulted.[52] Inmates also turned on each other, with their fists or with makeshift weapons. By generating rising expectations and undermining bureaucratic morale, Judge Justice created a temporary power vacuum that prison gangs quickly filled. The tragic result was a series of riots and violent episodes that left fifty-two inmates dead within two years.[53]

Accountability Battles

Three important trends have characterized accountability battles in recent years: a sharpening of conflicts within state government, as funding shortages have required difficult tradeoffs; a rethinking of intergovernmental controls, including devolution in some areas, stronger hortatory controls in others; and growing emphasis on performance measures as a technique for achieving accountability. In some policy domains, it seems that state administrative agencies enjoy more discretion, thanks to devolution and managing for results. In others, it appears that state administrative agencies are subject to tougher controls.

State Legislatures versus Governors

Accountability battles between state legislatures and governors have erupted in recent years. Some of the most bitter disputes have focused on the amount of money individual agencies and programs receive. In his autobiography, former president Bill Clinton recalls one such battle, over transportation funding, when he was governor of Arkansas. The Arkansas Highway Department promoted a new roads program, to be financed by new taxes, and managed to win over key business and farm leaders and the state legislature. Having promised the voters not to support a major tax increase, Clinton vetoed the bill, only to have his veto overridden by the state legislature. It was the only veto override in Clinton's twelve years as governor.[54] Many governors enjoy line-item veto authority, which permits them to veto a particular appropriation rather than an entire bill. Wisconsin even authorizes the governor to veto words or letters. A resourceful governor can use this power to restructure almost any program. In 2005, for example, Gov. Jim Doyle diverted $330 million to Wisconsin's public schools through creative use of the line-item veto.[55]

In recent years, governors and state legislatures have clashed over how to spend tobacco settlement funds awarded to forty-six states under the Master Settlement Agreement (MSA) of 1998. In Massachusetts, Gov. Mitt Romney allocated only $1.7 million to tobacco control in his budget for fiscal year (FY) 2004. The state legislature objected and restored tobacco control spending to $2.5 million.[56] In Michigan, Gov. John Engler preferred to spend MSA funds on college scholarships, and the state legislature agreed. When Gov. Jennifer Granholm, Engler's successor, proposed redirecting tobacco funds from scholarships to health programs in her FY 2004 budget, the state legislature objected. These battles, of course, have important implications for the funding available to health agencies, education agencies, and other agencies that have been authorized to spend MSA funds.

Legislative vetoes have aroused considerable conflict between state legislatures and governors, even when the same party controls both branches of government. Executive orders also have triggered conflict between state legislatures and governors. Tensions between state legislatures and governors can be stressful for administrative agencies, especially when the two branches of government are controlled by different political parties. During a bitter budget battle between Republican governor John Engler and Democrats in the Michigan state legislature in 1991, the child care licensing division was threatened with extinction and licensors received pink slips. A strong grassroots lobbying campaign managed to save the division, but the experience was extremely unpleasant for state agency officials.⁵⁷

Federal versus State Officials

State bureaucracies routinely are asked to implement federal statutes, such as environmental protection statutes. Often these federal statutes contradict state statutes or the policy preferences of the state's governor. Under such circumstances, a showdown is likely, with the federal government citing the "commerce clause" or the "take care clause" of the U.S. Constitution while the state government cites the Tenth Amendment.

The U.S. Supreme Court and other federal courts have usually sided with the federal government in accountability battles where the allocation of federal funds is at issue. If states accept federal funding, they also must accept the conditions the federal government attaches to those funds. However, many intergovernmental disputes do not involve federal funding but a federal effort to preempt state activity in a particular policy domain. Here, also, the U.S. Supreme Court has sided with the federal government, although with occasional exceptions.

In *National League of Cities v. Usery,* the Supreme Court surprised many observers by rejecting the federal government's attempt to extend minimum wage and maximum hour provisions to municipal employees.⁵⁸ In doing so, the Court said that the Tenth Amendment prohibited any federal action that impaired "the State's freedom to structure integral operations in areas of traditional governmental functions." Thus, a key provision of the 1974 Fair Labor Standards Act Amendments was ruled unconstitutional. The decision was an important victory for both state and local governments.

In subsequent cases, the Supreme Court wrestled gamely with the "traditional governmental functions" criterion and offered further clarification. For example, in *Hodel v. Virginia Surface Mining and Reclamation Association,* the Court articulated a threefold test for determining when Tenth Amendment claims shall prevail.⁵⁹ Specifically, the Court extended protection to the states if federal regulations regulate the states as states; address matters that are indisputably attributes of state sovereignty; and impair the states' ability to structure integral operations in areas of traditional function. In *Hodel*—a strip-mining case involving a partial preemption statute—the Court concluded that Congress had acted properly and with restraint. Similarly, in *Federal Energy Regulatory Commission v. Mississippi,* the Court applauded Congress for imposing modest constraints on state public utility commissions, when it could have preempted the field entirely.⁶⁰

Finally, after years of painful efforts to distinguish between "traditional government functions" and other functions, the Supreme Court abandoned that doctrine outright in *Garcia v. San Antonio Metropolitan Transit Authority*.[61] Writing for the majority, Justice Harry A. Blackmun concluded that "State sovereign interests . . . are more properly protected by procedural safeguards inherent in the structure of the federal system than by judicially created limitations on federal power."[62] In effect, the states would have to protect themselves through vigorous lobbying on Capitol Hill. The Supreme Court no longer would invoke a rule that was "unsound in principle and unworkable in practice."[63]

If the *Garcia* decision left state and local governments discouraged about the future of intergovernmental relations, a more recent decision has left them jubilant. In *U.S. v. Lopez*, the Supreme Court ruled that Congress had exceeded its constitutional authority in prohibiting the possession of a gun within 1,000 feet of a school.[64] In effect, the Court ruled that the commerce clause, which has justified numerous federal mandates in the past, cannot be equated with national supremacy. In *U.S. v. Morrison* (2000), the Supreme Court struck down the Violence Against Women Act on similar grounds.[65] Under the current regime, a regulated activity must "substantially affect" interstate commerce if the law authorizing the regulation is to be upheld as constitutional.

Some intergovernmental disputes can become quite heated, even if they do not spill over into the courts. Some governors, distressed by the high cost of drugs, and unimpressed by the federal government's cost containment efforts, have proposed that states should be free to import drugs from Canada, a policy opposed by the federal Department of Health and Human Services and the Food and Drug Administration (FDA). While these battles rage, some state agencies have moved ahead and provided information about Canadian drugs to citizens. For example, the Minnesota Department of Human Services includes detailed information about Canadian pharmacies and their drug price lists on its Web site. An angry FDA has demanded that the agency shut down its Web site.[66]

Managing for Results

In recent years, state governments have turned to "managing for results" as a technique for achieving greater accountability in state government. Although the precise elements vary from state to state, the most mature systems include the following elements: strategic plans that clarify important public goals; performance measures that demonstrate progress toward these goals; and linkages between performance measures and other important decisions, such as budgeting decisions.[67]

As one might expect, some states have moved rapidly to promote managing for results, whereas other states have lagged behind. When *Governing* magazine first produced a fifty-state report card on government performance in 1999, it awarded the following letter grades for managing for results: two As, twenty Bs, twenty Cs, seven Ds, and one F.[68] In a more recent report, published in 2005, *Governing* dropped its letter grades but continued to find sharp disparities. At one end of the spectrum, Missouri, Utah, and Virginia earned high marks for taking performance measures seriously. For example, the Missouri house of representatives used performance information for 25 percent of its budgeting decisions for FY 2006. In Virginia, Gov. Mark Warner established performance contracts for top officials, which he personally reviewed, along with agency scorecards. At the other end of the spectrum, New Hampshire, North Carolina, and Tennessee struggled to institutionalize performance measures. In New Hampshire, the state legislature abandoned its support for performance measures after state agency officials proved incapable of developing or using them.[69]

When managing for results works, state governments learn from performance measures and use that information to alter practices, programs, and policies. In Florida, for example, the Department of Environmental Protection established a performance management system in which the secretary periodically designated certain problems as "focus" or "watch" areas based upon worsening trends. This system enabled Florida to make progress in reducing petroleum leaks from underground storage tanks, in reducing health hazards at shellfish processing plants, and in deliberately burning trees and vegetation in state parks to help prevent large, uncontrolled fires.[70] In Oregon, the Department of Environmental Quality determined that point source pollution (for example, from power plants) was responsible for a declining proportion of Portland's ozone problem. Armed with this information, the department shifted resources to area and mobile sources (for example, automobiles), where pollution was worsening at a rapid rate.[71] These examples illustrate how managing for results is supposed to work: the state agencies used performance measures to document worsening problems; managerial changes and resource shifts ensued.

Conclusion

State administrative agencies once enjoyed considerable autonomy. Ignored by virtually everyone but clientele groups, they were "semisovereign" entities. In the early 1970s that began to change. As state budgets grew and state bureaucracies increased in importance, this era came to a close. To make state agencies more accountable, politicians and judges institutionalized a wide variety of reforms. Through direct and indirect means, they attempted to bring state bureaucracies under control.

Ironically, this occurred at precisely the same time as the growing professionalization of state agencies. Thanks to civil service reforms, budget increases, rising education levels, and growing pressure for specialization, state bureaucracies acquired greater experience and expertise. Today, they are more adept at problem solving than ever before and arguably more deserving of discretion. Thus, they chafe at external pressure, particularly when it is highly coercive.

General agreement exists that state agencies ought to be accountable. Even state bureaucrats cheerfully concede that point. However, consensus on the need for bureaucratic accountability has given way to "dissensus" on lines of authority. If governors and state legislators both claim an electoral mandate, who is right? If federal and state politicians both cite constitutional prerogatives, who is correct? If judges and politicians disagree on spending priorities, who deserves the power of the purse?

In the early twenty-first century, state agencies are more accountable to their sovereigns than they used to be. Yet, accountability has become a murky concept. Principal-agent theories of politics work only when the principal's identity is clear to the agent.[72] In numerous policy areas, state bureaucratic agents face dual principals or even multiple principals.

Thus, accountability battles rage, as competing sovereigns press their claims. As one might expect in a federal system, different actors have won accountability battles in different settings and at different times. A kinder, gentler quest for accountability could emerge if managing for results becomes more fully institutionalized at the federal and state levels. Thus far, however, the concept of managing for results has been grafted onto a wide array of other accountability mechanisms, ranging from catalytic to hortatory to coercive controls. So long as this situation persists, state administrative agencies will continue to be buffeted about by powerful pressures from politicians, judges, and interest groups, at both the state and federal levels.

Notes

1. John Hird, *Power, Knowledge and Politics: Policy Analysis in the States* (Washington, D.C.: Georgetown University Press, 2005), 62.
2. *Immigration and Naturalization Service v. Chadha*, 462 U.S. 919 (1983); L. Harold Levinson, "The Decline of the Legislative Veto: Federal/State Comparisons and Interactions," *Publius* 17 (Winter 1987): 115–132.
3. Julia Melkers and Katherine Willoughby, "The State of the States: Performance-Based Budgeting Requirements in 47 out of 50," *Public Administration Review* 58 (January–February 1998): 66–73.
4. Alan Greenblatt, "A Rage to Reorganize," *Governing*, March 2005, 30–35.
5. Ibid., 31.
6. Larry J. Sabato, *Goodbye to Good-time Charlie: The American Governorship Transformed* (Washington, D.C.: CQ Press, 1983).
7. Melkers and Willoughby, "The State of the States," 66–73.
8. John Miller and Abigail Thernstrom, "Losing Race," *New Republic*, June 26, 1995, 17–20.
9. *Rutan v. Republican Party of Illinois*, 497 U.S. 62 (1990).
10. Mathew McCubbins and Thomas Schwartz, "Congressional Oversight Overlooked: Police Patrols versus Fire Alarms," *American Journal of Political Science* 28 (February 1984): 180–202.

11. William Gormley Jr., "The Representation Revolution: Reforming State Regulation through Public Representation," *Administration and Society* 18, no. 2 (August 1986): 179–196.
12. Involuntary bill inserts later were ruled unconstitutional in a California case that effectively invalidated a key provision of the Wisconsin law. See *Pacific Gas and Electric v. Public Utilities Commission of California*, 106 S. Ct. 903 (1986).
13. Beth Givens, *Citizens' Utility Boards: Because Utilities Bear Watching* (San Diego, Calif.: Center for Public Interest Law, University of San Diego Law School, 1991).
14. William Gormley Jr. and Helen Cymrot, "The Strategic Choices of Child Advocacy Groups," *Nonprofit and Voluntary Sector Quarterly* (forthcoming).
15. Regulatory federalism also may be used to describe the relationship between state and local governments. For more on the growing burdens placed by state governments on local governments, see Catherine Lovell and Charles Tobin, "The Mandate Issue," *Public Administration Review* 41 (May–June 1981): 318–331. See also Joseph Zimmerman, "Developing State-Local Relations: 1987–1989," in *The Book of the States, 1990–1991* (Lexington, Ky.: Council of State Governments, 1990), 533–548.
16. Advisory Commission on Intergovernmental Relations, *Regulatory Federalism: Policy, Process, Impact and Reform* (Washington, D.C.: Advisory Commission on Intergovernmental Relations, 1983).
17. Timothy Conlan, "And the Beat Goes On: Intergovernmental Mandates and Preemption in an Era of Deregulation," *Publius* 21 (Summer 1991): 43–57.
18. Ibid., 50.
19. Anne Cammisa, *From Rhetoric to Reform? Welfare Policy in American Politics* (Boulder, Colo.: Westview Press, 1998).
20. Chung-Lae Cho and Deil Wright, "The Devolution Revolution in Intergovernmental Relations in the 1990s: Changes in Cooperative and Coercive State-National Relations as Perceived by State Administrators," *Journal of Public Administration Research and Theory* 14 (October 2004): 447–468.
21. Michael Dobbs, "NEA, States Challenge 'No Child' Program," *Washington Post*, April 21, 2005, 21; Anita Kumar, "States Leave No Child Law Behind," *St. Petersburg Times*, September 4, 2005, 1.
22. Ann McColl, "Tough Call: Is NCLB Constitutional?" *Phi Delta Kappan*, April 2005, 604–610.
23. Chad Foster and Gary Cordner, "Terrorism's Impact on Law Enforcement," *State News* 48 (March 2005): 28–35.
24. *Wyatt v. Stickney*, 324 F. Supp. 781 (M.D. Ala. 1971).
25. *Newman v. Alabama*, 349 F. Supp. 278 (M.D. Ala. 1972).
26. *James v. Wallace*, 406 F. Supp. 318 (M.D. Ala. 1976); and *Pugh v. Locke*, 406 F. Supp. 318 (M.D. Ala. 1976).
27. *Youngberg v. Romeo*, 102 S. Ct. 2452 (1982).
28. 111 S. Ct. 2321 (1991).
29. Wendy Parker, "The Decline of Judicial Decisionmaking: School Desegregation and District Court Judges," *North Carolina Law Review* 81, no. 4 (May 2003): 1623–1658.
30. Douglas Reed, *On Equal Terms: The Constitutional Politics of Educational Opportunity* (Princeton: Princeton University Press, 2001).
31. Dennis Farney, "Insufficient Funds," *Governing*, December 2004, 26–29.
32. William Gormley Jr., *Taming the Bureaucracy: Muscles, Prayers, and Other Strategies* (Princeton: Princeton University Press, 1989).
33. David Godschalk and Bruce Stiftel, "Making Waves: Public Participation in State Water Planning," *Journal of Applied Behavioral Science* 17, no. 4 (October–December 1981): 597–614.
34. Judy Rosener, "Making Bureaucrats Responsive: A Study of the Impact of Citizen Participation and Staff Recommendations on Regulatory Decision Making," *Public Administration Review* 42 (July–August 1982): 339–345.

35. Administration on Aging, U.S. Department of Health and Human Services, *National Summary of State Ombudsman Reports for U.S. Fiscal Year 1982* (Washington, D.C.: Government Printing Office, 1983).
36. Abraham Monk, Leonard Kaye, and Howard Litwin, *National Comparative Analysis of Long Term Care Programs for the Aged* (New York: Brookdale Institute on Aging and Adult Human Development and the Columbia University School of Social Work, 1982).
37. William Gormley Jr., *The Politics of Public Utility Regulation* (Pittsburgh: University of Pittsburgh Press, 1983).
38. Paul Teske, *After Divestiture: The Political Economy of State Telecommunications Regulation* (Albany: State University of New York Press, 1990), 63–85.
39. Ibid.
40. Gerald Thain and Kenneth Haydock, *A Working Paper: How Public and Other Members of Regulation and Licensing Boards Differ: The Results of a Wisconsin Survey* (Madison: Center for Public Representation, 1983).
41. James Q. Wilson, ed., *The Politics of Regulation* (New York: Basic Books, 1980).
42. On citizen participation: Cheryl Miller, "State Administrator Perceptions of the Policy Influence of Other Actors: Is Less Better?" *Public Administration Review* 47 (May–June 1987): 239–245; on interest group intervention: Glenn Abney and Thomas Lauth, *The Politics of State and City Administration* (Albany: State University of New York Press, 1986).
43. David Rafter, "Policy-Focused Evaluation: A Study of the Utilization of Evaluation Research by the Wisconsin Legislature" (Ph.D. diss., University of Wisconsin, 1982).
44. Hird, *Power, Knowledge and Politics,* 139.
45. Kenneth Meier, "Executive Reorganization of Government: Impact on Employment and Expenditures," *American Journal of Political Science* 24 (August 1980): 396–412; and Karen Hult, *Agency Merger and Bureaucratic Redesign* (Pittsburgh: University of Pittsburgh Press, 1987).
46. Doug Roederer and Patsy Palmer, *Sunset: Expectation and Experience* (Lexington, Ky.: Council of State Governments, 1981).
47. Evelyn Brodkin and Michael Lipsky, "Quality Control in AFDC as an Administrative Strategy," *Social Service Review* 57, no. 1 (March 1983): 1–34.
48. Eric Black, "Why Regulators Need a Don't-Do-It-If-It's-Stupid Clause," *Washington Monthly* 16, no. 12 (January 1985): 23–26.
49. Don Phillips, "Federal Speed Limit, Set in 1974, Repealed," *Washington Post,* November 29, 1995, 1.
50. Douglas Stencel, "Analysis of Joint Committee for Review of Administrative Rules Caseload, 1985–1986" (Madison, Wis., 1987).
51. Tinsley Yarbrough, *Judge Frank Johnson and Human Rights in Alabama* (Tuscaloosa: University of Alabama Press, 1981).
52. James Marquart and Ben Crouch, "Judicial Reform and Prisoner Control: The Impact of *Ruiz v. Estelle* on a Texas Penitentiary," *Law and Society Review* 19, no. 4 (1985): 557–586.
53. Aric Press, "Inside America's Toughest Prison," *Newsweek,* October 6, 1986, 46–61.
54. Bill Clinton, *My Life* (New York: Knopf, 2004), 319.
55. Phil Brinkman, "Lawmakers Question Veto-Changed Budget," *Wisconsin State Journal,* July 27, 2005, 1.
56. Frank Sloan and others, "States' Allocations of Funds from the Tobacco Master Settlement Agreement," *Health Affairs* 24 (January-February 2005): 220–227.
57. Ted DeWolf, Michigan Department of Social Services, interview by author, July 13, 1993.
58. *National League of Cities v. Usery,* 426 U.S. 833 (1976).
59. *Hodel v. Virginia Surface Mining and Reclamation Association,* 452 U.S. 264 (1981).
60. *FERC v. Mississippi,* 456 U.S. 742 (1982).

61. *Garcia v. San Antonio Metropolitan Transit Authority,* 105 S. Ct. 1005 (1985).
62. Ibid., at 1018.
63. Ibid., at 1016.
64. *U.S. v. Lopez* 514 U.S. 549 (1995); Ann Devroy and Al Kamen, "Clinton Says Gun Ruling Is a Threat," *Washington Post,* April 30, 1995, 1.
65. *U.S. v. Morrison,* 529 U.S. 598 (2000).
66. Marc Kaufman, "FDA, States at Odds over Drugs," *Washington Post,* February 22, 2004, 11.
67. Maria Aristigueta, *Managing for Results in State Government* (Westport, Conn.: Quorum Books, 1999), 19–23.
68. Katherine Barrett and Richard Greene, "Grading the States," *Governing,* February 1999, 17–90.
69. Katherine Barrett and Richard Greene, "Grading the States: A Management Report Card," *Governing,* February 2005, 24–90.
70. William Gormley Jr., "Environmental Performance Measures in a Federal System" (Research Paper 13, National Academy of Public Administration, Washington, D.C., 2000), appendix A.
71. Ibid.
72. Jonathan Bendor and Terry Moe, "An Adaptive Model of Bureaucratic Politics," *American Political Science Review* 79 (September 1985): 755–774.

7

State Government Finances
A Review of Current Conditions and the Outlook

Henry A. Coleman

The United States is a federal system of government in which the responsibility for providing and financing public services is shared among three levels of government. The 87,576 units of government in the U.S. federal system include the federal government, 50 state governments, and more than 87,500 local units of government.[1] Each of these jurisdictions provides public services to its citizens and raises revenue to support those services. Economists define fiscal capacity as a jurisdiction's revenue-raising ability relative to the spending needs that it faces. A jurisdiction's fiscal capacity is influenced by many factors. The state's economy and tax system affect its ability to raise revenues. Its income, population, and demographic mix influence public service demand. Where a jurisdiction's spending needs outstrip its revenue-raising ability, a fiscal crisis looms.

The system of federalism in the United States is both diverse and dynamic. At any point in time, fiscal capacity may differ significantly among units of government. It is dynamic in that considerable changes in fiscal capacity are often evident over time, both within and among units of government.

Within the U.S. federal system, the national government often seems to dominate in regard to the level of spending and taxation, and its ability to influence fiscal activities at other levels of government. Local governments are highly visible due to the sheer number of units and to the widely held view that they are the level of government closest to the people. However, state government finances play an important role in the U.S. federal system, although they may be the least visible entities within the federal system. For several reasons, state governments are likely to face an even more expanded role in providing domestic services in the future.

First, in a trend that started during the Reagan administration and was heightened in the aftermath of September 11, the national government is increasingly focused on national defense and homeland security. As such, more traditional domestic service responsibilities will rest with state and local governments.[2] However, the future role of local government is itself in doubt, as some scholars hold that local governments need a primary own-source of tax revenue, such as the property tax, to remain viable.[3] Other analysts note that the property tax is being undermined as a major revenue source for local governments through tax revolts, tax incentives, tax exemptions, and many school financing controversies around the country.[4] So serious concerns have been raised about the extent to which local government can step in to fill the void left by the federal government in providing domestic services. As such, whether through the devolution of responsibilities from the federal government or by default through limitations on local governments, states may be forced to assume more importance within the federal system. This expanded role for state government should not obscure the fact that significant differences in taxing and spending patterns among individual states may exist.

Whether state governments rise to the occasion is a function of their collective willingness and ability to assume an expanded role.[5] Throughout much of the current decade, state governments in aggregate have experienced a fiscal crisis, which may greatly affect their ability to assume a larger role within the federal system. The fiscal crisis confronting states has been sustained and significant, with estimates of the deficits totaling nearly $200 billion for fiscal years 2002–2004. Initial state budget projections for fiscal year 2005 showed that $40 billion in shortfalls had to be addressed.[6]

It has also been argued that the current fiscal crisis (fiscal years 2002–2005) has been both more sustained and more severe than the previous crisis of the early 1990s, which lasted for only three years. Moreover, states have been much more reluctant to raise taxes, and much more inclined to cut services, in responding to the current crisis. Even though state revenues have recently shown signs of renewed growth, they are still well below the level necessary to restore services to the level that prevailed at the start of the 1990s.[7]

The nature of the fiscal crisis facing states varies by cause, severity, and appropriate policy responses. For example, the deficit confronting a particular state may be caused by downturns in the overall economy, which is called a cyclical deficit, or by more chronic long-term disparities between revenues and spending, which is referred to as a structural deficit. In other words, a cyclical budget shortfall occurs when, during an economic downturn, state revenues fall while spending pressures increase. Revenues decline because personal income decreases, consumption by individuals and businesses decreases, and business profits decline, thus reducing the revenue yield from the state's personal income tax, general and selective sales taxes, and corporate income taxes, respectively. Spending increases because poverty and unemployment increase, which leads to increased demand for public assistance, housing assistance, health care assistance, and so forth. Because most states are required to spend no more than they raise in revenues—to balance their budget—these cyclical imbalances are a cause for concern. However, cyclical deficits are generally temporary and will likely be reduced or eliminated as the economic recovery occurs.

Structural deficits are said to exist when recurring revenues are not adequate to cover recurring spending needs. These deficits are considered chronic, or long-term, and often indicate that the state's revenue system is not responsive to the need for more revenues as the costs of providing needed public services increase. Perhaps more important, structural deficits are believed to result because the tax system for many states has not adapted to reflect evolving economic, demographic, or technological conditions.

Of course, a state may suffer from any one or combination of these budget deficits. Because of their chronic nature, structural deficits are considered to represent the most serious threat to the ability of state government to play an expanded role in the U.S. federal system. A summary of several recent studies suggests that between twenty-seven and forty-four states were experiencing significant structural gaps in their budgets.[8]

The remaining sections of this chapter present a brief discussion of state budget processes, a review of state government spending and revenue-raising activities, and an examination of the major fiscal policy issues confronting state finances at the beginning of the twenty-first century.

Overview of Budget Processes

Budgets are important because they describe the context in which state spending and revenue decisions are made and any limitations imposed on policymakers in making changes to state tax or spending policies.[9] Several aspects of state government budget processes will be discussed, including balanced-budget requirements; limitations on taxes, spending, and indebtedness; and reserves available to help deal with unexpected economic downturns or other emergencies.

Balanced-Budget Requirements

Most states operate on a fiscal year that runs from July 1 to June 30.[10] Twenty-nine states operate on an annual budget cycle and twenty-one on a biennial budget cycle.[11] Within the prevailing budget cycle, states are required to balance spending and revenues, although the nature of the balanced-budget requirement varies significantly.[12] The economists Brian Knight, Andrea Kusko, and Laura Rubin have observed the following:

> While all states except Vermont have some form of balanced budget requirement, the manner in which state governments must correct shortfalls in operating budgets depends on the requirements' details, which vary substantially across states. These rules are either stated explicitly in the state's constitution or are part of the laws of the state, and some states have multiple provisions that require a balanced budget. Balanced budget requirements can be placed into the following five categories, according to the state's most stringent provision:
> 1. governor must submit a balanced budget—that is, one that contains no projected shortfall (1 state);
> 2. legislature must pass a balanced budget (5 states);
> 3. state must correct any shortfall in the next fiscal year (7 states);
> 4. no carryover of shortfall into the next biennial budget cycle (7 states); and
> 5. no carryover of shortfall into the next fiscal year (29 states).[13]

These authors further note that other factors, such as bond ratings and public expectations, may also contribute to fiscal discipline within a state. For example, bond-rating agencies often take a skeptical view of fiscal "gimmicks"—such as deferring expenditures, accelerating tax payments, selling assets, or one-shot revenues—and respond to such proposals by downgrading the state's bond rating. This increases the costs of borrowing for the state. Thus, the threat of having its bond rating downgraded helps to instill fiscal discipline. Similarly, the fear that tax and spending policies may be seen as radical and generate an adverse public response—as reflected in opinion polls, unfavorable editorials, or public demonstrations—also prompts adherence to more mainstream policies, which contributes to fiscal discipline.

Tax and Expenditure Limitations

Many states impose some type of restriction on spending or revenue raising. Indeed, thirty states have some type of tax or expenditure limitation, or both. Two-thirds of those states restrict spending growth to some index of inflation. In addition, twelve states require approval by a supermajority (such as two-thirds majority vote margin) in the state legislature for an increase in taxes or fees, and another three states require voter approval.

Debt Limits

In financing many capital activities, states can choose a pay-as-you-go system or the issuance of debt. Two types of debt issues are generally available—revenue bonds or general obligation bonds. With revenue bonds, the repayment of the principal and interest is contingent on the successful completion of the project. The full taxing authority of the issuing jurisdiction is pledged to the repayment of the principal and interest of general obligation debt, which is also called full faith and credit debt. Several states do not issue general obligation debt, and other states that issue general obligation debt do not limit the amount.[14] Each of the remaining states has some type of limitation on the amount of general obligation debt, with the limitation generally based on a formulaic relationship with either the general revenues or appropriations of the state. Alternatively, some debt limits are stated as fixed dollar amounts.

Budget Reserves

The effects of recessions on state budgets were noted earlier. Although the onset of a cyclical downturn is often difficult to predict with any precision, states also have to deal on occasion with unforeseen emergencies due to natural or man-made disasters. To help in dealing with the financial impacts of unexpected emergencies or downturns in the economy, states maintain contingency and stabilization funds. Budget stabilization funds—so-called Rainy Day Funds—allow states to spend during an economic downturn without having to resort to raising existing taxes or introducing new ones.

Some forty-five states (all but Arkansas, Kansas, Montana, Oregon, and Utah) now have such funds. Although these instruments have been helpful in staving off more drastic adjustments during short-term crises, they are seldom capitalized sufficiently to withstand a significant and sustained economic downturn. Among the fifty states all but two (Michigan and Mississippi) have contingency funds—reserves set aside for unexpected emergencies, such as natural disasters.

Again, these budget processes help to provide a context for the adjustments that state governments must make in response to problems brought on by a fiscal crisis. This is an important, but only partial, part of the story. In order to get a more complete picture, information on how states raise and spend money is needed. The following sections shed further light on these aspects of state finances.

How Do States Spend Money?

State governments are major players in the federal system. Total general expenditures for state governments in 2001 were $1.045 trillion, up significantly from the 1990 total of $508 billion. Per capita state general spending grew from $2,048 in 1990 to $3,671 in 2001. Per capita state general expenditures varied significantly among states, with the top states being Alaska ($13,232), Vermont ($5,221), Hawaii ($5,008), Delaware ($4,959), and Wyoming ($4,718). The lowest per capita spending states were Texas ($2,723), Nevada ($2,798), Florida ($2,846), Arizona ($2,926), and Tennessee ($2,981).[15]

Within the state budget, spending takes place via several funds. Fund accounting is used by nonprofit organizations that receive funds whose use is restricted to a specific purpose. The accounting system is organized so that the use of the dedicated funds is separately identified and monitored.[16]

Although it varies somewhat from state to state, four types of funds are used in state budgeting. The "general fund" is the largest and most flexible fund, and the one generally considered to most closely reflect state preferences and priorities. "Federal funds" are funds received from the federal government, generally in the form of grants-in-aid. "Bond funds" are established with the proceeds from the sale of bonds and used primarily for capital investment purposes. Finally, "other state funds" are used to fund spending from revenues that are restricted by state statute or constitution. For example, casino taxes in New Jersey are dedicated to providing services for the elderly and the disabled. Similarly, the gas tax in many states is earmarked for road construction, maintenance, or improvements. In 2003 general fund spending was almost 44 percent of total state expenditures, followed by federal funds (29 percent), other state funds (24 percent), and bond fund spending (3 percent).

State spending in general is spread among seven functional categories, including elementary and secondary education, higher education, public assistance, Medicaid, corrections, transportation, and all other areas. (See Table 7–1.) Elementary and secondary education is the largest area of total

Table 7–1 State Government Expenditures, Fiscal Year 2003

Functional area	% of total spending	2002–2003 % change	% of general fund spending	2002–2003 % change
Elem. and sec. educ.	22	6	36	1
Medicaid	21	8	17	4
Higher education	11	3	12	(2)
Transportation	8	4	1	(12)
Corrections	3	2	7	2
Public assistance	2	2	2	(3)
All other	32	2	26	(3)

Source: National Association of State Budget Officers, *2003 State Expenditure Report* (Washington, D.C.: NASBO, 2004), 4, http://www.nasbo.org.

Note: ( ) = decrease; totals may not equal 100% due to rounding.

state spending, followed by Medicaid. Medicaid was the fastest growing area of total spending for each of the last two years. The spending pattern for total state expenditures parallels that for the general fund, except for transportation spending. These general patterns mask several significant changes in relative spending over time, and significant differences in relative spending among individual states. For example, higher education was the second largest area of state spending until the late 1980s, when Medicaid emerged as the second largest area. The proportion of total state spending accounted for by elementary and secondary education, Medicaid, and corrections has increased significantly over the last decade and a half. Significant differences in spending among states reflect variations in the allocation of service responsibilities between the state and local governments, the costs of providing services, service preferences, the quality of services provided, and state financial resources.

How Do States Raise Money?

State government general revenue totaled about $1.1 trillion in fiscal 2001, almost double the 1990 level of $517 billion. Per capita general revenue increased from $2,085 in 1990 to $3,685 in 2001. Per capita general revenue varied considerably by state, with the top five states being Alaska ($9,532), Delaware ($5,595), Wyoming ($5,520), Vermont ($5,068), and Hawaii ($4,927). The bottom five states included Florida ($2,699), Nevada ($2,753), Texas ($2,835), Arizona ($2,858), and Tennessee ($2,964).

State revenues are generally categorized as either own-source—reflecting a variety of state-imposed taxes, fees, and charges—or intergovernmental revenue—indicating revenues received from another level of government. State general fund revenues best describe own-source revenues. In 2003 general fund revenues totaled $491 billion. See Table 7–2.

Table 7–2 State General Fund Revenues, Fiscal Year 2003

Revenue source	% of total general fund revenues
Personal income tax	37
Sales tax	33
Corporate income tax	6
Gaming tax	1
Other taxes and fees	23

Source: National Association of State Budget Officers, *2003 State Expenditure Report* (Washington, D.C.: NASBO, 2004), 94, http://www.nasbo.org.

Of this total, personal income taxes represented the largest share, followed by sales taxes and all other taxes and fees, which include cigarette and tobacco taxes, alcoholic beverages taxes, insurance premium taxes, severance taxes, licenses and fees for permits, inheritance taxes, and charges for state-provided services. Forty-one states impose a broad-based personal income tax (all but Alaska, Florida, Nevada, New Hampshire, South Dakota, Tennessee, Texas, Washington, and Wyoming), and forty-five states (all but Alaska, Delaware, Montana, New Hampshire, and Oregon) impose a broad-based sales tax. All states impose selective excise taxes on items such as alcohol, tobacco, and gasoline.

Major Fiscal Policy Issues Confronting States

State governments are in a truly precarious fiscal position. By devolution or default, they are poised to assume a greater role in providing domestic services within the U.S. federal system at the same time that they are confronting significant fiscal problems resulting from a fiscal crisis, especially as it relates to the structural deficits being experienced by as many as forty-four states. The issues discussed below are illustrative of the kinds of issues that states must confront and address if they are to deal fairly and effectively with their citizens in adjusting to an expanded role in the federal system

Pressures for Spending Increases

Several factors may accelerate the trend toward increased state spending, including school financing, Medicaid, public employee retirement systems, and limitations on the use of labor-saving technologies in providing public services. The first three of these factors represent large areas of state spending that may continue to experience rapid growth. In addition, political and institutional constraints (such as collective bargaining agreements) may make it difficult to reduce or even control spending in these areas.

Schools

States (and their local school districts) face pressures to increase school funding to deal with a variety of concerns. These include projected enrollment increases, court-ordered requirements to reduce disparities in school funding, public demands for smaller class sizes to address school quality, declining and outmoded quality of school facilities, demands for higher teacher salaries to remain competitive with other occupations, and dealing with federal mandates regarding educational services for pupils with disabilities. Although the extent to which these school-spending pressures will be shared with local school districts will surely vary from state to state, it is safe to assume that much of the additional spending will fall on state budgets. Hawaii, for example, has a statewide school system with no local districts, so all additional costs will accrue to the state.

Medicaid

As noted earlier, Medicaid is already one of the largest areas of state spending, and the fastest growing. Medicaid spending is likely to increase even more because of growing health care costs, which regularly exceed the overall rate of inflation, and the shift in the costs of providing health services for the elderly and disabled from the fully federal-funded Medicare program to the joint federal-state-funded Medicaid program. Iris Lav describes how this shift occurs:

> Changing medical practices have shortened the length of time that people are hospitalized and have increased the use of prescription drugs and ambulatory care. While these medical advances can reduce overall health care costs and improve quality of care, they have the paradoxical effect of increasing Medicaid expenditures while lowering Medicare costs. Furthermore, Medicaid covers long-term care, whereas Medicare does not. A majority of the Medicaid expenditures for seniors and people with disabilities are for long-term care services. . . . As a result of these circumstances and trends, Medicaid has been financing a growing share of health insurance costs for the aged and disabled.[17]

Pensions

Rising state commitments to retired public employees have the potential to dwarf the fiscal concerns related to cyclical and structural deficits, with shortfalls projected to reach several hundred billion dollars.[18] There are three sources of funding for state retirement systems—employee contributions, employer contributions, and investment earnings. Employee and employer contributions are about equal to distributions currently paid out by retirement systems. However, investment earnings are well below the level necessary to meet future obligations. This current situation is made even more tenuous in some states because of enhanced benefits still being provided by policymakers, changes in pension fund asset allocations in favor of riskier investments, and significant future payouts as more workers age and become eligible for benefits.

Limitations of the Use of Technology

In an often-cited article written in 1967, the noted Princeton University professor William Baumol described a theory of how inflation could affect the costs of delivering public services.[19] The public sector competes with the private sector to attract and retain workers, primarily by offering comparable wage increases. However, because of technological changes that are introduced in the private sector, productivity increases offset the costs of higher wages paid to private sector workers, thereby keeping overall costs under control. Since it is more difficult to introduce labor-saving technology into the service-driven public sector, no offsetting productivity increases take place, with the result that increased wages mean increased costs for the delivery of any given quantity or quality of public services. In short, the more limited ability to introduce technological changes into the public sector will contribute to higher costs of services, even with no increase in either the quantity or quality of those services.

Outdated State Revenue Systems

Several researchers have argued that the tax system currently in place in most states is not adequate to address the revenue needs of those states. The tax systems were established when the economy, technology, and demographics were very different from those of today. These tax systems have not been modernized to reflect current circumstances.[20]

For example, the general sales and use tax is a major source of revenue for state government, representing slightly more than a third of general fund revenues in 2003. The state sales tax, which was first introduced in the 1930s, was established when the U.S. economy (and that of most states) was a goods-based economy, and most sales transactions were conducted face to face. Today's economy is a services-based economy, with more and more transactions taking place through remote means, such as over the Internet or through mail-order catalogs. State sales and use taxes have not been revised to reflect this new economic reality.

The Institute on Taxation and Economic Policy noted that "in 2003, services represented almost 60 percent of personal consumption nationally. Few states have successfully adapted to this change in consumption: only Hawaii, New Mexico, and South Dakota [tax] services comprehensively."[21] Similarly, policy analyst Michael Mazerov notes that " a majority of the states apply their sales tax to less than one-third of 164 potentially taxable services. Eight of the 45 states with sales taxes impose them on fewer than 20 service categories."[22] He goes on to note that "full taxation of 'readily available' services could generate sales tax revenue equal to 25 to 35 percent of current sales tax collections in about three-fourths of the forty-five states currently levying a sales tax. The total revenue yield nationally would be approximately $57 billion a year."[23]

Similarly, remote sales—including sales through the Internet, mail-order catalogs, and direct marketing—have cost states significant amounts of forgone sales tax revenues. Whenever the resident of a state makes a purchase from an out-of-state vendor but the good in question is to be primarily consumed within the state of residence, a "use" tax obligation is incurred. Because of the U.S. Supreme Court decisions in *National Bellas Hess vs. Illinois Department of Revenue* and *Quill Corporation vs. North Dakota,* the state of residence cannot force the out-of-state vendor to collect and remit the taxes generated by the transaction.[24] Donald Bruce and William Fox estimate that the loss of sales and use tax revenues due to such remote transactions primarily involving the Internet could grow from $15 billion in 2003 to somewhere between $22 billion and $34 billion by 2008.[25] The Streamlined Sales Tax Project (SSTP) was initiated by several organizations—including the Federation of Tax Administrators, the Multi-State Tax Commission, the National Conference of State Legislatures, and the National Governors Association—to address the concerns raised by the Supreme Court so that states may be able to compel out-of-state vendors to collect sales and use taxes, but Congress has shown little interest or inclination to enact legislation that embodies the work of the SSTP.

Other policies in the state tax system are similarly in need of updating. For example, many states with a personal income tax provide for special treatment of retirement income, without applying any type of means test to the taxpayer.[26] When this special treatment was introduced, retirement income was a relatively small component of personal income. As the population ages and more individuals reach retirement age, income from pensions and other retirement accounts has become a more significant portion of total personal income. It now represents a significant personal income tax loss to the states.

The corporate income tax has also declined considerably as a source of revenue for state governments. This has occurred in part because states are attempting to reduce business taxes in order to encourage economic development. Policy analyst and *State Tax Notes* columnist David Brunori holds that

> corporations have long sought to lower their state tax burdens, and have generally done so using a three-pronged approach: they employ really smart lawyers and accountants to plan around paying taxes; they secure all kinds of tax incentives to do essentially what they would be doing anyway; and ... they have continued their assault on the traditional way that corporate taxes are levied in the United States.[27]

Expanding Reliance on Gambling Revenues

In addressing their needs for more revenue, many states are looking to nontax revenue sources, such as fees and charges and gambling—including

Table 7–3 Casino Tax Revenue by State, 2004

State	Tax revenues (millions)
Nevada	$887
Illinois	802
Indiana	761
New Jersey	471
Louisiana	437
Missouri	403
Mississippi	333
Michigan	279
Iowa	253
Colorado	100
South Dakota	12

Source: American Gaming Association, *2004 State of the States: The AGA Survey of Casino Entertainment,* (American Gaming Association, Washington, D.C., 2005), 4, http://www.americangaming.org.

state-sanctioned lotteries, casinos, and racing. A recent report by the Institute on Taxation and Economic Policy finds the following:

> Some form of government-sanctioned gambling is now allowed in all but two states (Utah and Hawaii). By far the most popular forms of legalized gambling are lotteries and casinos: 37 states and the District of Columbia have state lotteries, and more than half the states have some form of casino gambling. Many states also allow "pari-mutuel" gaming, wagering on live events such as horse racing and greyhound racing. Advocates of state-sponsored gambling typically see it as a painless, voluntary tax—and one that is at least partially paid by residents of other states.[28]

Although states have shown a greater interest in all forms of nontax revenues, gambling revenues have been especially popular in the last several years. For example, in 2003 total lottery ticket sales increased to $43.5 billion from $2.4 billion in 1980, and net income to states increased to almost $14 billion from $978 million in 1980. See Table 7–3.

Casino tax revenue in 2004 ranged from a high of $887 million in Nevada to a low of $12 million in South Dakota. Note also that the casino industry pays other forms of state and local taxes, such as corporate income taxes, sales taxes, and local property taxes.[29] However, the potential of gambling revenues to help in addressing state fiscal problems should not be overstated. Although these revenues allow states to increase spending, they will play only a small role in the overall state budget context.[30]

In many instances, the financial benefits of gaming revenues to the states are overstated. First, it is important to distinguish between gross revenues generated by state-sponsored lotteries and the net revenues available to states to fund services. A significant portion, up to 50 percent, of lottery proceeds must be devoted to administration (including the costs of promoting the lottery) and to pay the cash prizes to lottery winners. When these "net" revenues are considered, the fiscal benefits are much more modest. More generally, with the possible exception of revenues in Nevada, gambling revenues amount to a relatively small portion of total state revenues. As the late economist Steven Gold once observed,

> Nevada's gambling and casino entertainment taxes in 1991 produced $348 million, along with another $57 million from licenses for slot machines and other games. These taxes brought in about 24 percent of Nevada's tax revenue. When other business taxes and the tourism it produces are counted, the gambling industry accounts for about half of Nevada's state tax revenue. But Nevada is unique. It combines a small population with a huge gambling industry. Gambling could not have nearly as much impact on state finances in a large state. Consider, for example, New Jersey, where the state's take in 1991 was $246 million in casino gross revenue taxes, along with another $50 million from licenses for casinos and slot machines. New Jersey's total state tax revenue was $11.6 billion, so these taxes and licenses were only about 2.5 percent of total state tax revenue.[31]

In addition, the growth in lottery revenues noted above reflects more states adopting lotteries, rather than more revenue from existing lotteries. Lottery revenues have grown very modestly if adjustments are made for revenues from lotteries adopted in additional states.[32] Indeed, the success of a state's lottery depends on attracting nonresidents to play a state's lottery. As more states introduce their own lottery, fewer out-of-state players are attracted to the lottery outside of their home state. Similarly, playing the lottery (or engaging in any form of state-sponsored gambling) is an alternative to participating in other activities that could generate sales or excise revenues. That is, as individuals devote more of their income to playing games of chance, less income is available to purchase goods and services that generate sales and excise tax revenues. This may have a significant adverse impact on states that rely more heavily on consumption taxes than on personal income taxes.[33]

It is also fair to say that gambling is not always a voluntary activity, at least for some portion of the population. This means that problems of gambling addiction and gambling-related crimes could increase as a result of the introduction of state-sponsored lotteries or state-sanctioned casinos. In determining the true benefits to a state, the costs of dealing with the increased social ills, which may result in increased state spending, should be considered. Finally, low-income individuals constitute a disproportionate share of participants in state-sponsored gambling. Therefore, gambling is said to be regressive in its impacts. In view of this litany of concerns, the Institute on Taxation and Economic Policy concludes that "there is growing evidence that state-sponsored gambling is both inequitable and inadequate as a long-term revenue source—and that the associated social costs of encouraging destructive gambling behavior may offset much of the revenue gains enjoyed by states in the short run."[34]

Interstate Competition and Tax Expenditures

Competition among states for economic development has grown significantly, and both targeted and broad-based tax incentives have been provided more frequently by individual states.[35]

All taxes are ultimately paid by individuals, either through reduced compensation to or employment of workers, through higher prices to consumers, or through reduced dividends and other compensation to shareholders. Still, the initial or legal incidence of much of the taxes imposed by states falls on businesses as legal entities. Businesses pay a variety of taxes, including property taxes, sales and use taxes, corporate income taxes, payroll taxes, and gross receipt taxes.[36] It has been estimated that businesses paid 43 percent of all state and local taxes in 2003, approximately $400 billion. It has also been estimated that businesses paid 65 percent of the increased taxes imposed by state and local government between 2002 and 2003.[37] Other evidence indicates that businesses pay about 40 percent of sales and use taxes.[38] This would suggest that businesses pay a significant and fair share of all state and local taxes.

Still, some analysts argue that taxes paid by businesses over the last several decades have not kept pace with the growth in business revenues, profits, or costs imposed on society. Noted law professor and tax analyst Richard Pomp argues that as a result of reduced federal tax burdens dating from the early to mid-1980s, businesses focused more on reducing their state tax liability.[39] Whether through more skillful tax planning, changes in their corporate status, or efforts to induce direct or indirect tax decreases, businesses have seen their corporate income tax liability fall dramatically. For example, there has been a significant increase in the number of businesses organized as pass-through entities—that is, as limited liability corporations, limited liability partnerships, or sub-chapter S corporations. For state tax purposes, this means that these corporations are taxed as individuals according to their state's personal income tax, rather than corporate income tax, rules.

Similarly, many states allow multistate companies to engage in strategic tax avoidance behavior by deviating from the formula developed for apportioning the income of companies that do business in several states. The Uniform Distribution of Income for Tax Purposes Act (UDIPTA) formula provides for the apportionment of business income of multistate companies among states based on an equal weighting of the relative amounts of payroll, property, and sales in each state. By increasing the weight applied to the so-called sales factor, states attempt to provide an advantage for those companies that create more jobs and invest more in physical facilities within that state. Many states also allow for separate entity accounting, which treats parent companies and their subsidiary companies as unrelated. This policy permits companies to concentrate profits in the state offering the most preferential tax treatment. Companies therefore have an incentive to shop around for the best tax location, even when that location differs from the one indicated by more traditional market factors, such as proximity to the marketplace or quality of the workforce available. Thus, as states engage in destructive competition for jobs and business investment, the result is often a needless loss of tax revenues.

Perhaps the most significant threat to the flow of state tax revenues from businesses is the proliferation of so-called tax expenditures. Tax expenditures are revenues forgone by the state, often as tax incentives—an inducement for a business to locate or expand within a particular state. Tax expenditures have grown significantly as more states engage in interstate competition for economic development. Tax expenditures differ from overall reductions in state business taxes—through rate reductions and other concessions—in that they represent favorable tax treatment provided to a single or limited number of firms.

Thirty-three states now provide some type of tax expenditure reporting, and more states have also introduced greater accountability measures into tax incentive packages provided to businesses. Still, many analysts believe that these tax expenditures represent a significant loss of potential state revenues.[40] Estimating the total amount of revenue loss by all states from tax expenditures is difficult, in large part because only about two-thirds of the states engage in some form of tax expenditure reporting, and these reports differ significantly in regard to the (state or local) taxes covered, the frequency of the reporting, and the methodology used to estimate revenue loss.[41] However, recent analysis by McIntyre and Nguyen helps to shed some light. These researchers examined 252 Fortune 500 companies over the 2001–2003 period. They calculated an average statutory state corporate income tax rate of 6.8 percent, which, when applied to the $981 billion in pretax profits realized by this group of firms, should have produced $67 billion in state corporate tax revenue. However, the actual amount of state corporate tax revenue paid by these 252 companies was $25 billion, indicating nearly $42 billion in lost state tax revenues over the three-year period.[42]

Federal Fiscal Policies

Federal policies have both positive and negative effects on state finances, many of which may be difficult to measure or quantify. Whatever the total impact of federal policies on state governments, available evidence indicates that the negative impacts have increased since about 2000, thereby contributing to the state fiscal crisis. According to Iris Lav, "a conservative estimate suggests that federal policies are costing states and localities about $185 billion over the four-year course of the state fiscal crisis, from state fiscal year 2002 through fiscal year 2005."[43] The primary means of adverse effects on state finances have been through changes in federal tax policies, unfunded federal mandates, shifts in health care coverage from Medicare to Medicaid, reduced federal grants-in-aid to states and localities, and federal limitations on state taxing authority.

Federal Tax Cuts

Federal taxes form the basis for many state-level taxes. For example, the

Federation of Tax Administrators notes that

> All states have structured their inheritance/estate taxes to be coordinated with the federal state death tax credit. At the present time, 38 states and the District of Columbia provide that the only state death tax is a "pick-up" or "sponge" tax in which the state death tax is an amount equal to the state death tax credit allowed for federal purposes. . . . Repeal of the federal estate tax will have the effect of repealing the state death tax in those jurisdictions that rely only on the pick-up or sponge tax.[44]

The Federation of Tax Administrators estimated the state death tax revenues (and therefore the potential loss of revenues facing states) at $7.5 billion in 1999. Moreover, they noted that the "repeal of estate tax may have implications for other taxes as it changes expected taxpayer behavior" regarding the transfer of property, charitable donations, and realization of capital gains.[45]

Similarly, many states link their corporate income tax to the counterpart federal tax. In 2002 the federal government enacted "bonus depreciation," which had significant adverse revenue implications for states that remained coupled to the federal tax. Under the bonus depreciation provision, federal law

> allows a business to claim an immediate tax depreciation of up to 30 percent of the cost of new equipment, rather than following the standard accounting approach of depreciating the full cost gradually over several years as under previous federal law. The bonus is effective retroactive to September 2001. . . . It expires in September 2004 . . . [and] states stand to lose more than $14 billion in corporate and individual tax revenue over three years.[46]

Changes in other provisions of the federal tax code, such as Section 179, provided immediate tax relief for small and medium-sized companies that bought equipment, with costs to state coffers that were estimated to total more than $1 billion over fiscal years 2004 and 2005.[47]

Federal tax cuts may also pose more indirect threats to state finances. For instance, Robert McIntyre contends that "by 2006, Bush's tax cuts would double the number of taxpayers affected by the AMT [Alternative Minimum Tax] from fewer than 9 million to almost 19 million. . . . Once in the AMT, taxpayers can no longer claim deductions for state and local taxes."[48] This reduces the ability of state and local governments to "export" a portion of their tax burdens and will likely have a limiting effect on the willingness to impose taxes, especially more progressive ones. In addition, the federal government may be inclined to reduce grants-in-aid to states and their localities to help offset the costs of the tax cuts, the war effort, and stepped-up homeland security.

Federal Grants to States and Localities

Even in the absence of the need to finance federal tax cuts, federal grants to states and local governments have been on the decline. Federal grants peaked in 1980 at 40 percent of state and local government expenditures from their own sources and bottomed out in 1990 at 25 percent. Perhaps more important, Medicaid constituted a growing proportion of federal grants, with other grants-in-aid declining precipitously in relative terms.

The conversion of grants that were previously open-ended matching grants to block grants may also produce long-term fiscal difficulties for states. For example, the old public assistance program, Aid to Families with Dependent Children (AFDC), was a joint federal- and state-funded program, with the federal share being an inverse function of the level of personal income in the state. That is, the federal government funded approximately $0.78 of each AFDC grant benefit dollar in a poor state such as Mississippi, but only $0.50 of each dollar expended in a wealthy state like New Jersey. Moreover, the total spending level was not capped. Therefore, as the number of eligible individuals increased, program spending increased. The new program, Temporary Assistance to Needy Families, is administered as a block grant, whereby a fixed sum of money is given to a state to provide the needed assistance. If caseloads—the number of eligible recipients—increase, states must either reduce the level of benefits provided or absorb the costs of providing the expanded benefits in their own budgets; the federal government provides no additional funding.

Federal Mandates

Federal requirements for additional spending in several areas will prove costly to state governments. Iris Lav and Andrew Brecher estimate that the No Child Left Behind Act, which imposes additional testing and other requirements on school pupils, represents an unfunded federal mandate of about $32 billion over the four-year period of the state fiscal crisis.[49] The Help America Vote Act, designed to help modernize voting technologies, could cost another $1 billion over that same period. The Individuals with Disabilities Education Act fell short of federal funding commitments by $40 billion over the fiscal crisis period. Finally, state and local spending related to homeland security requirements imposed by the federal government could produce annual costs for states that range between $6.5 billion and $17.5 billion.[50]

Federal Limits on State Taxing Authority

Limitations on state taxing authority are not new, and they have taken several forms.[51] For example, the Internet Tax Freedom Act of 1998 (renewed in 2001) precludes states from taxing Internet access. The cost to states in forgone revenue over the crisis period is estimated at $4.5 billion.[52] The Railroad Revitalization and Regulatory Reform Act of 1976, which places restrictions on state tax treatment on railroad property, has also limited the ability of states to raise revenues.[53] Finally, as noted earlier, the failure by Congress to give states the authority to force out-of-state vendors to collect and remit sales taxes has proved very costly to states.

The Distribution of State Revenue Burdens

Another major concern in state and local public finance is the extent to which tax burdens are distributed fairly among taxpayers within the state, based on either a benefits-received or an ability-to-pay principle. The benefits-received principle holds that the distribution of tax burdens should reflect the benefits that taxpayers receive from the services provided, without regard for redistribution among taxpayers at the state (and local) government level. Alternatively, the ability-to-pay principle holds that taxpayers should pay for public services based on some measure of income or wealth, with better-off taxpayers paying a larger share of the costs of public services. Public finance specialists have frequently noted the limitations on subnational units of government in pursuing redistributive tax or spending policies because of the mobility of taxpayers among jurisdictions.[54]

Because of the incentives for tax avoidance that result when redistribution policies are implemented at the state or local level, the conventional wisdom is that progressive taxes that reflect the ability to pay should be used by higher levels of government. Where tax burdens rise with increases in income or wealth, taxes are said to be progressive. Where a larger portion of the income of low-income individuals must be devoted to meeting their tax obligations, the taxes are said to be regressive.

State and local tax systems are generally regarded as regressive, reflecting the relatively large role played by property taxes and various types of general and selective sales taxes.[55] Indeed, as noted above, although personal income taxes currently generate more revenue than general sales taxes, more states (forty-five) employ a general sales tax than employ a personal income tax (forty-one), whereas all states employ selective excise taxes. In fact, sales taxes amount to almost 50 percent of total state tax revenues. Moreover, when combined with the various nontax revenues, which are also generally regarded as being regressive, state tax systems are likely to be mildly to highly regressive in their total impact.

Andrew Reschovsky notes that states are concerned about the impacts of their major revenue sources:

> Most of the 42 states that levy an individual income tax have taken various steps to achieve at least some degree of tax progressivity. The majority of states have a system of graduated rates, with nominal rates rising as income rises. Even states with a flat rate generally build some degree of progressivity into their tax structure through the use of deductions, exemptions, or credits. Of the 45 states that levy a general sales tax, most exempt the purchase of various goods and services with the explicit goal of reducing the burden of the tax on those with limited incomes.[56]

Several actions taken by state policymakers in the last decade have likely increased the regressivity of state revenue systems. For example, some analysts argue that the failure to include most services in the sales tax base or the inability to capture most forms of remotes sales makes the sales tax even more regressive, because low-income taxpayers consume relatively more goods than services and generally have less access to remote means of purchase (such as the Internet). As these components of consumption and remote transactions grow in importance, the sales tax will become more regressive. Moreover, as consumption taxes become a larger component of the overall revenue system for states, the system becomes more regressive.

A disturbing pattern has emerged regarding policy changes in the distribution of state tax burdens. Many states throughout the 1990s made their tax systems less progressive. During periods of economic downturn, when states raised taxes to meet recession-induced budget shortfalls, they predominantly raised those taxes that fall most heavily on low- and moderate-income households. During those periods when stronger economies allowed taxes to be cut, much of the benefit was targeted on higher income families.[57]

Personal income taxes accounted for just 32 percent of the net increases enacted in 1990 through 1993 but 74 percent of the net decreases enacted in 1994 through 1997. By contrast, sales and excise taxes accounted for 46 percent of the tax increases in the early 1990s but just 0.5 percent of the net tax cuts in the mid-1990s.[58]

Similarly, as more states adopt nontax revenue sources and they contribute a larger portion of the total revenues used to finance public services, low-income taxpayers will face an ever-increasing portion of the relative tax burden. As such, one by-product of an expanded role for state government may be relatively heavier fiscal burdens for low- and moderate-income households.

Conclusion

Although the fiscal outlook is improving for many states, the fiscal crisis that extended from fiscal 2002 to 2005 exacted a toll on state finances. States experienced both short-term cyclical fluctuations and more chronic disruptions in their budgets. These tough fiscal times occurred just as more fiscal responsibilities were being loaded onto the states. More fiscal perils lie ahead if current predictions regarding pension finances hold true.

Clearly, states contributed to their own fiscal misery by adopting policies that limit their flexibility to respond to budget crises and through some of the policy choices they made. By failing to modernize their major tax instruments, engaging in destructive interstate competition for economic development, and resorting to gambling revenues that are likely to prove illusory as a long-term solution, states have at least exacerbated their fiscal difficulties.

Federal policies must also share responsibility for the current difficulties of states. Significant problems for the states have resulted from the federal government's mandating additional state spending, undermining state revenue sources, and imposing significant limitations on the authority of states to tax significant economic activities.

If states are to assume the expanded role in the U.S. federal system, they must be more mindful of the changing economic, demographic, and technological circumstances going on around them and take the necessary policy actions to accommodate the new world in which they are operating. In addition, the states will need more cooperation from the federal government if they are to fulfill their new destiny.

Notes

1. U.S. Bureau of the Census, *Statistical Abstract of the United States, 2004–2005* (Washington, D.C.: Government Printing Office, 2005).
2. Daphne A. Kenyon, "The Federal Impact on State and Local Government Finances at the Beginning of the 21st Century," *State Tax Notes*, December 17, 2001, 932.
3. Therese J. McGuire, "Alternatives to Property Taxation for Local Government," *State Tax Notes*, May 15, 2000, 1715.
4. David Brunori, "To Preserve Local Government, It's Time to Save the Property Tax," *State Tax Notes*, September 10, 2001, 815.
5. See Henry A. Coleman and Colin L. Wood, "America's Intergovernmental System: An Expanded Role for the States," in *Research in Urban Economics: The Changing Economic and Fiscal Structure*, ed. Robert D. Ebel, 187–204 (Greenwich, Conn.: JAI Press, 1984).
6. Iris J. Lav and Andrew Brecher, "Passing Down the Deficit: Federal Policies Contribute to the Severity of the State Fiscal Crisis" (Washington, D.C.: Center on Budget and Policy Priorities, 2004), 1.
7. Robert Zahradnik, Iris J. Lav, and Elizabeth McNichol, "Framing the Choice," Report by the Center on Budget and Policy Priorities, Washington, D.C., 2005, http://www.cbpp.org.
8. Iris J. Lav, Elizabeth McNichol, and Robert Zahradnik, *Faulty Foundations: State Structural Budget Problems and How to Fix Them* (Washington, D.C.: Center on Budget and Policy Priorities, 2005).
9. This section draws heavily from the National Association of State Budget Officers, *Budget Processes in the States* (Washington, D.C.: NASBO, 2002).
10. The exceptions are Alabama and Michigan (October 1 to September 30), New York (April 1 to March 31), and Texas (September 1 to August 31).
11. However, in Kansas, twenty state agencies are on a biennial (two-year) budget, and the remaining agencies are on an annual budget cycle. Similarly, in Missouri, the state has the authority to operate on either an annual or a biennial budget cycle. Since the 1994 fiscal year, the state's operating budget has been on an annual cycle and its capital budget on a biennial cycle. The remaining states operate exclusively on a biennial budget cycle.
12. For states with biennial budgets, revenues and expenditures need not be equal for each year, as long as they are in balance over the course of the budget cycle.
13. Brian Knight, Andrea Kusko, and Laura Rubin, "Problems and Prospects for State and Local Governments," *State Tax Notes*, November 3, 2003, 391.
14. See National Association of State Budget Officers, *Budget Processes in the States*, 24, 36.
15. See U.S. Bureau of the Census, *Statistical Abstract of the United States, 2004–2005* (Washington, D.C.: GPO, 2005).
16. Robert N. Anthony and Regina E. Herzlinger, *Management Control in Nonprofit Organizations*, rev. ed. (Homewood, Ill.: Richard D. Irwin, 1980), 92.
17. Iris J. Lav, "Piling on Problems: How Federal Policies Affect State Fiscal Conditions," *National Tax Journal* 56, no. 3 (September 2003): 545.
18. J. Fred Giertz, "The Impact of Pension Funding on State Government Finances," in "State Fiscal Crises: Causes, Consequences, Solutions," ed. Therese J. McGuire and C. Eugene Steuerle, special supplement, *State Tax Notes*, November 3, 2003, 433–439.

19. William J. Baumol, "Macroeconomics of Unbalanced Growth: The Anatomy of Urban Crisis," *American Economics Review* 57 (June 1967), 415–426.
20. George F. Break, "The New Economy and the Old Tax System," *State Tax Notes*, March 6, 2000, 767–771.
21. See Institute on Taxation and Economic Policy, "Should Sales Taxes Apply to Services?" Policy Brief no. 3, 2004, http://www.ctj.org/itep/.
22. Michael Mazerov, "Expanding Sales Taxation of Services: Options and Issues," *State Tax Notes*, July 21, 2003, 183.
23. Ibid., 190.
24. *National Bellas Hess v. Illinois Department of Revenue*, 386 U.S. 753 (1967); *Quill Corporation v. North Dakota*, 112 S. Ct. 1904 (1992).
25. See Donald Bruce and William F. Fox, "State and Local Sales Tax Revenue Losses from E-Commerce: Estimates as of July 2004," *State Tax Notes*, August 16, 2004, 511–518.
26. Lav, McNichol, and Zahradnik, *Faulty Foundations*.
27. David Brunori, "Corporate Tax Discombobulation Continues," *State Tax Notes*, March 26, 2001, 1087.
28. Institute on Taxation and Economic Policy, *The ITEP Guide to Fair State and Local Taxes* (Washington, D.C.: ITEP, 2005), 44–45, http://www.itepnet.org.
29. Ranjana G. Madhusudhan, "What Do We Know about Casino Taxation in the United States," *Proceedings of the 91st Meetings of the National Tax Association* (Washington, D.C.: National Tax Association, 1998), 85.
30. Steven D. Gold, "Gambling Is No Panacea for Ailing State Budgets," *State Tax Notes*, October 18, 1993, 909.
31. Ibid., 908.
32. Ibid.
33. Ibid., 908–909.
34. Institute on Taxation and Economic Policy, "Uncertain Benefits, Hidden Costs: The Perils of State-Sponsored Gambling," Policy Brief no. 19, 2005, http://www.itepnet.org.
35. Robert S. McIntyre and T. D. Coo Nguyen, *State Corporate Income Taxes, 2001–2003: A Joint Project of Citizens for Tax Justice and the Institute on Taxation and Economic Policy* (Washington, D.C.: CTJ and ITEP, 2005), 5.
36. Robert Cline, William Fox, Tom Neubig, and Andrew Phillips, "Total State and Local Business Taxes: A 50-State Study of the Taxes Paid by Business in Fiscal 2003," *State Tax Notes*, March 1, 2004, 737–750.
37. Ibid.
38. Raymond J. Ring Jr., "The Proportion of Consumers' and Producers' Goods in the General Sales Tax," *National Tax Journal* 42 (June 1989): 167–180.
39. Richard D. Pomp, "The Future of the State Corporate Income Tax: Reflections (and Confessions) of a Tax Lawyer," in *The Future of State Taxation*, ed. David Brunori, 49–71 (Washington, D.C.: Urban Institute Press, 1998).
40. See Good Jobs First at http://www.goodjobsfirst.org/pdf/nmcs.pdf for a sample of relevant individual state studies.
41. John L. Mikesell, "Tax Expenditure Budgets, Budget Policy, and Tax Policy: Confusion in the States," *Public Budgeting and Finance*, Winter 2002, 34–51.
42. McIntyre and Nguyen, *State Corporate Income Taxes, 2001–2003*, 1.
43. Iris J. Lav, "Federal Policies Contribute to the Severity of the State Fiscal Crisis," Report by the Center on Budget and Policy Priorities, Washington, D.C., October 22, 2003, 1.
44. Federation of Tax Administrators, "Repeal of Federal Estate Tax Would Have Effect on States," *State Tax Notes*, March 12, 2000, 903.
45. Ibid., 906.

46. Nicholas Johnson, "States Can Avoid Substantial Revenue Loss by Decoupling from New Federal Tax Provision," *State Tax Notes,* April 1, 2002, 79.
47. Nicholas Johnson, "Federal Tax Changes Likely to Cost States Billions of Dollars in Coming Years," *State Tax Notes,* June 9, 2003, 909.
48. Robert S. McIntyre, "The Effects of the Bush Tax Cuts on State Tax Revenues," *State Tax Notes,* May 14, 2001, 1694.
49. Iris J. Lav and Andrew Brecher, "Passing Down the Deficit: Federal Policies Contribute to the Severity of the State Fiscal Crisis," Report by the Center on Budget and Policy Priorities, Washington, D.C., 2004, http://www.cbpp.org.
50. Ibid., 9.
51. See Henry A. Coleman, "External Limits on State Taxation of Business Activities," in *Economic Union in Federal Systems,* ed. Anne Mullins and Cheryl Saunders, 193–211 (New South Wales: Federation Press, 1994).
52. Lav and Brecher, "Passing Down the Deficit."
53. Coleman, "External Limits on State Taxation of Business Activities."
54. Andrew Reschovsky, "The Progressivity of State Tax Systems," in *The Future of State Taxation,* ed. David Brunori (Washington, D.C.: Urban Institute Press, 1998), 161–189.
55. See Institute on Taxation and Economic Policy, *Who Pays: A Distribution Analysis of the Tax System in All Fifty States,* 2nd ed. (Washington, D.C.: ITEP, 2003), http://www.itepnet.org.
56. Reschovsky, "Progressivity of State Tax Systems," 161.
57. Nicholas Johnson and Iris Lav, "Are State Taxes Becoming More Regressive?" Report by the Center on Budget and Policy Priorities, Washington, D.C., 1997, 1, http://www.cbpp.org.
58. Ibid., 8.

8

State Education Policy in the New Millennium
Margaret E. Goertz

In the United States, the authority for public elementary and secondary education resides in the states, a "reserved" power arising from the Tenth Amendment of the U.S. Constitution.[1] All state constitutions contain provisions requiring states to create a system of free public schools. Although states historically delegated considerable authority to their local communities, states now play a major role in the funding and regulation of education, and education dominates the state policy agenda. With states providing nearly half of all public school revenues, elementary and secondary education commands the largest share of state budgets. About one-third of state general fund expenditures are devoted to this function.[2] Legislators must grapple annually (or biennially) with the size of the state education aid budget; the allocation of these funds to local districts; and the consequences of these decisions for the level of local education spending, state and local taxes, and funds available for other public services. States have also assumed greater authority in many nonfiscal areas of education, ranging from teacher certification to the establishment of student performance standards to sanctions for poorly performing schools and school districts, extending the power of the state to areas that were once the sole responsibility of local school boards.

State education policy discussions and resolutions reflect the changing environment of American education, the national education agenda, and the competing reform values of equity, excellence, efficiency, and choice. *Equity* focuses on equalizing or distributing educational resources and opportunities to meet moral or societal goals. *Excellence* focuses on the use of these resources to support professional or publicly determined standards of quality or proficiency. *Efficiency* focuses on holding educators accountable for the performance of their schools and students and rendering schools more productive. As used in this chapter, *choice* refers broadly to policies that place the control of education in the hands of schools, parents, or private contractors.[3]

The Environment of State Education Policy

Education policy has been shaped by fundamental changes in its social, economic, and political environment. Declining test scores throughout the 1970s undermined public confidence in the country's public school system and led business leaders to question the quality of the nation's future workforce. An eroding U.S. position in the international economy turned policymakers' attention and energies to issues of efficiency, excellence, and choice in education and away from earlier concerns with equity. Policy leadership thrust upon the federal government by the Russian *Sputnik* launching in the late 1950s, the Supreme Court's desegregation rulings in the 1950s, and the War on Poverty of the 1960s shifted back to the states in the 1970s, where fragmented and diffuse interest groups compete for control of the education agenda. Today, states are struggling to define and support a rigorous educational program that meets the postindustrial needs of American business at a time when the school-age population is growing in numbers and in cultural diversity; the public is questioning the cost, quality, and efficiency of public education; and the federal government is holding states accountable for significant gains in student learning.

The Social Environment of Education

The social environment of education encompasses the nature of the population to be educated and society's expectations for its schools. The percentage of children under age eighteen living in poverty decreased from 26.5 percent in 1960 to 15.8 percent in 2001, due largely to the War on Poverty programs of the late 1960s. But poverty rates differ considerably by race and ethnicity and by family structure. In 2001, 30 percent of African American children and 27 percent of Hispanic children were poor, compared with 13 percent of white children.[4] Some of these differences are related to family structures. Single-parent households, especially those headed by members of racial or ethnic minorities, are more likely to live in poverty. In 2001, 18 percent of white, 27 percent of Hispanic, and 55 percent of African American children lived in single-parent households, and one-third of white and half of minority single-parent households had incomes below the poverty line.[5] However, minority children living in two-parent households also had poverty rates that were twice those of their white peers.

The educational problems of children from poor families are confounded by their growing racial and economic isolation from mainstream society. Between 1976 and 2002, the proportion of white, non-Hispanic students in American public schools declined from 76 percent to 60 percent of the student population, while the proportion of African American students increased slightly (15.5 percent to 17.3 percent), and the proportion of Hispanic students nearly tripled (6.4 percent to 17.8 percent).[6] Although the *Brown v. Board of Education* decision and the civil rights movement significantly increased the number of African American students attending school with white students, schools remain segregated in all regions of the country. Prior to the *Brown* decision in 1954, virtually all African American students in southern and border states and a majority of African American students in other areas of the country attended "intensely segregated" schools—that is, 90 percent or more minority. In 2001 about 40 percent of African American and a similar percentage of Hispanic students were in these kinds of schools.

Nearly three-quarters of African American and Hispanic students attended schools that were more than 50 percent minority.[7] One reason for concern about the racial and ethnic composition of schools is the strong link between racial and economic segregation. Eighty percent of predominantly minority schools (having more than 70 percent minority students) had concentrated poverty—that is, more than half of the students participated in the federal free lunch program—whereas fewer than 25 percent of predominantly white schools had this level of poverty.[8]

States are affected differentially by the concentration of poor, minority, and limited-English-proficient students. Southern and southwestern states had the highest school-age poverty rates in the country. Eleven states were racially homogeneous—they had 15 percent or fewer minority youth in 2002—whereas five states, including the country's two largest, California and Texas, had "majority-minority" school-age populations (see Table 8–1). Half of the nation's English-language learners are educated in schools in the West, where such students make up 16 percent of all students compared with about 7 percent nationally. Still, during the 1990s the number of English-language learners in the Midwest doubled, and that in the South increased almost 50 percent.[9]

These demographics have three major implications for education policy.[10] First, schools are faced with an "imperiled generation" of children who are at risk of failure in school. A large achievement gap exists between white and nonwhite students, and between students from poor and nonpoor families. For example, 75 percent of white fourth grade students, but only 40 percent of African American and 44 percent of Hispanic fourth graders, scored at or above Basic on the 2003 National Assessment of Educational Progress reading test. Similarly, only 45 percent of students eligible for the free and reduced-price lunch program reached a Basic level of proficiency, compared with three-quarters of students who were not eligible for the program.[11] School curricula, programs, and structure need to be redesigned to meet the needs of children who come from multiple language and cultural backgrounds, are potential low achievers, change schools frequently, and have health and family problems. Second, the link between education and financial and career success in adulthood has grown stronger as the number of jobs in the middle of the economic range—primarily in manufacturing—continues to decline. If educational services for poor and minority students are not improved, these individuals will become increasingly concentrated in the nation's low-paying service economy. Third, there is a growing gap between those who benefit from public services and those who pay for them. Those population groups with the largest vested interest in education are those with limited political power—low-income and minority citizens. As poor and minority students become increasingly concentrated in inner-city and rural schools, white middle-aged, middle-class suburban dwellers have become less willing to pay for these public schools, leading state legislators to resist school finance reforms that raise taxes or redistribute education resources.[12] In addition, as the nation's

Table 8–1 Economic and Racial/Ethnic Make-up of the States (percent)

State	Persons aged 5 to 17 below the poverty line (2000)	Public school students by race or ethnicity (2002)			
		White[a]	Black[a]	Hispanic	Other[b]
United States	15.1	59.5	17.3	17.8	5.5
Alabama	20.7	60.2	36.3	1.8	1.7
Alaska	11.1	59.4	4.7	3.7	32.2
Arizona	18.5	50.0	4.8	36.5	8.7
Arkansas	20.7	70.5	23.2	0.8	1.5
California	19.1	34.0	8.3	45.5	12.2
Colorado	10.7	65.7	5.7	24.3	4.2
Connecticut	10.0	69.0	13.6	14.1	3.3
Delaware	11.5	58.4	31.4	7.2	2.9
District of Columbia	31.2	4.3	83.7	10.4	1.7
Florida	17.2	51.6	24.7	21.4	2.3
Georgia	16.7	53.0	38.2	6.2	2.7
Hawaii	13.6	20.4	2.4	4.6	72.7
Idaho	13.2	85.9	0.8	10.9	2.4
Illinois	13.8	58.3	21.1	16.9	3.7
Indiana	11.2	82.2	12.2	4.3	1.3
Iowa	10.2	89.0	4.3	4.4	2.3
Kansas	11.0	76.8	9.1	10.4	3.7
Kentucky	20.0	86.9	10.8	1.4	1.0
Louisiana	25.8	48.5	47.8	1.7	2.0
Maine	12.9	95.9	1.6	0.7	1.8
Maryland	10.3	51.5	37.5	5.8	5.1
Massachusetts	11.9	75.1	8.8	11.2	4.9
Michigan	13.3	72.4	20.3	3.8	3.5
Minnesota	9.3	81.1	7.4	4.2	7.4
Mississippi	26.4	47.3	50.9	1.0	0.9
Missouri	15.0	77.9	18.2	2.3	0.6
Montana	17.9	85.4	0.7	2.0	12.0
Nebraska	11.8	80.6	7.0	9.2	3.2
Nevada	13.1	52.7	10.5	28.7	8.1
New Hampshire	7.4	94.4	1.5	2.2	1.9
New Jersey	10.9	58.6	17.8	16.6	7.0
New Mexico	24.1	33.6	2.4	51.7	12.3
New York	19.6	54.2	20.0	19.0	6.7
North Carolina	15.4	59.2	31.4	5.9	3.5
North Dakota	12.8	88.6	1.1	1.3	9.0
Ohio	13.4	79.7	16.9	7.0	19.4
Oregon	13.7	78.1	3.0	12.5	6.4
Pennsylvania	14.2	77.1	15.5	5.2	2.3
Rhode Island	16.1	72.2	8.4	15.6	3.8
South Carolina	18.4	54.4	41.5	2.7	0.4
South Dakota	16.1	85.3	1.5	1.6	11.6
Tennessee	17.1	71.3	24.8	2.4	1.4
Texas	19.8	39.8	14.3	42.7	3.2

Table 8-1 *(continued)*

State	Persons aged 5 to 17 below the poverty line (2000)	Public school students by race or ethnicity (2002)			
		White[a]	Black[a]	Hispanic	Other[b]
Utah	9.5	84.1	1.1	10.4	4.4
Vermont	10.8	95.8	1.3	0.7	2.2
Virginia	11.9	61.8	27.2	6.2	4.8
Washington	12.9	72.6	5.6	11.6	10.2
West Virginia	23.4	94.4	4.5	0.5	0.7
Wisconsin	10.6	79.5	10.4	5.4	4.8
Wyoming	13.4	86.7	1.3	7.7	4.2

Sources: Poverty data calculated from U.S. Bureau of the Census, table P87, http://factfinder.census.gov. Racial and ethnic data from Lee Hoffman, Jennifer Sable, Julia Naum, and Dell Gray, *Public Elementary and Secondary Students, Staff, Schools, and School Districts: School Year 2002–2003*, NCES 2005-314 (Washington, D.C.: U.S. Department of Education, National Center for Education Statistics, 2005), table C-3.

a. Excludes persons of Hispanic origin.
b. Includes Asian or Pacific Islander and American Native/Alaska Native.

population ages, fewer individuals have a direct stake in the public education system. Only one-third of households in 2000 had children under eighteen; senior citizens made up 21 percent of all households, a number that will increase as the baby boomers reach retirement age.[13]

Social values about education are also important in framing education policy. In the 1960s the civil rights movement heightened public awareness of inequities in society, and passage of the Elementary and Secondary Education Act in 1965 focused attention on issues of equality of educational opportunity. Title I of the act (now Title I of the No Child Left Behind Act) provides financial support for the education of economically disadvantaged students. Enactment of the Bilingual Education Act of 1968 and the Education for All Handicapped Children Act of 1975 (now called the Individuals with Disabilities Education Act) expanded educational access to students not proficient in the English language and to those with disabilities. The education reform movement of the 1980s and 1990s, however, redirected attention to excellence, efficiency, and choice. The educational policies of these decades emphasized higher educational standards for students and teachers, greater accountability for school and student performance, and increasing parental choice. Although the focus on standards, accountability, and choice continues, there is renewed interest in issues of equity as well. State and federal policy, such as the No Child Left Behind Act of 2001, address the values of both equity and excellence by requiring that rigorous standards be applied to *all* students. Plaintiffs have initiated an unprecedented number of school finance court cases, most of which are focused on ensuring that school districts have an adequate level of resources to meet these higher academic standards.

The Economic Environment of Education

The education reform movement of the last twenty years has been dominated by economic concerns: declining U.S. competitiveness in an international economy; low industrial productivity; and changes in the skill level, size, and composition of the nation's labor force. Worker productivity must continually increase if the United States is to compete successfully in the global economy. Yet employers in large and small businesses alike decry the lack of preparation for work among high school students. At a time when workforce skills are growing increasingly complex and undergoing rapid change, too many students lack the necessary reading, writing, mathematical, and problem-solving skills to meet entry-level job requirements.[14] Performance on national assessments of reading has shown little change since the National Assessment of Educational Progress test was first administered in 1971, and only one-third of fourth- and eighth-grade students met the proficiency standards in 2003.[15] Scores on mathematics assessments improved slightly between the mid-1970s and 1990 and then increased steadily through 2003. Improvement was concentrated in the basic skills areas, however, and by 2003 only one-third of students met or exceeded the proficient level.[16] In addition, although the performance gap between white and nonwhite students has narrowed, a substantial disparity remains. As poor and minority individuals constitute a larger and larger portion of the labor force, "business leaders have come to understand that the emerging labor supply problem is essentially an educational problem."[17]

Another aspect of the economic environment that affects state education policy is the availability of fiscal resources to support public education. Whereas per pupil spending (adjusted for inflation) on elementary and secondary education grew 27 percent in the 1970s and 38 percent in the 1980s, it rose only 16 percent in the 1990s, reflecting a weak economy at the beginning of that decade and growing enrollments.[18] The environment for increases in school revenue in the first decade of the twenty-first century is not favorable. State support for education will be limited by slow economic growth, the rising cost of health programs, particularly Medicaid, high levels of debt, and an aversion to raising state taxes (see Chapter 7).[19]

The Political Environment of Education

Until the late 1960s, state education policy was the province of broadly based education interest groups (state education departments, schools of education, superintendents, administrators, and teachers) and a small number of legislators who specialized in education policy. Groups like the Educational Conference Board in New York and the Princeton Group in New Jersey sought to build consensus among these educational interests on the policy goals and legislative priorities in their states. This structure fit the limited state role in education at the time. Three factors have contributed to the growing complexity of education politics today: the changing roles of the federal and state governments in education policy, the growing political and programmatic fragmentation of education, and the emergence of noneducation interests into the education policy arena.

The involvement of the federal and state governments in public education expanded rapidly in the late 1960s and early 1970s. Although the federal government had always played a modest role in public education, concern over national security and poverty led it to support the development of curricular innovations in mathematics and science, to design and fund equal educational opportunity programs, and to support the expansion and professionalization of state departments of education throughout the country. In times of state fiscal constraint it continues to fund the majority of department of education positions in many states.[20] Starting in the late 1980s, the federal focus began to shift from student access to additional services to the quality of the services provided and educational accountability. As discussed in greater detail later, the Improving America's Schools Act of 1994 and its successor, the No Child Left Behind Act of 2001 (NCLB), have required states to adopt rigorous academic standards, implement testing aligned with these standards, accept greater accountability for the performance of all students, and ensure the placement of "highly qualified" teachers in all classrooms as conditions for receiving funds under these laws. Thus, although federal aid to education represents less than 10 percent of all spending on elementary and secondary education, the impact of its financial contribution has become far-reaching.

Expansion of the state role in education policy was driven in part by its role in the implementation of the new federal programs of the 1960s and 1970s, but also by the expanding fiscal role of states (caused by exploding school populations and the first round of school finance court cases) and a corresponding call for accountability in the use of these new state education dollars. As state courts called for greater equalization of education funding, both the state share of local education expenditures and the absolute level of state education spending rose substantially. This growth led many states to implement minimum competency testing and other policies in the 1970s to hold educators accountable for the operation and performance of their schools. A national call for higher academic standards in the 1980s, now incorporated in the provisions of federal laws, expanded the state role further in the setting of student, teacher, and school standards.

The broadened roles of state and federal government in education policy changed state education politics in two ways. First, the state education agenda expanded. With state education aid a major component of state budgets, legislators became preoccupied with the increasingly contentious job of raising and allocating state dollars to local school districts. Every year, policymakers have to balance a complex equity, political, and economic agenda, as school finance decisions become intertwined with the politics of redistribution and taxation. On the nonfiscal policy side, the push for higher education standards and increased accountability has thrust governors and legislators in the role of defining and measuring the goals and elements of a quality education, areas that had been the province of education professionals and local school boards. In recent years these issues have become controversial, as the conservative right challenges both the substance and the value-orientation of state standards and related policies.

Second, the number of actors interested and involved in shaping education policy decisions grew, transforming the political structure from a statewide monolith to a fragmented system of education politics.[21] The growth of collective bargaining for teachers, the civil rights movement, and the creation of interest groups organized around new federal programs for special needs students shattered the old consensus-building structures, replacing them with competing centers of power—teacher unions; administrator groups; and bilingual, Title I, and special education advocates.

In the early 1980s business groups emerged as powerful new voices in shaping education policy as the focus of education policy shifted to quality of education and educational outcomes, and business has remained a stalwart supporter of standards-based reforms. The politics of education also grew more complicated (and sometime contentious) as governors emerged as major players in education policy, sometimes leading, sometimes challenging, traditional legislative prerogatives. Some governors began to play a visible role in education policy in the 1970s, when many became leaders in school finance reform in their states. Their role increased dramatically in the 1980s, when a group of reform-minded governors undertook an education reform movement that sought to respond to calls by the public, the business community, and the president for improved education. Reform activities by individual governors coalesced in 1989 when President George H. W. Bush and the nation's governors embraced the concept of national education goals at a historic education summit, and many governors continue to work with the business community in support of standards-based reform through a bi-partisan organization, Achieve Inc.[22]

What was unique about the politics of state education reform in the 1980s was the relatively unimportant role of education interest groups in the formulation of new state policies. Although opposed to specific aspects of the new reforms, education groups were stymied. Strong public and business support ensured backing from governors and state legislators.[23] In many states, traditional education groups have found it difficult to regain their previous influence in state education policy, as Republican governors and legislatures mobilize the public and the business community around an agenda of testing, accountability, and choice. Religious organizations and some inner-city parents also champion choice programs, particularly those that give parents vouchers for private schools. In a few states where voters can enact fiscal and programmatic policy through ballot initiatives and referenda, vocal interests take their political agendas directly to the electorate, and in some instances they have succeeded in imposing changes such as tax limitations or antibilingual education policies.

Major Issues in State Policy

Although the fifty states are socially, economically, and politically diverse, policymakers in every state must direct five major areas of education policy: curriculum and instruction, accountability, teachers, governance, and finance.

Curriculum and Instruction

States have used a variety of measures over the years to influence the content of the school curriculum, not the least of which was minimum competency testing. But until the 1990s, most state activity focused on instructional time or required courses or credits, or both. All states mandate the minimum number of days students must attend school, and the majority of states (thirty-four) have set this minimum at 180 days or longer. Another eleven states have mandated shorter school years, generally between 170 and 175 days. Forty states also mandate the minimum length of the school day. Districts may extend their school year and school day beyond these minimum times, and many do.[24]

In 1983, in response to poor student performance on national and international assessments, the National Commission on Excellence in Education recommended that high school students take more courses in the "New Basics"—English, mathematics, science, social studies, and computer science. Specifically, high school graduates should complete four years of English, three years of mathematics, three years of science, three years of social studies, and one-half year of computer science. Two years of a foreign language were strongly recommended for college-bound students.[25] Forty-four states mandate the number and type of courses students must complete for high school graduation, and most of these states raised their course work standards after the publication of the commission's report, *A Nation at Risk*. Yet, twenty years later, only half of these states had enacted policies that met the National Commission's recommendations. In 2003–2004 thirty-seven states required four or more years of English, and thirty states required three or more years of social studies; fewer required three years of mathematics (twenty-four) or three years of science (twenty-one). In addition, few states specified which mathematics and science courses students must take, such as Algebra 1 (seventeen), geometry (seven), biology (fourteen), or physical science (eleven).[26]

Course work and instructional time requirements provide little substantive guidance in developing appropriate curricula. The standards-based reform movement, which emerged in the late 1980s and early 1990s through the work of a group of education leaders, governors, businessmen, researchers, and organizations such as the National Council of Teachers of Mathematics and the American Association for the Advancement of Science, was designed to address this shortcoming. Under the theory of standards-based reform, states establish challenging content and performance standards for all students and align key state policies affecting teaching and learning—curriculum and curriculum materials, preservice and inservice teacher training, and assessment—to these standards. Then, states give schools and school districts greater flexibility to design appropriate instructional programs in exchange for holding schools accountable for student performance.[27]

These ideas initially received the support of President George H. W. Bush who, in the aftermath of the 1989 education summit, unsuccessfully proposed a system of voluntary national standards and tests. The Clinton administration subsequently took a "carrot and stick" approach to promote and support nascent state standards-based reform efforts. The Improving America's School Act of 1994 called for states to develop challenging standards in at least reading and mathematics, create high-quality assessments to measure performance against these standards, and have local districts identify low-performing schools for assistance. The Goals 2000 legislation and programs like the National Science Foundation's State and Urban Systemic Initiatives provided funds for states and localities to design the components of a standards-based system and to build the capacity of local districts to implement these reforms.

The NCLB Act requires states to establish challenging learner outcomes in, at a minimum, mathematics, reading, writing, and science, but the federal government does not review or approve the content of these standards. Federal law forbids its agencies from mandating, directing, or controlling the specific instructional content, curriculum, programs of instruction, or academic achievement standards and assessments of states, school districts, or schools, although it can and does use grants to support the adoption of instructional programs with a particular focus.[28] Thus, states determine the substance of academic standards.

In 2004 all but one state had developed content standards in reading and mathematics, and all but two in science and social studies as well.[29] States have not adopted common standards, however. Although many states have aligned their mathematics and science, and to a lesser extent their reading, standards to those developed by the professional organizations in these fields, states differ in the coverage, rigor, specificity, and clarity of their curricular framework. One evaluation reported that content standards in only five of the thirty states reviewed were clear and specific and covered what the reviewers considered essential reading and math skills in each grade.[30] Other analyses also showed variation in the quality of standards both across and within states.[31] Some states have developed both professional and community consensus for the content of the standards. Other states have faced philosophical battles over what should be taught (for example, evolution or the content of social science courses) and how (for example, different approaches to teaching mathematics and reading). For example, after gaining control of the Kansas State Board of Education, religious conservatives have voted twice to change that state's science standards to include alternatives to the teaching of evolution. The teaching of mathematics became the subject of heated controversy in many states, with traditionalists (including university mathematics professors) battling reformers over appropriate pedagogy (teacher-directed versus student-constructed knowledge) and curricular emphasis—process (problem-solving and mathematical reasoning) versus content (facts, computation, and algorithms). Similar fights took place over reading curriculum policy: what is the best way to teach reading—through the direct instruction of phonics and skills, using controlled text, or indirect instruction through students' interaction with authentic literature, in an approach called "whole language?"[32]

Accountability and Assessment

States historically used systems of school accreditation as a means of monitoring and regulating education in their communities. Traditionally, accreditation has focused on compliance with input standards (for example, the proportion of certified staff and number of books in the library) and with process standards (for example, the method of handling student complaints). Districts were monitored periodically through a combination of district self-reports and site visits by state department of education personnel. In line with their increased attention to student standards and use of incentives and sanctions to improve school performance, states began revising their accountability systems in the 1990s to focus more heavily on student performance. Prior to the enactment of NCLB, however, state accountability and assessment systems differed in many ways: who was held accountable (students, schools, or school districts), how performance was measured (for example, the grades and subjects assessed), measures of progress and performance goals, and the consequences of not meeting state goals (ranging from public scrutiny to state takeover for schools).[33]

In response to this variation the NCLB Act standardized state accountability and assessment policies. The law requires states to test all students in grades 3–8 and once in high school in reading and mathematics by 2005–2006, and to test students once per grade span in science by 2007–2008. Although the federal government cannot dictate the form or content of a state assessment, it will determine whether assessments are aligned with state standards. States also must establish annual goals and objectives for student performance (called Adequate Yearly Progress, or AYP) so that all students are proficient on state standards by 2014. States and school districts must report on the progress of districts, schools, and specific subgroups of students (racial and ethnic, impoverished, disabled, and limited English proficient). Schools and school districts that receive Title I funds and whose students, including any of the specified subgroups, fail to show AYP, are subject to an increasingly punitive set of sanctions, beginning with granting parents the right to choose another public school and possibly culminating with school closing or state takeover. Each state's accountability and assessment plans must be approved by the federal government.

There has been considerable debate about the type and extent of flexibility states have in responding to the accountability requirements of the NCLB Act. Some provisions allow no flexibility: states must hold schools and districts accountable separately for progress in reading and mathematics, they must calculate AYP separately for all students and all subgroups of students in a school and school district, and states must follow the NCLB provisions for establishing "starting points" for the AYP targets, as well as timelines for implementing specified sanctions to Title I schools. Areas of flexibility include setting state content and performance standards, designing assessments, establishing the growth trajectory for improvement and the minimum number of students required for inclusion in accountability calculations, and determining whether NCLB sanctions should be applied to schools that do not receive Title I funds. And states may choose how to incorporate NCLB accountability requirements into their state accountability systems.

All states have developed accountability policies that meet the requirements of NCLB. About half of the states will use the NCLB model of AYP as their state accountability system.[34] Some of these states did not have a statewide accountability system (beyond public reporting) before the enactment of NCLB. Other states replaced their prior definition of AYP. Twenty-three states, however, will include criteria in addition to those required under NCLB provisions in their state accountability systems. At least eleven states will apply two or more ratings to their schools, generally the federal AYP rating and a separate state rating. These separate state accountability systems share a set of design features that distinguish them from the provisions of NCLB: they use performance indexes that average test scores across subject areas, give differential weight to subjects or performance levels, or include nonacademic indicators; they apply student or school growth measures; or they fail to consider subgroup performance in their rating systems.[35]

State accountability policies—particularly the use of growth models and lack of subgroup accountability—identify fewer schools in need of improvement and therefore fewer schools eligible for assistance and possibly subject to sanctions under federal and state laws. In Florida, for example, although close to 75 percent of the state's schools failed to make AYP under the federal guidelines in 2003–2004, only 9 percent of the schools were given grades of "D" or "F" under the state system. Nearly half of the schools received a grade of "A." About 60 percent of the schools in North Carolina that met the "state growth goals" failed to make AYP. These disparate ratings have created a public relations nightmare for states, particularly in suburban school districts that receive high ratings under state measures, and have led some states to request that their state accountability policies replace those required by federal law.

The NCLB Act focuses on school and school district accountability. Many states have developed high-stakes accountability systems for students as well as schools. Eight states have promotion policies for students in elementary and middle grades that incorporate state tests. Half of the states require (twenty) or plan to require (five) students to pass a state examination to graduate from high school, an increase of seven states since 1992. Most state high school exit examinations assess a student's general knowledge of English and language arts and of mathematics and often of science and social studies as well. Whereas most of the older graduation tests focused on basic skills, nearly all these states have revised their examinations to align with more rigorous state standards and to assess content taught in the early high school grades. Five of the states (Maryland, Mississippi, New York, Tennessee, and Virginia) require students to pass a specified number of end-of-course examinations for graduation.[36] Another handful of states administer end-of-course examinations but use them for other purposes, such as students' grades (for example, North Carolina).

There appears to be widespread support at the state and school district level for the basic premises of NCLB—that having a uniform accountability system based on content and performance standards and focusing attention on subgroup performance and achievement gaps will positively affect student achievement.[37] At the same time, provisions of the law have generated criticism from state and local policymakers, educators, and some members of Congress. First, policymakers have contested the cost of implementing such NCLB requirements as expanding their state assessment systems and providing support to low-performing schools and students. State studies have predicted that the cost of teaching all students to standards could require states to raise spending 20 to 40 percent, or a total of $137 billion nationally.[38] Although federal appropriations for NCLB grew 50 percent between 2001 and 2006, this represented an increase of only $4.6 billion and fell about $7 billion short of authorized spending. This mismatch between projected costs and federal funding led Connecticut and school districts in other states to sue the federal government, charging that the NCLB Act imposes unfunded requirements. The Utah legislature similarly ordered state officials to ignore provisions of the law that conflict with state goals or require state financing. A second concern involves how NCLB applies testing and accountability provisions to students with disabilities and English-language learners. States question whether students with special needs can and should be expected to meet the same proficiency standards as other students.

Finally, high-stakes school and student accountability policies raise the question of whether educational institutions have the kinds of human and fiscal resources they need to improve schools and to provide all students the opportunity to learn to high standards. Passing rates on high school exit exams show persistently lower achievement for racial and ethnic minority students, English-language learners, and students with disabilities. Although states are taking steps to help teachers prepare students for exit examinations through curriculum alignment, professional development, and test preparation materials, few states target funds to student remedial services. Similarly, many districts, particularly in low-wealth communities, report that they lack the resources and technical assistance they need to support schools that have been identified for improvement through state or NCLB accountability policies.[39]

Teacher Policy

A growing body of research shows that effective teachers can raise student achievement.[40] There is less agreement about the background characteristics of a good teacher (for example, level and type of preparation, test scores, years of experience, or certification) or about ways to increase the supply of quality teachers (such as raising salaries, expanding pathways into the teaching profession, or changing the salary structure). Yet states and school districts are under pressure to place better-trained teachers in every classroom, particularly those of poor, minority, and low-achieving students. States have had minimum requirements for entrance into the teaching profession for decades, but the substance of these policies differed considerably. For example, prior to the enactment of NCLB, only half of the states required teachers to major in the subject they planned to teach; another eleven states allowed prospective teachers to have either a major or a minor in their teaching field. As a result, only two-thirds of secondary teachers reported in 2000 that they had majored in the subjects they taught. One-third of students in high-poverty schools took at least one core academic course with a teacher who did not have an academic major or a minor in that subject.[41]

The NCLB Act addresses teacher quality by requiring that all teachers of core academic subjects be "highly qualified" by 2005–2006. In addition to being fully licensed or certified by their state, new public elementary school teachers must pass a state test demonstrating subject knowledge and teaching skills in reading, writing, mathematics, and other areas of the basic elementary school curriculum. New middle or secondary school teachers must complete an academic major (or equivalent coursework), have a graduate degree, or have advanced certification or credentialing, or pass an examination, in each of the academic subjects they teach. Veteran teachers must meet these same requirements or demonstrate competency in all subjects taught through an evaluation designed by their state.

Although NCLB has introduced some consistency into teacher certification requirements, there is still considerable variability within and across states in how teachers are trained, licensed, and supported. Although all new teachers must now have a subject major in their teaching area, decentralized higher education governance systems make it difficult for most states to influence the content of either subject matter or education courses. Therefore, the content and quality of teacher preparation programs can, and do, vary widely within as well as across states. In addition, forty-four states allow individuals with a college degree to seek licensure through an "alternative route," such as Teach for America or Troops to Teachers. Instead of enrolling in a teacher education program, alternative route participants earn their teaching certificates in an abbreviated period of time, often while they are in the classroom. Alternative routes now produce about 35,000 new teachers each year and account for nearly one-quarter of newly hired teachers in New Jersey and Texas.[42] One way that states ensure that prospective teachers have a minimum level of knowledge and skills, regardless of how or where they are prepared, is to test them in basic skills, subject matter knowledge, or professional knowledge prior to issuing a license. The federal Higher Education Act of 1998 also requires states to report the percentage of teaching candidates in traditional preparation programs who pass these examinations, by higher education institution, as a way of monitoring program quality. The performance of new teachers cannot be compared across the states, however, because states select their own assessments and establish different passing scores.

An expanding area of teacher policy is induction. Induction programs aim to orient beginning teachers to their school and professional communities and help them strengthen their teaching and classroom management skills. Half of the states require beginning teachers to participate in some type of induction program, usually as a condition of receiving a standard license. But the programs range in length from one to three years and from informal mentoring and feedback to more intensive, structured support and formal evaluation. In most cases, states regard induction and mentoring as a local school district responsibility, even when they mandate these activities.

States also regulate the recertification of teachers but generally base recertification on years of teaching experience, completion of additional formal education, or in-service training. The requirements in most states do not specify that this additional training be in the individual's teaching area, and individual teachers, and sometimes their schools, usually determine the content of the training. States play a limited role in teacher professional development generally. They may require districts to provide in-service opportunities and educators to develop plans for continued professional growth, and many states establish guidelines for or approve in-service activities used for recertification, although these guidelines rarely mention content. Most districts must rely on local funds or federal categorical aid programs, such as NCLB or Individuals with Disabilities Education Improvement Act, to support professional development activities. The "high objective uniform state standard of evaluation" (HOUSSE) provisions of NCLB are designed to ensure that veteran teachers have the content knowledge necessary to teach their subjects. But the law permits state HOUSSE plans to vary in both form and rigor. In 2004 thirty states used some version of a point system, in which teachers earn points for completion of additional course work or professional development. Another seven states used a version of their regular teacher performance evaluation to document teachers' content knowledge.[43]

In the early 1980s many states set out to raise teacher salaries to make teaching more competitive with other professions. By 1986 at least thirty states had set minimum teacher salaries.[44] In addition to upgrading salaries, state policymakers also experimented with incentive systems, such as merit pay programs and career ladders, to reward teachers for more, or better, performance. The trend in the 1990s was to transform these programs into less controversial, school-based incentive programs. Kentucky and North Carolina, for example, provide financial rewards to schools if student performance on state tests meets or exceeds state-determined improvement goals. In other plans teachers receive pay increases for demonstrating knowledge and skills that excellent teachers should have. Some states and school districts, for example, grant pay increases to teachers who achieve National Board for Professional Teaching Standards certification. There is renewed interest in differentiated pay systems as new accountability policies place pressure on schools to raise student achievement. Governors, legislatures, and the business community are discussing policies that would tie increases in salaries to student performance, teacher skill levels, and employment in shortage areas or low-performing schools, but tight state budgets have stalled action on these proposals.[45]

Governance

Local school districts are creations of their state; states define their boundaries, governance structures, and responsibilities.[46] The standards-based reform movement, with its focus on student outcomes, and political demands for the decentralization and deregulation of schooling have led many states to place greater authority in the hands of schools and parents. Site-based management, charter schools, and vouchers and contracting are policies designed to give schools, their communities, and parents greater control over education so they have the freedom and flexibility to improve student performance.

Most schools report that they have some type of advisory body, but its influence is generally limited to matters of school planning, parent involvement, and fund-raising. In its various forms, site-based management provides greater school-site autonomy over some combination of budget, personnel, and program decisions. Most site-based management plans also include a school-based governance structure that involves parents and teachers (and sometimes community members) in the decision-making process. The Kentucky Education Reform Act, for example, requires all schools to establish school-site councils and assigns these bodies responsibility for curriculum, instructional materials, personnel, and other policies, many of which had previously been under the purview of the local school board. The Chicago Reform Act of 1988 required that city to reallocate the resources of the system to the school level and created local school councils at each school, which were responsible for adopting a school improvement plan, devising a budget to implement that plan based on a lump sum allocation, and hiring and firing the principal.

States also began experimenting with the deregulation of state education policy in the mid-1980s as a way of promoting school-based innovation. Initially, states permitted schools to seek waivers from regulation, but the early waiver programs were limited in their eligibility criteria and in the rules that could be exempted. Not surprisingly, the programs had limited impact on school practice.⁴⁷ The deregulation movement then evolved to the creation of charter schools. Charter schools operate under contract with sponsoring agencies (for example, local school boards, universities, state boards of education), which specify the outcomes and how they will be measured and the nature and extent of the schools' freedom from state and district regulation. Although charter schools are schools of choice, they are publicly funded and, in most states, may not have selective admissions policies.

The degree of autonomy granted charter schools by state legislatures varies widely across the states. A few states grant superwaivers to charter schools, limiting state regulation to health, safety, and civil rights issues, whereas other states specify what state and local rules may be waived. Most states, however, require charter schools to negotiate personnel, service, and budget decisions with their districts, and many limit the number of charters permitted.⁴⁸ The charter school movement has grown rapidly since Minnesota authorized the first charter school in 1992. By 2005, 3,000 charter schools served nearly 740,000 students, although half of these schools were concentrated in five of the forty states with charter school laws.⁴⁹ The number of charter schools may grow under NCLB, which requires districts to restructure Title I schools that have failed to make AYP for five consecutive years. The law lists conversion to a charter school as one restructuring option.

More radical forms of deregulation and decentralization place the control of education in the hands of a private contractor or directly in the hands of the parents. Over the years, school districts have privatized many education support activities, such as transportation and food service, but in the mid-1990s districts and states began to contract out the management of entire schools. Maryland, for example, contracted the management of Baltimore's three lowest-performing schools to a private company. Philadelphia assigned the operation of many of its low-performing schools to private contractors, nonprofit community organizations, and local universities. Like charter schools, private contractors or other providers are given leeway in how they manage schools in exchange for promises of raising student achievement.

Proposals to use parental choice as a way of improving the quality of public education date back more than two hundred years. Proponents argue that giving parents the power (and the dollars) to choose their schools will produce educational programs and schools that are more responsive to the needs and concerns of parents and their children and that the system will use resources more efficiently. Charter schools provide one option for parents who are dissatisfied with traditional public schools, but nearly all states offer other forms of public school choice. These laws allow students to attend other public schools within their district (intradistrict choice) or in other districts (interdistrict choice), take courses in postsecondary institutions, or attend public or private specialized schools. In 1999, 25 percent of districts provided intradistrict choice, and 14 percent of public school students (and nearly one-quarter of African American students) exercised that choice option.⁵⁰ It is expected that public school choice options and attendance will increase, as NCLB requires districts to offer public school choice to students who attend failing Title I schools. By 2005, however, few students had made use of this provision, perhaps because they have few options in small school districts, face competition for a limited number of seats in higher-performing schools in urban districts, or already participate in a choice program.

The most controversial parental choice policy is the tuition voucher program. Although privately funded voucher programs serve students in a small number of districts, by 2003 only four states had enacted state-financed tuition or voucher programs that allow students to attend nonsectarian or religious schools of their choice. These programs are limited to students attending the states' lowest-performing schools or to students with special needs or from low-income families, and, in two states, to specific school districts. Advocates of voucher programs predict that more states will adopt voucher plans in the aftermath of the U.S. Supreme Court decision in *Zelman v. Simmon-Harris*, which allows states to include private religious schools in choice plans under certain conditions.[51] State constitutions and courts will determine whether more states extend school choice to religiously supported schools and how these plans will interact with civil rights laws, such as court-ordered desegregation of schools.

At the same time that states are allocating greater authority to schools and parents, they have increased their oversight of low-performing schools and school districts and expanded their powers to intervene in the operation of these entities. The level and type of state control in takeovers vary across states, however, and include relieving local school boards of their duties, installing a state-appointed superintendent, and placing governance authority in the hands of a city's mayor. The NCLB requirement that Title I-funded schools that fail to meet student performance goals for five consecutive years be restructured could prompt states to get more directly involved in the operation of low-performing schools and school districts.

School Finance

The state role in education finance dates to 1647 when the General Court of Massachusetts passed the Old Deluder Satan Act, requiring every town to set up a school or pay a sum of money to a larger town to provide educational services. By the mid-nineteenth century several states had created not only statewide systems of public education but mechanisms for funding these schools. In New York State, for example, an 1849 statute provided for a state share of school funding of 52 percent. Yet the fixed appropriation could not keep up with rising school costs, and local real property taxes had to bear an increasing share of the burden. Thus more than 150 years ago state legislators faced the same vexing problems as legislators today: how to alleviate wealth-based disparities in education spending and taxation among school districts in their state.

School districts receive revenues from three sources: the federal government (7.9 percent), state government (49.3 percent), and local taxes (42.8 percent).[52] These national averages for the 2001–2002 school year mask major differences in sources of revenues across the states. As shown in Table 8–2, state support for elementary and secondary education ranges from a low of 31.5 percent in Nevada to 89.1 percent in Hawaii. Similarly, the local share of education funding varies from 62.4 percent to 1.9 percent in these two states, respectively. The level of local education revenues is driven by the interaction of the wealth and tax effort of a community. This close relationship between wealth and revenues makes it possible for a rich district to raise more revenue for education than a poor district, even though both are applying the same education tax rate. For example, a community with property wealth of $100,000 per student can raise only $1,000 per student in local tax revenues with a ten-mill tax rate, whereas a wealthier neighboring community with a tax base of $500,000 per student can raise five times as much, or $5,000 per student, with that same tax effort. Although most state aid systems are designed to compensate for these wealth-based disparities in education spending, state aid is generally insufficient to offset these differences in community wealth. The result of these school finance systems is that poor school districts cannot generate sufficient revenue for an adequate education program, or one that matches their more fortunate neighbors.

Wealth-based disparities in education spending evident in the 1960s led to a series of legal challenges to state education finance systems. This first wave of litigation, which continued into the 1970s and early 1980s, was characterized by *equity* cases that focused on the relationship between school district wealth and spending. The remedies were designed to equalize spending among school districts by providing additional state aid to low-wealth communities. This new judicial activism spurred states to restructure and expand their education funding systems; state education revenues rose by one-third, and the state share of funding rose from 40 to 49 percent, between 1971 and 1981.[53] School finance activity abated in the 1980s as state policymakers turned their attention to issues of excellence in education. The equity issue appeared to be dead until four new school finance decisions were issued in 1989 and 1990 in Kentucky, Montana, New Jersey, and Texas. These decisions led to a second wave of school finance cases, which have focused on issues of *educational adequacy* as well as equity. School finance cases were filed in forty-one states between 1989 and 2004. Thirty-six court decisions were handed down, twenty-one of which declared their state's school-funding systems unconstitutional. Cases are pending in the other five states.[54]

The school finance equity cases emphasized whether school districts of different wealth and tax effort received similar levels of funding. In contrast, adequacy cases consider whether that level of funding is sufficient to prepare all students for higher education, skilled employment, and other experiences of adult life. Whereas issues of educational adequacy are often raised in equity cases to illustrate the negative effects of inadequate funding on educational opportunities, educational adequacy claims relate the level of education re-

Table 8-2 Educational Expenditures per Pupil and Revenues by Source and State, 2001–2002

State	Current expenditures per pupil	Source of revenues (percent)		
		Federal	State	Local
United States	$7,734	7.9	49.3	42.8
Alabama	6,029	10.4	58.7	30.9
Alaska	9,563	16.8	56.6	26.6
Arizona	5,964	10.3	49.7	40.0
Arkansas	6,276	10.7	55.5	33.7
California	7,434	9.3	59.4	31.3
Colorado	6,941	6.0	42.2	51.8
Connecticut	10,577	4.6	42.7	52.7
Delaware	9,284	8.6	64.3	27.1
Florida	6,213	10.0	45.3	44.6
Georgia	7,380	7.2	49.2	43.7
Hawaii	7,306	9.1	89.1	1.9
Idaho	6,011	8.8	61.1	30.1
Illinois	7,956	7.7	33.9	58.4
Indiana	7,734	6.1	50.9	43.1
Iowa	7,338	7.0	48.0	45.0
Kansas	7,339	7.9	57.8	34.3
Kentucky	6,523	10.5	59.6	29.8
Louisiana	6,567	12.5	49.2	38.3
Maine	8,818	8.2	44.2	47.7
Maryland	8,692	6.4	37.2	56.4
Massachusetts	10,232	5.5	43.2	51.4
Michigan	8,653	7.3	64.6	28.1
Minnesota	7,736	5.5	61.4	33.1
Mississippi	5,354	15.0	54.1	30.9
Missouri	7,135	7.6	36.3	56.2
Montana	7,062	13.2	47.9	38.9
Nebraska	7,741	7.8	35.5	56.6
Nevada	6,079	6.1	31.5	62.4
New Hampshire	7,935	4.7	51.8	43.4
New Jersey	11,793	4.2	42.9	52.9
New Mexico	6,882	14.2	72.0	13.8
New York	11,218	6.3	48.2	45.5
North Carolina	6,501	8.5	64.5	27.1
North Dakota	6,709	14.0	38.2	47.8
Ohio	8,069	5.9	45.6	48.5
Oklahoma	6,229	11.9	56.7	31.5
Oregon	7,642	8.3	55.9	35.7
Pennsylvania	8,537	7.0	37.8	55.2
Rhode Island	9,703	6.2	42.1	51.8
South Carolina	7,017	9.1	51.0	39.9
South Dakota	6,424	14.1	36.4	49.5
Tennessee	5,959	9.5	43.6	46.9
Texas	6,771	9.3	40.8	49.8
Utah	4,900	8.3	59.0	32.7
Vermont	9,806	6.3	69.5	24.2

(continued)

Table 8–2 *(continued)*

State	Current expenditures per pupil	Source of revenues (percent)		
		Federal	State	Local
Virginia	7,496	6.3	40.9	52.9
Washington	7,039	8.5	62.4	29.1
West Virginia	7,844	10.5	60.9	28.5
Wisconsin	8,634	5.6	53.7	40.8
Wyoming	8,645	8.3	48.8	42.8

Source: Crecilla Cohen and Frank Johnson, *Revenues and Expenditures for Public Elementary and Secondary Education: School Year 2001–2002*, NCES 2004-341 (Washington, D.C.: U.S. Department of Education, National Center for Education Statistics, 2004), tables 5 and 2.

sources provided to students to some measure of an adequate education, as defined by the state in its constitution, in a court's interpretation of that constitution, or in a state statute. In the *Abbott v. Burke* decision, for example, the New Jersey Supreme Court defined the state's constitutional obligation as ensuring that students in poor urban communities have the opportunity to compete in, and contribute to, the society entered by their relatively advantaged peers.[55] Courts in Alabama, Kentucky, and Massachusetts defined their states' obligation in terms of broad educational outcomes, such as "sufficient mathematical and scientific skills to function in [their state] and at national and international levels, . . . sufficient understanding of the arts to enable each student to appreciate his or her cultural heritage and the cultural heritage of others, . . . [and] sufficient support and guidance so that every student feels a sense of self-worth and ability to achieve."[56]

Ongoing school finance litigation and the new focus on educational adequacy create a large number of education finance policy issues for states. First, although early rounds of litigation decreased inequities, many states must address continuing disparities in education spending that separate their poor and wealthy communities. They must decide how, and how much, to equalize these spending differences and how to raise the revenues to pay for greater equalization. In addition, states must find ways to fund programs for the growing number of students with special needs—those with disabilities, limited English proficiency, and economic and social needs. Second, states face growing opposition to the use of property taxes to fund education. Most taxpayers want the state to bear a larger portion of education funding, yet they are often unwilling to support higher state taxes. Michigan reduced its reliance on local property taxes to pay for schools but raised the state sales tax two cents on the dollar to pay for the increased state share. In contrast, New Jersey cut its state income tax, forcing local communities to bear a larger share of education and municipal costs. Other states have responded to taxpayer pressures by capping local property taxes, but often without replacing this lost local revenue with sufficient state aid.

In addition to these traditional school finance issues, state policymakers face new challenges in responding to the new "adequacy" decisions by the courts. The first issue is how to define and measure an adequate education. Should states use input standards, such as minimum class size, number of computers in a school, or minimum facilities standards, or should they determine what kinds of programs are necessary to help students achieve the outcome standards being established by state boards of education, legislatures, and courts? States have begun to define the parameters of an adequate education as they issue content and student performance standards in academic disciplines. It is unclear, however, what level and mix of educational services and resources are needed to enable all students to meet these new standards. Once a state determines the basis of an adequate education, it must determine the cost of this education for students with differing needs and design a state school finance system that supports an adequate education. In New Jersey, the state supreme court addressed the issue by using the expenditure levels of wealthy (and usually high-performing) school districts as its benchmark for a constitutionally adequate education. Other states, such as Maryland and New York, convened panels of education experts to identify and cost out instructionally appropriate programs and services.

Other finance issues are raised by nonfinance reform initiatives. As states encourage changes in governing structures for education, such as site-based management, choice, and charter schools, they must consider how to allocate resources to school sites and parents, as well as, or instead of, school districts. Districts will have to develop school-based fiscal accounting systems that provide these sites with detailed information on revenues, budgets, and expenditures. As states turn to outcome-based accountability systems, policymakers have become increasingly interested in the use of fiscal incentives to improve school performance. Incentive funding is still in the early stages of development, however, and little is known about how incentives work or how the allocation of incentive dollars will affect equalization policy.

Finally, considerable spending disparities exist across, as well as within, states. In 2001–2002 the average per-pupil expenditure nationally was $7,734 but ranged from a low of $4,900 in Utah to a high of $11,793 in New Jersey (see Table 8–2). These interstate expenditure differences raise the question of adequacy at a national level—what is the level of spending needed to bring all students to a proficient level of performance, as required under the No Child Left Behind Act?

Conclusion

State education policy in the new millennium will be shaped by many forces. These include the changing demographics of the student population, the changing structure of the nation's economy, the national education reform agenda, and a more complex and fragmented education policymaking structure. At a time when workforce skills are growing increasingly complex and undergoing rapid change, students in general, and students of color or of limited English proficiency in particular, are not learning the high level of skills needed for a postindustrial society. Education reformers argue that dramatic improvements in student learning will require a more systemic approach to education policy, an approach promoted by the federal government. Most states have responded to the current wave of reform by developing more ambitious student outcomes, curricular frameworks, and assessment systems but have been slower to redesign their teacher preparation, professional development, and school finance policies in support of higher student standards.

State policymakers face many challenges, reflecting the continuing tensions between the reform values of equity, excellence, efficiency, and choice. As state courts increasingly link school finance reform to guarantees of an "adequate" education, policymakers must define and fund the mix of educational services and resources required to bring all students up to these new high standards. As most students nationally perform well below these standards, the new finance reforms will require new funds or a redistribution of existing state aid. Both are politically unacceptable alternatives. Conservatives, who have gained power in many statehouses and state boards of education, as well as in Congress, argue that increased parental choice and a market-driven education system are more appropriate ways to improve the nation's schools, and will continue to push for more charter schools and vouchers. Although the No Child Left Behind Act calls for more uniformity in state assessment, accountability, and teacher policy systems, considerable variation remains across states in the substance of these policies, particularly measures of student proficiency. The jury is out on whether standards-based education reform, greater choice, and a stronger federal role will ensure that no child is left behind in a global economy. But education will remain center stage in state policy for years to come.

Notes

1. This chapter addresses only elementary and secondary education policy. It does not include a discussion of public higher education, which is also a responsibility of state government.
2. National Association of State Budget Officers, *2003 Expenditure Report* (Washington, D.C.: National Association of State Budget Officers, 2004), figure 6, http://www.nasbo.org/Publications/PDFs/2003ExpendReport.pdf (accessed October 25, 2004).
3. Frederick M. Wirt, Douglas Mitchell, and Catherine Marshall, as cited in Frederick M. Wirt and Michael W. Kirst, *Schools in Conflict* (Berkeley, Calif.: McCutchan Publishing, 1989), 260; and James W. Guthrie, "United States School Finance Policy, 1955–1980," in *School Finance Policies and Practices: The 1980's: A Decade of Conflict,* ed. James W. Guthrie (Cambridge, Mass.: Ballinger, 1980), 3–46.
4. *Digest of Education Statistics, 2002,* NCES 2003–060 (Washington, D.C.: U.S. Department of Education, National Center for Education Statistics, 2003), table 21.
5. Ibid., tables 19 and 21.

6. Data from 1976 are drawn from the U.S. Department of Education, Office of Civil Rights 1976 Elementary and Secondary School Civil Rights Survey; 2002 data are reported in Lee Hoffman, Jennifer Sable, Julia Naum, and Dell Gray, *Public Elementary and Secondary Students, Staff, Schools, and School Districts: School Year 2002–03*, NCES 2005-314 (Washington, D.C.: U.S. Department of Education, National Center for Education Statistics, 2005), table C-3.
7. Gary Orfield and Chungmei Lee, *Brown at 50: King's Dream or Plessy's Nightmare?* (Cambridge, Mass.: Harvard University Civil Rights Project, 2004).
8. Ibid.
9. *English Language Learner Students in U.S. Public Schools: 1994 and 2000*, NCES 2004–035 (Washington, D.C.: U.S. Department of Education, National Center for Education Statistics, 2004), table 1.
10. James Gordon Ward, "The Power of Demographic Change: Impact of Population Trends on Schools," in *Who Pays for Student Diversity? Population Changes and Educational Policy*, ed. James Gordon Ward and Patricia Anthony (Newbury Park, Calif.: Corwin Press, 1992), 1–20.
11. *The Nation's Report Card: Reading Highlights, 2003*, NCES 2004-452 (Washington, D.C.: U.S. Department of Education, National Center for Education Statistics, 2003).
12. See, for example, "States Resist Meeting K-12 Spending Levels Ordered by the Courts," *Education Week*, April 6, 2005, 1.
13. Frank Hobbs and Nicole Stoops, U.S. Bureau of the Census, *Demographic Trends in the 20th Century*, Census, 2000 Special Reports, Series CENSR-4 (Washington, D.C.: GPO, 2002).
14. Council for Economic Development, *Investing in Our Children: Business and the Public Schools* (New York: Council for Economic Development, 1985); *Rising to the Challenge: Are High School Graduates Prepared for College and Work?* (Washington, D.C.: Achieve, 2005); Jean Johnson and Ann Duffelt, "Public Agenda: Reality Check 2002," *Education Week*, March 6, 2002.
15. *The Nation's Report Card: Reading Highlights, 2003*.
16. *The Nation's Report Card: Mathematics Highlights, 2003*, NCES 2004–451 (Washington, D.C.: U.S. Department of Education, National Center for Education Statistics, 2003).
17. Michael Timpane, "Business Has Rediscovered the Public Schools," *Phi Delta Kappan* 65 (February 1984): 390.
18. Total expenditures per pupil expressed in constant 2001–2002 dollars. Thomas D. Snyder, Alexandra G. Tan, and Charlene M. Hoffman, *Digest of Education Statistics, 2003*, NCES 2005–025 (Washington, D.C.: U.S. Department of Education, National Center for Education Statistics, 2004), table 166.
19. National Governors Association/National Association of State Budget Officers, *The Fiscal Survey of States* (Washington, D.C.: National Governors Association/National Association of State Budget Officers, December 2003); Nicholas W. Jenny, "State Tax Revenue Shows Slight Improvement," *Rockefeller Institute State Fiscal News* 3, no. 8 (November 2003).
20. U.S. General Accounting Office, *Education Finance: Extent of Federal Funding in State Education Agencies*, GAO/HEHS-9-53 (Washington, D.C.: GAO, 1994).
21. Wirt and Kirst, *Schools in Conflict*.
22. The education summit led to the adoption of six national education goals that addressed school readiness, high school completion, competency in nine academic areas, preparation for responsible citizenship and productive employment, and school safety. In 1994 Congress codified these six goals and added two more that are directed at teacher professional development and parental involvement in the schools. *The National Education Goals Report: Building a Nation of Learners, 1994* (Washington, D.C.: National Education Goals Panel, 1994).
23. Susan H. Fuhrman, "State Politics and Education Reform," in *The Politics of Reforming*

School Administration: The 1988 PEA Yearbook, ed. Jane Hannaway and Robert Crowson (Philadelphia: Falmer Press, 1988), 61–75.
24. Laura Cavell and others, *Key State Education Policies on PK–12 Education: 2004* (Washington, D.C.: Council of Chief State School Officers, 2005).
25. National Commission on Excellence in Education, *A Nation at Risk: The Imperative for Educational Reform* (Washington, D.C.: National Commission on Excellence in Education, 1983).
26. Cavell and others, *Key State Education Policies on PK–12 Education: 2004.*
27. Marshall S. Smith and Jennifer O'Day, "Systemic School Reform," in *The Politics of Curriculum and Testing,* ed. Susan H. Fuhrman and Betty Malen (London: Falmer Press, 1991), 233–267.
28. Susan H. Fuhrman, "Less Than Meets the Eye: Standards, Testing and Fear of Federal Control," in *Who's in Charge Here? The Tangled Web of School Governance and Policy,* ed. Noel Epstein (Washington, D.C.: Brookings Institution Press, 2004), 131–163.
29. "Quality Counts, 2005: No Small Change," special issue, *Education Week* 24, no. 17 (January 6, 2005).
30. Richard W. Cross, Theodor Rebarber, and Justin Torres, *Grading the Systems: The Guide to State Standards, Tests, and Accountability Policies* (Washington, D.C.: Thomas B. Fordham Foundation, 2004).
31. "Quality Counts, 2005"; Robert Rothman, "Benchmarking and Alignment of State Standards and Assessments," in *Redesigning Accountability Systems for Education,* ed. Susan. H. Fuhrman and Richard F. Elmore (New York: Teachers College Press, 2004), 96–137.
32. See, for example, P. David Pearson, "The Reading Wars," *Educational Policy* 18 (January and March 2004): 216–252, and Alan H. Schoenfeld, "The Math Wars," *Educational Policy* 18 (January and March 2004): 253–286, respectively, on controversies regarding reading and mathematics curriculum; and Suzanne M. Wilson *California Dreaming: Reforming Mathematics Education* (New Haven, Conn.: Yale University Press, 2003).
33. Margaret E. Goertz and Mark C. Duffy, *Assessment and Accountability Systems in the 50 States: 1999–2000,* CPRE Research Report Series RR-046 (Philadelphia: University of Pennsylvania, Consortium for Policy Research in Education, 2001).
34. Lynn Olson, "In ESEA Wake, School Data Flowing Forth," *Education Week,* 23, no. 15 (December 10, 2003): 1.
35. Margaret E. Goertz, "Implementing the No Child Left Behind Act: Challenges for the States," *Peabody Journal of Education* 80, no. 2 (2005): 73–89.
36. Center on Education Policy, *State High School Exit Exams: A Maturing Reform* (Washington, D.C.: Center on Education Policy, 2004).
37. Center on Education Policy, *From Capitol to the Classroom: Year 2 of the No Child Left Behind Act* (Washington, DC: Center on Education Policy, 2004).
38. William J. Mathis, "The Cost of Implementing the No Child Left Behind Act: Different Assumptions, Different Answers," *Peabody Journal of Education* 80, no. 2 (2005): 90–119.
39. Goertz, "Implementing the No Child Left Behind Act."
40. See, for example, Eric A. Hanushek and Steven G. Rivkin, "How to Improve the Supply of High Quality Teachers," in *Brookings Papers on Education Policy, 2004,* ed. Diane Ravitch (Washington, D.C.: Brookings Institution Press, 2004), 7–44.
41. Analysis by Richard Ingersoll, "Quality Counts, 2003: If I Can't Learn From You," special issue, *Education Week* 22, no. 17 (January 9, 2003): 14.
42. C. Emily Feistritzer, *Alternative Teacher Certification: A State-by-State Analysis, 2005* (Washington, D.C.: National Center for Education Information, 2005).
43. Kate Walsh and Emma Snyder, *Searching the Attic* (Washington, D.C.: National Council on Teacher Quality, 2004).
44. Linda Darling-Hammond and Barnett Berry, *The Evolution of Teacher Policy* (Santa Monica, Calif.: RAND, 1988).

45. See, for example, *Teaching at Risk: A Call to Action* (New York: Teaching Commission, 2004).
46. This section is drawn from Thomas Corcoran and Margaret Goertz, "The Governance of Public Education," in *The Public Schools,* ed. Susan Fuhrman and Marvin Lazerson (New York: Oxford University Press, 2005), 25–56.
47. Susan H. Fuhrman and Richard F. Elmore, *Ruling Out Rules: The Evolution of Deregulation in State Education Policy* (New Brunswick, N.J.: Rutgers University, Consortium for Policy Research in Education, 1995).
48. For detailed information on state charter school laws, see Center for Education Reform, *Charter School Laws Across the States: Ranking and Scorecard,* 8th ed. (Washington, D.C.: Center for Education Reform, 2004).
49. US Charter Schools, *State by State #'s,* http://www.uscharterschools.org (accessed April 19, 2005).
50. Kerry J. Gruber and others, *Schools and Staffing Survey, 1999–2000: Overview of the Data for Public, Private, Public Charter, and Bureau of Indian Affairs Elementary and Secondary Schools,* NCES 2002-313 (Washington, D.C.: U.S. Department of Education, National Center for Education Statistics, 2002); Stacy Bielick and Christopher Chapman, *Trends in the Use of School Choice: 1993 to 1999,* NCES 2003-031 (Washington, D.C.: U.S. Department of Education, National Center for Education Statistics, 2003).
51. *Zelman v. Simmon-Harris* 536 U.S. 639 (2002).
52. Crecilla Cohen and Frank Johnson, *Revenues and Expenditures for Public Elementary and Secondary Education: School Year 2001–02,* NCES 2004–341 (Washington, D.C.: U.S. Department of Education, National Center for Education Statistics, 2004).
53. Deborah A. Verstegen, "The New Wave of School Finance Litigation," *Phi Delta Kappan* 76 (November 1994): 243–250.
54. Author's calculations based on data from ACCESS, a project of the Campaign for Fiscal Equity, http://www.schoolfunding.info; and "Quality Counts, 2005: No Small Change." Lawsuits are pending in an additional six states that had court decisions rendered between 1989 and 2004.
55. *Abbott v. Burke,* 119 N.J. 287, 363 (1990).
56. *Harper v. Hunt,* Opinion of the Justices, 624 So. 2d 107 (Ala. 1993).

9

State Welfare Policy
Irene Lurie

Few public functions are as closely shared by state and federal governments as the provision of financial assistance to needy families with children. From colonial times until the early twentieth century, local governments and private charities bore primary responsibility for poor relief. Between 1910 and 1930, most states introduced welfare programs for poor mothers and their children, although local governments continued to pay a large share of their cost. With passage of the Social Security Act of 1935, the federal government lifted some of this burden from state and local governments by contributing to the cost of state welfare programs. Over the next six decades, Aid to Families with Dependent Children (AFDC) was operated by the states with federal financing and, increasingly, under federal laws and regulations that constrained the states in designing their programs. Federal control over policy design increased until the Personal Responsibility and Work Opportunity Reconciliation Act of 1996 (PRWORA) eliminated AFDC and created the Temporary Assistance for Needy Families (TANF) block grant, which devolved authority for designing programs back to the states.[1]

The shifting balance of control between the federal government and the states reflects the varying strength of centralizing and decentralizing forces. The federal government's greater capacity to finance the cost of welfare programs has long been a centralizing force. Another centralizing force has been the wide differences in the generosity of state welfare programs, which caused liberals in Washington to distrust the states. Conservatives favoring decentralization attributed the expansion in welfare programs to undue mandates and pressure from the federal government. If states had greater authority, they believed, they would have flexibility to design programs that better met the needs of their residents and to test innovative approaches to reducing welfare dependency. Liberals suspected their real motive in asking for flexibility was to reduce the generosity of their programs.

What tipped the balance in favor of devolution in 1996? How have states responded to their new authority to design welfare programs? What have been the effects of TANF on poor families? To answer these questions, we first discuss the dilemmas that make welfare reform so difficult. A brief history of welfare reform then illustrates how the federal government and the states wrestled with these dilemmas and how state pressure for more authority culminated in TANF. A discussion of the main provisions of TANF and the variety of states' responses to them is followed by a summary of the effects of

TANF on low-income families. This provides some insight into the further reforms proposed by the Bush administration.

Fundamental Dilemmas in Designing Welfare Programs

The repeated reforms of the welfare system stem from dilemmas inherent in designing a system paying benefits to poor families. The system can be described by five parameters: the amount of the benefit paid to a family with no income; how the benefit varies with a family's earnings, other income, and assets; the definition of a family; how the benefit varies with the size of a family; and whether the benefit is in cash or in kind (that is, goods and services). Defining these parameters requires difficult tradeoffs between the goals of efficiency and equity that economists generally use to judge government policies.

In the context of welfare policy, promoting efficiency means designing programs to minimize effects on people's behavior that society considers to be undesirable. Each of the five parameters of program design may potentially alter people's behavior in undesirable ways by distorting the incentives they face. By paying higher benefits to a family with no income, welfare reduces the incentive for parents to work and for a single parent to seek child support from an absent parent. By scaling benefits to the level of earnings, it reduces the reward for earning additional income. By defining an eligible family as one that is deprived of a breadwinner, generally the father, it may encourage parents to divorce, separate, or never marry. By limiting eligibility to people with children and raising benefits when another child is born, it rewards childbearing. A program paying benefits in cash maximizes the flexibility of families to decide how to spend their money, but they may not spend it in ways judged wise by the rest of society. Uncertainty about the magnitude of families' responses to these incentives creates fertile ground for reform.

Designing programs to promote equity raises disagreements about the meaning of equity. Most people agree that government policies should give equal treatment to equals, treating people the same if they are in similar circumstances. This concept of horizontal equity can be difficult to achieve in practice, but it is widely accepted as fair. Designing government policies that treat low-income people more generously than high-income people requires judgments about vertical equity, or fairness among people in different circumstances. Because members of society hold various values about vertical equity, designing policies like welfare, which redistribute income from higher- to lower-income families, is contentious and has been resolved differently at different times and places.

When the federal government assumed partial responsibility for welfare in 1935, it left the states with the important power to set the amount of welfare benefits paid to their residents. States have made vastly different decisions about benefit levels (see Table 9–1). In 2003 the most generous state in the lower forty-eight, California, paid $679 per month to a family of three with

Table 9–1 Welfare Caseloads and Benefit Levels, by State

	Welfare caseloads		Three-person family, March 2003	
State	Families on TANF, December 2004[a]	Percent change in families on welfare, August 1996 to December 2004	Maximum monthly benefit	Maximum monthly income for eligibility
Alabama	20,839	-49	$164	$204
Alaska	4,577	-62	923	1,245
Arizona	45,917	-26	347	585
Arkansas	8,771	-60	204	278
California	466,597	-47	679	913
Colorado	15,076	-56	356	510
Connecticut	20,086	-65	543	834
Delaware	5,723	-46	338	427
District of Columbia	17,324	-32	379	538
Florida	65,175	-68	303	392
Georgia	46,065	-63	280	513
Hawaii	8,474	-61	570	1,362
Idaho	1,887	-78	293	635
Illinois	38,667	-82	377	466
Indiana	49,549	-4	288	591
Iowa	17,866	-43	426	1,061
Kansas	17,441	-27	403	518
Kentucky	35,569	-50	262	973
Louisiana	17,184	-75	240	359
Maine	9,863	-51	485	1,022
Maryland	24,919	-65	472	589
Massachusetts	49,481	-42	633	707
Michigan	81,007	-52	459	773
Minnesota	29,569	-49	532	976
Mississippi	17,272	-63	170	457
Missouri	41,007	-49	292	558
Montana	4,743	-53	494	858
Nebraska	9,916	-31	364	692
Nevada	7,116	-48	348	694
New Hampshire	6,076	-33	600	749
New Jersey	46,441	-54	424	635
New Mexico	18,083	-46	439	901
New York	144,012	-66	577	810
North Carolina	36,466	-67	272	1,489
North Dakota	2,873	-40	477	2,071
Ohio	84,937	-58	373	979
Oklahoma	13,691	-62	292	704
Oregon	19,836	-34	460	615
Pennsylvania	96,642	-48	403	676
Rhode Island	11,141	-46	554	1,277
South Carolina	16,056	-64	204	577
South Dakota	2,842	-51	469	675
Tennessee	71,824	-26	185	979

(continued)

Table 9–1 (continued)

	Welfare caseloads		Three-person family, March 2003	
State	Families on TANF, December 2004[a]	Percent change in families on welfare, August 1996 to December 2004	Maximum monthly benefit	Maximum monthly income for eligibility
Texas	95,259	-61	208	416
Utah	4,672	-67	474	573
Vermont	4,672	-47	629	988
Virginia	10,439	-83	320	411
Washington	56,930	-42	546	1,091
West Virginia	13,607	-63	453	1,130
Wisconsin	21,121	-59	673	1,401
Wyoming	331	-92	340	539
U.S. total/median	1,955,631	-55	$403	$692

Sources: Column 1: http://acf.hhs.gov/programs/ofa/caseload/2004/family04tanf.htm; column 2: http://www.acf.hhs.gov/news/stats/afdc.htm; columns 3 and 4: U.S. Department of Health and Human Services, Administration for Children and Families, *Temporary Assistance for Needy Families Program (TANF) Sixth Annual Report to Congress* (Washington, D.C.: Department of Health and Human Services, 2004), table C.

a. Excludes 172,566 families aided by separate state programs financed with Maintenance of Effort funds. Most of these families reside in California, New York, and Virginia.

no other income, four times the benefit of $164 paid by Alabama, the least generous state. From a state perspective, these benefits reflect the values its residents hold about redistributing income and their financial ability to finance welfare benefits. From a national perspective, these differences can be criticized as being both inefficient and horizontally inequitable: inefficient by providing an incentive for residents of lower-benefit states to migrate to a higher-benefit state and inequitable by paying different amounts to families in similar circumstances.

A welfare system paying such widely varying benefits is criticized by economists like Richard Musgrave, who argued that welfare should be a responsibility of the federal government. In enumerating the appropriate roles of each level of government in a federal system, Musgrave counted income distribution as a federal-level function. "The heart of fiscal federalism," argued Musgrave, lies in the proposition that the distribution and stabilization functions "require primary responsibility at the central level."[2] The federal government has more capacity to impose taxes and can transfer income to poor families more equitably. States levying high taxes risk driving away high-income taxpayers, and states paying high welfare benefits risk becoming "welfare magnets" to the poor. Research on the welfare magnet hypothesis reaches conflicting conclusions, although recent research finds some evidence that welfare influences migration.³ Regardless of the strength of these effects, analysts argue that states keep their welfare benefits low at least in part to avoid becoming welfare magnets, and political leaders certainly use welfare magnet rhetoric to argue against raising benefits.⁴

Additional spending to mitigate these problems is hindered by the public's perception that welfare is costly and absorbs a large share of federal and state budgets. In fact, the cost of TANF is modest compared with other major federal and state programs transferring income to families and individuals. TANF used $29 billion of federal and state funds in 2003. Social Security, in contrast, paid $471 billion in cash benefits to elderly, widowed, or disabled people. Medicare financed $276 billion in health care for the elderly and disabled. Unemployment insurance, which like Social Security calculates benefits on the basis of previous earnings rather than current income, paid out $41 billion to unemployed workers. Among the programs that base benefits on current income, the largest and fastest growing is Medicaid, which spent $215 billion to assist low-income individuals and families with their medical expenses in 2001. The Supplemental Security Income (SSI) program paid $35.6 billion to low-income elderly, blind, or disabled individuals in 2003. The Food Stamp program, which is federally financed but administered by the states, gave low-income households $21 billion to purchase food in 2003. The federal Earned Income Tax Credit (EITC), which supplements the wages of low-income workers through the tax system, raised incomes by $39 billion. The TANF program looks small in this context.⁵

The shares of federal and state budgets devoted to welfare were similarly small. In 2003 the TANF block grant was less than 1 percent of federal outlays, and state expenditures for public assistance averaged only 2.2 percent of total state expenditures. Expenditures for public assistance ranged from 6.2 percent of total state expenditures in California to 0.3 percent in Alabama, Idaho, Mississippi, and South Carolina. The bulk of state spending was for other functions: 21.7 percent for elementary and secondary education, 10.8 percent for higher education, 21.4 percent for Medicaid, 8.2 percent for transportation, 3.5 percent for corrections, and 32.2 for remaining functions. State expenditures for public assistance included not only TANF but also the states' share of SSI and state and locally funded general assistance and emergency assistance. TANF spending alone was 1.5 percent of state expenditures.⁶

From AFDC to TANF

Such inefficiencies and inequities raised little public concern until the 1960s, when the War on Poverty focused public attention on the plight of poor families. Many states responded by increasing the level of welfare benefits. More important, in 1970 the U.S. Supreme Court ruled that welfare benefits were "a matter of statutory entitlement for persons qualified to receive them."⁷ As a result of this and other court decisions, more families became eligible for assistance and a greater proportion of families who had been eligible

Figure 9–1 Families on Welfare

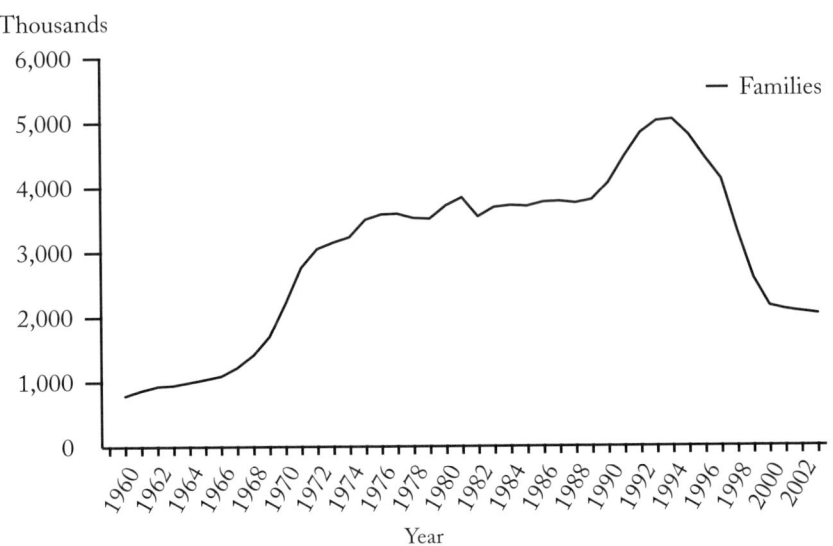

Source: U.S. Department of Health and Human Services, Administration for Children and Families, http://www.acf.hhs.gov/newsstats/3697.htm.

for assistance but had not received benefits participated in the program.[8] Between 1967 and 1972, AFDC caseloads soared from 1.2 to 3.0 million families (see Figure 9–1).

The Search for Solutions

Although the increases in benefit levels and program participation improved equity, the increase in caseloads focused attention on the perverse incentives in the welfare system. The search for solutions to these perverse incentives generated a stream of reforms and proposed reforms in the AFDC program. From 1967 to 1981, these reforms increased the control of the federal government over state policies, particularly policies to encourage welfare recipients to work. Proposals for further reform debated throughout the 1970s would have increased federal control still further by creating a minimum nationwide benefit, but they failed in Congress. Instead, in response to reforms proposed by President Ronald Reagan in 1981, Congress turned the initiative back to the states.

The first federal legislation requiring states to encourage welfare recipients to work was the Work Incentive (WIN) program enacted in 1967. WIN authorized states to offer recipients a range of education and training activities, including basic education, institutional and on-the-job training, unpaid work experience, public jobs, and job placement services. WIN funds also financed child care for program participants. Complementing the education and training, the 1967 legislation created a financial incentive for recipients to work by changing the way benefits were scaled to the level of earnings. Instead of reducing a recipient's benefits by $1 for each dollar of earnings, leaving the recipient with the same total income regardless of his or her work effort, the law required states to disregard a portion of the recipient's monthly earnings—$30 plus one-third of earnings above $30—so that work effort would be rewarded by an increase in total income. Legislation in 1971 added the requirement that all recipients, except those specifically excluded by law, register for the WIN program when they applied for welfare and accept a job if one was available. For the first time, recipients of AFDC could be required to work and, if they refused, could be sanctioned by a reduction in their welfare benefit. Yet despite WIN services, the financial work incentive, and the states' authority to impose a work requirement, welfare caseloads continued to rise.

Amid this concern with work incentives was a growing perception that the AFDC program was inherently flawed in additional ways and needed more sweeping reform. Critics argued that limiting welfare eligibility to single-parent families, generally headed by mothers, was inequitable and also might encourage out-of-wedlock births and marital instability. The War on Poverty questioned the wide differences in the welfare benefits offered by the states, pointing to a greater federal role. In response to these criticisms, Presidents Richard Nixon and Jimmy Carter each proposed liberal welfare reforms that would have extended eligibility to all low-income families with children, including intact families with a working parent, thereby eliminating the incentives for out-of-wedlock births and marital instability. Importantly, their proposals would have provided a minimum nationwide welfare benefit, improving the horizontal equity of the welfare system and discouraging interstate migration. But these reforms would have further increased caseloads and costs and extended AFDC's financial work disincentive to two-parent families. Members of Congress, particularly southern senators from low-benefit, low-wage states who feared a minimum benefit would put upward pressure on wages, prevented enactment of these reforms.

After a decade of fruitless debate about these liberalizing reforms, the election of President Reagan in 1980 reversed the direction of presidential proposals. Reagan's 1981 budget gave states new options for toughening their welfare employment programs. States could operate a "workfare" program, in which a recipient works without wages in a public or nonprofit agency in exchange for the welfare grant. States could also require both AFDC applicants and recipients to search for a job, and they could pay a recipient's benefit to an employer to subsidize his or her wages.

Given these new options, many states seized the opportunity to design a welfare employment program that met the state's own vision of welfare reform. The optional nature of these initiatives gave states a sense of ownership of these programs, facilitating the changes needed to implement them.[9] New names helped to highlight the reforms and put each state's individual stamp on its program. GAIN (Greater Avenues for Independence) in California, MOST (Michigan Opportunity and Skills Training) in Michigan, REACH (Realizing Economic Achievement) in New Jersey, and PEACH (Positive Employment and Community Help) in Georgia are just a few examples. Evaluations by independent research organizations found these programs were feasible to operate and yielded benefits that, while typically small, were generally positive.[10]

The Reagan years (1981–1988) were also notable for a shift in attitudes away from those of the late 1960s and early 1970s, when legal challenges to the states turned AFDC into an entitlement program. The rise in labor force participation among married women with children, the rapid growth in the number of families headed by single mothers, and the continued rise in the number of welfare dependents led many political leaders, policy analysts, and scholars to argue that government should place greater demands on single parents. Government has an obligation to give financial assistance to poor parents, they argued, but parents have an obligation to help themselves become economically self-sufficient.[11] The idea that welfare involves a set of *mutual* obligations gained popularity in statehouses and Congress. Supported by the National Governors Association and its chair, Gov. Bill Clinton, Congress sought to put this idea into place with the Family Support Act of 1988.

The design of the Family Support Act was grounded in the states' initiatives permitted by Reagan's 1981 budget. When these initiatives proved effective, the governors worked with Congress to eliminate WIN and create a welfare employment program required of all states, the Job Opportunities and Basic Skills Training Program (JOBS).[12] JOBS increased federal funding for education, training, and employment services; increased funds for child care; and set clear goals that states must meet to receive their full share of federal funds. It also strengthened the financial incentive for recipients to take a job by continuing to finance their child care and Medicaid coverage for a year after they earned enough to become ineligible for welfare. But many governors were reluctant to spend the increased state money required by the law and were not aggressive in implementing the program. Although expenditures for the JOBS program and child care increased, inadequate funding slowed the pace of implementation. The JOBS program succeeded in giving more poor mothers the opportunity to go to school and training programs, but it did not reduce caseloads. To the contrary, perhaps because many recipients went to school instead of searching for work, caseloads increased sharply from 3.7 million in 1988 to 5.0 million in 1994.

State-Initiated Waivers

As states were implementing the JOBS program, a few governors, most notably John Engler in Michigan and Tommy Thompson in Wisconsin, began to make national names for themselves with campaigns to cut welfare dependency. Both governors proposed that the JOBS program be supplemented with additional approaches to reducing welfare caseloads and costs. These approaches called for changing the rules determining AFDC eligibility and benefits to increase the incentive for recipients to work and prepare for work and to place pressure on them to change their behavior in ways that would reduce the cost of welfare. Perhaps most important, states sought to restructure their programs not only to increase the incentive to work but to make work a necessity.

To implement these changes, states needed waivers from the federal law governing the structure of the program. Section 1115 of the Social Security Act, an amendment enacted in 1962, permits the federal government to grant waivers from certain sections of the act to states wishing to operate demonstration or experimental projects. Initially, because states requested waivers for their intended purpose of conducting research on alternative welfare policies, use of the waiver process generated little controversy. But waivers began to serve another purpose in 1992, when President George H. W. Bush encouraged the states to request them by promising to streamline the process for approving waiver applications and to approve a wide range of projects. Under the guise of research, the demonstrations gave states the opportunity to pursue their own version of welfare reform. Many governors, both Republicans and Democrats, responded to the challenge.

Some of the waivers eased restrictions on eligibility and benefits, whereas others tightened restrictions. To ease restrictions that may discourage recipients from working, some states increased the amount of earnings disregarded in calculating the AFDC benefit. To encourage continued employment by people who earned their way off welfare, some states extended the number of months of subsidized child care and Medicaid that a family could receive after leaving welfare from the standard limit of twelve months. Many states increased the dollar limit on the value of a welfare family's automobile to facilitate employment requiring transportation. To give mothers and fathers more equal access to education and training, some states made noncustodial fathers eligible for JOBS services. Some states increased the amount of assets an eligible family may hold to encourage recipients to save for their education and training. Several states "cashed-out" food stamps by giving money instead of stamps, so that recipients had a greater choice in their spending. To give welfare agencies flexibility in assisting families in crisis—for example, a breadwinner risking job loss as a result of a car breakdown—waivers in some places permitted "welfare diversion": a one-time payment to welfare applicants that addressed their immediate problem—in this example, lack of funds for car repairs—so they did not need to become welfare recipients.

Many waivers restricted eligibility and benefits as a means of altering recipients' behavior. Some states imposed a "family cap" so that a mother could not receive an increased benefit when she had another child. States with "learnfare" decreased benefits when children or teen parents failed to attend school or increased benefits by giving bonuses for good school attendance. Some states also fingerprinted recipients to prevent welfare fraud or required recipients to perform unpaid community service as a condition of eligibility. Immunizations against childhood diseases were made a condition of eligibility in several states. A few states also exercised the option in existing law to require mothers under age eighteen to live with their parents. Although thwarted by the courts, some high-benefit states also attempted to discourage in-migration by implementing a "Welcome, stranger" policy that gave recent immigrants into the state the amount of welfare paid by their previous state of residence. Finally, and most controversial, were the waivers that permitted states to impose a time limit on a family's eligibility for AFDC benefits.

Welfare waivers quickly became fashionable, attracting even states where welfare reform was usually a low priority. By 1995 the U.S. Department of Health and Human Services had approved the applications of more than thirty states. The timing of these waiver applications is curious because President Bill Clinton had campaigned on a promise to "end welfare as we know it"—welfare reform was already back on the federal agenda. States could have been expected to wait for Congress to act on Clinton's proposal before making reforms of their own; instead, they took the initiative. What were their motivations in requesting these waivers? And why did the federal government approve them?

Certainly some governors had given careful thought to welfare reform and believed they could create an alternative that was superior to the current system. Other factors may also have led to a desire for reform, such as a recognition that the JOBS program was neither cheap nor rapid in its payoff, that welfare caseloads were continuing to rise, and that the incidence of teenage out-of-wedlock childbearing was increasing. But to a greater degree the waiver movement was an appeal to voters. Once started, this show of toughness generated a bandwagon effect among governors, legislators, and welfare officials, who wanted to avoid being seen as easy on welfare.

As demonstrated during the years since Reagan's 1981 budget, governors, legislators, and welfare commissioners prefer to take the initiative in seeking welfare reform than to respond to mandates imposed by the federal government. During the 1980s many state leaders were enthusiastic in designing their own welfare employment programs and claiming ownership of their creations. But when federal legislation in 1988 forced states to implement the JOBS program, which consisted of services that many states were already providing, state officials saw it as another federal mandate requiring program changes and additional expenditures. Some state leaders, rather than spending political capital by increasing expenditures for the JOBS program, chose to generate political capital by restricting welfare eligibility and benefits. One state welfare commissioner explained that officials stood to benefit from this tough approach because "the public blames the welfare system for problems in their own life."[13] At low cost to the majority of voters, a hard-line stance on welfare policy offers state leaders an easy opportunity for political gain. The waiver movement overtook the Clinton administration's proposal to reform the welfare system. Clinton's proposal was tough, with a time limit on the receipt of cash assistance, but it contained the safety net of subsidized jobs for people exhausting their time-limited benefits. Republicans took control of Congress in the 1994 elections for the first time in forty years. Enacting welfare reform was a central component of their platform. However, it called for the kind of decentralized decision making used for the waivers, rather than a program designed in detail by Washington, and it limited federal spending for welfare to help balance the budget. Controls on federal welfare spending were acceptable to the governors, particularly the thirty Republican governors, but in exchange they wanted more flexibility in designing and operating their welfare programs. House leaders and governors quickly reached a compromise: a block grant that would limit federal spending while giving the states greater power over their welfare programs. Clinton vetoed the legislation twice but finally signed the Personal Responsibility and Work Opportunity Reconciliation Act of 1996, thereby ending the AFDC program and creating the Temporary Assistance for Needy Families block grant. Liberals felt betrayed, and three of Clinton's own appointees to the U.S. Department of Health and Human Services resigned in protest. In his memoirs, Clinton acknowledged their protest and wrote, "I decided to sign the legislation because I thought it was the best chance America would have for a long time to change the incentives in the welfare system from dependence to empowerment through work."[14]

The TANF Block Grant

The purposes of TANF as stated in the law are an instructive introduction to the program. First, they reflect the desire of governors to free their welfare programs from the federal strictures in AFDC. Second, they reveal the perception in Congress that welfare altered people's behavior in undesirable ways by distorting the incentives they faced. In addition to providing assistance to families, which was a stated purpose of AFDC, a purpose of TANF is to alter behavior regarding work, marriage, and childbearing. The block grant law begins:

> The purpose of this part is to increase the flexibility of States in operating a program designed to —
>
> (1) provide assistance to needy families so that children may be cared for in their own homes or in the homes of relatives;
> (2) end the dependence of needy parents on government benefits by promoting job preparation, work, and marriage;
> (3) prevent and reduce the incidence of out-of-wedlock pregnancies and establish annual numerical goals for preventing and reducing the incidence of these pregnancies; and
> (4) encourage the formation and maintenance of two-parent families.[15]

A block grant is a fixed payment to each state independent of the state's expenditures. In general, block grants represent a bargain between the federal government and the states: the federal government limits the amount of money it gives states and, in exchange, states get increased flexibility to operate their programs. In theory at least, greater flexibility will enable states to manage their programs within the funding limit. Block grants had been used before 1996, most notably by President Reagan, but had never replaced an entitlement program for the poor.

The TANF block grant replaced the open-ended matching grant for AFDC. Under the AFDC funding formula, the federal government financed a percentage of all the welfare benefits paid by the states, ranging from 50 percent of benefits in richer states to a potential 83 percent in poorer states. These grants were open-ended, with no statutory limit on the total amount, and depended only on the matching rates and the levels of state spending. In 1995, for example, the federal share was 50 percent for California and 78.58 percent for Mississippi. The federal government paid California $3,356 million, or 50 percent of its total spending of $6,713 million, and paid Mississippi $70 million, or 78.58 percent of its total spending of $90 million.

An open-ended matching grant for AFDC was appropriate for an entitlement program because federal funds automatically increased when welfare caseloads increased. Medicaid, funded by the same formula, and the federally funded food stamp program are also entitlement programs. A block grant is less appropriate for an entitlement program because it leaves the states paying the full cost of caseload increases and gives them a windfall if caseloads decrease. Consistent with block grant funding, TANF explicitly ended the statutory entitlement in AFDC by stating, "This part shall not be interpreted to entitle any individual or family to assistance under any State program funded under this part."[16] Welfare is now potentially like programs subsidizing child care and housing, where states use waiting lists to cope with insufficient funds for everyone who meets the eligibility criteria, and no longer an income safety net for all eligible families.

Congress set the total block grant at $16.6 billion per year from 1997 to 2002 and, in the absence of reauthorizing legislation, has extended this amount in subsequent years. The block grant to each state was based on the amount of its AFDC grant during the years between 1992 and 1995, when caseloads and hence federal funds were at a historic high. Because caseloads have declined since then, the block grants are larger than the matching grants states would have received under AFDC, giving states a financial windfall. Clearly, the rhetoric that TANF would help balance the federal budget has not become a reality. For the states, this windfall has been an important source of financing for child care, transportation, and other assistance to poor families.

Freezing federal grants at their historic levels protected the states against an immediate cut in funding, but they continued to put states with low benefits and small caseloads at a financial disadvantage relative to more generous states. More generous states received larger federal grants to assist their poor population, encouraging the perpetuation of the horizontal inequities among families living in high- and low-benefit states. The block grant to New York, for example, was $2,443 million, whereas the block grant to Texas, with roughly the same population and poverty rate, was $486 million. The PRWORA authorized supplemental grants to compensate for these disparities, but they were small, about 2 percent of the TANF block grant.

Congress anticipated that the block grant would cause states to cut back on their own spending, since they no longer faced the incentive of the federal match for each dollar of state expenditures. To limit this response, TANF required states to maintain their own spending at a level equal to 75 to 80 percent of their own spending in 1994.[17] These state dollars, termed Maintenance of Effort funds, are not subject to the same rules as federal funds and, as discussed below, have enabled states to avoid some of the restrictions imposed by the block grant. Maintenance of Effort funds have averaged about $10 billion per year since 1997.

Consistent with the rationale of block grants, TANF imposed fewer restrictions on state welfare programs than AFDC had done. States are free to design all five parameters of their welfare programs, not just the level of benefits. They can design their own policies to reward work by disregarding any amount of a family's earnings. They can define any needy family as qualified for assistance regardless of the marital status of the parents. They can impose a family cap and pay benefits in cash or in kind. They are also free to impose behavioral mandates on applicants and recipients as a condition of receiving assistance, like learnfare and mandatory immunizations. Essentially, the TANF block grant was the culmination of the waiver movement, devolving authority for many policy choices to the states

Although TANF gave states more flexibility, it imposed several momentous restrictions on their use of federal funds to provide assistance to poor families. First, federal funds cannot be used to assist an adult for more than sixty months over his or her lifetime. Second, states must require parents to work as soon as they are ready to work or within two years, whichever is earlier. If recipients fail to comply with the work requirement and other behavioral mandates, states have the authority to sanction them by reducing their assistance payment or even terminating assistance entirely.

TANF also embodied a management style that focused on performance. Additional funds were set aside for bonuses to states that achieve "high performance" and for bonuses to states that reduce out-of-wedlock births while also reducing "the rate of induced pregnancy terminations."[18] The law penalized states that failed to engage a minimum percentage of its caseload in a work-related activity. The mandated work participation rate was 25 percent in 1997, rising to 50 percent in 2002. Two-parent families were subject to a 75 percent work participation rate, rising to 90 percent. States failing to meet these participation rates were to be penalized by a cut in block grant funds.

Being the product of a bargain between Congress and the states, the law and the federal regulations elaborating on the law gave the states several escape hatches from these restrictions. The law lowered the work participation rate that each state must meet by a percentage point for each percentage point decline in the caseload since 1995, provided the caseload decline was not due to changes in the state's eligibility criteria. Giving states credit for reductions in their caseloads lessened the conflict a state would face in choosing between policies that encourage work participation and policies that reduce caseloads. As a result of the caseload reduction credit, virtually all states have met the work participation rate and none has been penalized.

A second escape hatch from these restrictions is through the use of Maintenance of Effort funds. States can use their Maintenance of Effort funds for a "separate state program" that is not subject to the TANF time limit or work rules. New York, for example, has used Maintenance of Effort funds to finance its "safety net" program for families exhausting the sixty-month time limit on assistance financed by the block grant. Numerous states have used a separate state program to assist two-parent families because the minimum work participation rate for these families of 90 percent was too high for them to reach.

Another escape hatch is through the definition of "assistance" in the federal regulations. A liberal decision was made by the U.S. Department of Health and Human Services to exclude from the definition certain expenditures for poor families, including work subsidies (that is, payments to employers to help cover the costs of employee wages, benefits, and training); supportive services, such as child care and transportation, provided to families who are employed; Earned Income Tax Credits; short-term benefits to deal with a specific crisis; and services such as counseling and job retention and advancement services.[19] Because these expenditures are not considered "assistance," they are not subject to TANF's restrictions.

Impacts of TANF

The decade of the 1990s brought a sea change to the welfare system. Welfare caseloads reached an all-time high of 5.1 million families in spring 1994 and then fell precipitously. Caseloads fell to 2.2 million families in 2000, a decline of more than 50 percent, and then declined more slowly, reaching 2.0 million by the end of 2003 (see Figure 9–1). The fall in caseloads was widespread across the states. Between the enactment of TANF in August 1996 and June 2003, caseloads declined in every state except Indiana. The decline was less than 30 percent in only five states and exceeded 70 percent in four states (see Table 9–1). Total caseloads changed little between 2000 and 2003, increasing in some states and decreasing in others.

Impacts on State Policy

The governors and state welfare administrators responded to TANF with the leadership and creativity they had shown in responding to Reagan's 1981 budget and in devising the waivers from the AFDC law. Free from the constraining rules in AFDC and subject to the new constraints and incentives in TANF, state elected and appointed officials made fundamental reforms in their welfare systems. Each state's TANF program became the product of the state's institutions, political culture, demographics, economic and financial conditions, and management systems. State AFDC programs had always differed in the generosity of their benefits and in other significant respects, but the diversity of state TANF programs is far greater. Instead of one welfare system, the nation now has fifty systems.

Of the three new purposes of TANF, states focused primarily on encouraging and requiring people to work. Many states adopted a "work first" process for people applying for assistance. Work first took several forms, from searching for a job to attending an orientation to learn about policies and services to encourage and support work. In Georgia, for example, TANF applicants were required to search for work for several weeks before the welfare agency would authorize assistance. Applicants met with staff from the Georgia Department of Labor, who asked about their education and prior work experience and referred them to employers with job openings. In Michigan, TANF applicants were required to attend an orientation to learn about work rules and the child care and transportation available to TANF recipients. Assistance was authorized only after the applicant attended the first day of a work-related activity, which was generally a program providing help in searching for a job. Given discretion in designing policy, states devised their own variant of work first.

Work first served several functions beyond the obvious one of helping applicants find work and thereby reducing their need for welfare. Work first sent a clear message to welfare applicants that they would need to participate in a work-related activity as a condition of receiving welfare, a prospect that discouraged some people from continuing their application. Requiring applicants to spend time searching for work or attending an orientation also served to identify people unable to do this because they were already working but not reporting their earnings to the welfare agency. Administrators described as "miracle jobs" the jobs that people found just at the moment they were expected to attend an activity required by the welfare agency.

With welfare no longer an entitlement, welfare agencies could also divert applicants from assistance by offering them a one-time cash payment on the condition they withdraw their application for ongoing assistance. A slim majority of states adopted a policy of diverting applicants by one-time payments.[20]

Once receiving assistance, recipients were under pressure to engage in a work-related activity. TANF required states to cut the benefits of recipients who failed to comply with work requirements without good cause. This sanction could be a portion of the welfare grant or, if a state chose, the full amount of the family's grant. A full family sanction for noncompliance with work requirements was elected by twenty states.[21] In addition to sanctions for failure to work, states sanctioned recipients for failure to cooperate with child support enforcement and for failure to comply with other rules, like immunizing their children and attending parenting classes.

In addition to penalizing recipients who do not work, many states increased the financial reward for recipients who work. States were no longer bound by a federal rule requiring them to disregard $120 of monthly earnings and one-third of the remainder in calculating welfare benefits.[22] Some states continued this policy but many were more generous, a few disregarding 100 percent of earnings during the first month or months of employment. With more stringent work requirements and more generous financial incentives to work, the number of welfare recipients who worked increased under TANF. In 2003, 21 percent of adults were employed in regular, unsubsidized jobs.[23]

States responded in numerous ways to the sixty-month time limit on the use of federal funds to provide assistance. Several states imposed a shorter lifetime limit: twenty-one months in Connecticut; twenty-four months in Arkansas, Idaho, and Indiana; thirty-six months in Utah; and forty-eight months in Delaware, Florida, and Georgia. Several states imposed an intermittent time limit; North Carolina, for example, imposed a sixty-month lifetime time limit and also limited assistance to twenty-four months followed by thirty-six months of ineligibility. Several states continued paying benefits to children after their parents reached the time limit. Some other states, including Massachusetts, Michigan, New York, Oregon, and Vermont, imposed no time limit and used their Maintenance of Effort funds or other state funds to finance benefits after sixty months. In most states, caseloads fell sharply before families began to hit the time limit, suggesting that a triggering of the limit was not the immediate cause of the decline. Knowing the limit was coming, however, might have motivated recipients to prepare themselves for a life without welfare by finding a job or finishing school. The time limit certainly motivated welfare offices to implement work first and other work-related activities.

Substituting a block grant for a matching grant provided an incentive for states to reduce the generosity of their welfare system, particularly the level of cash benefits. States that increased expenditures would now need to pay the full additional cost, whereas states that decreased expenditures would continue to receive their full block grant and could reallocate their own funds elsewhere, provided they met the Maintenance of Effort requirement. If policymakers believed that high welfare benefits were welfare magnets, encouraging the poor to migrate from low-benefit to high-benefit states, TANF could set off a "race to the bottom" in which states competed by lowering benefits to keep out the poor and lowering taxes to attract business.

A comparison of the cash benefits paid by the states in 1994 and 2003 shows that most states kept benefits stable. Only five states and the District of Columbia decreased the maximum monthly benefit paid to a family of three. Yet after taking into account the 22 percent inflation over this period, real benefits declined in every state except Louisiana, Maryland, Mississippi, West Virginia, and Wisconsin.[24] States did not race to the bottom, but inflation carried them in that direction. Moreover, the large differential among states in their levels of benefits, a horizontal inequity among poor families who are in similar circumstances, persists.

Although states focused attention on the work goals of TANF, they responded more warily to the law's family policy goals. The public generally accepts the idea that mothers on welfare should work, and much research demonstrates that effective welfare-to-work programs can be designed. Public sentiment for using the welfare system to discourage out-of-wedlock pregnancies and encourage the formation and maintenance of two-parent families is weaker, and far less is known about designing effective programs to achieve these goals. With the exception of programs to prevent teen pregnancy by teaching abstinence from sex until marriage, where special funds and restrictions spurred state action, state initiatives in family policy have trailed behind the rapid creation of work programs.[25]

Impacts on State Expenditures

The decline in caseloads relieved pressures for state spending on cash assistance, and because the block grant was fixed, states also received a windfall in federal funds. In addition to having these extra funds, states had more flexibility in spending them. TANF also allowed states to carry over federal funds from one year to the next, using the block grant for one year to finance spending in subsequent years. States were initially cautious in spending their TANF block grant funds, knowing they would not receive additional funds if caseloads rose in the future, and many states left some of their block grant in Washington to use later. This practice continued unchecked until Congress, seeing the unspent balances accumulate, threatened to cut the block grant. Recognizing that they needed to use it or lose it, states picked up the pace of spending the block grant.

As states prepared their budgets, each state knew the amount of its federal allocation for the year, plus unspent allocations from previous years and the amount it must spend to meet its Maintenance of Effort requirement. These two amounts became "pots" of money that states spent with considerable discretion. States spent these funds on other activities besides cash assistance, and the distinction between what is welfare and what is not welfare has become blurred.

Spending on cash assistance has declined substantially since the creation of TANF. In 1994, before caseloads began to drop, spending on cash assistance was $23 billion.[26] By 2003, reported spending on "basic cash assistance" was only $10.2 billion, or 35.2 percent of total TANF and Maintenance of Effort funds (see Table 9–2). Basic cash assistance is defined by the federal regulations as assistance to meet a family's ongoing basic needs.

With only 35.2 percent of funds used for basic ongoing cash assistance, funds were available for other types of services, cash payments, and in-kind assistance. Spending for services related to work used a large share of these funds. Work-related activities to help people find jobs and increase their earning capacity, such as job search and job placement, education and training, and subsidies to employers to help cover the costs of employing welfare recipients,

Table 9–2 Use of TANF and Maintenance of Effort Funds, Fiscal Year 2003

Use of funds	Amount (millions of $)	Total (%)
Basic assistance	10,218	35.2
Child care	5,258	18.1
Work-related activities	2,599	8.9
Work subsidies	31	.1
Education and training	494	1.7
Other work activities/expenses	2,074	7.1
Other nonassistance	2,889	9.9
Refundable earned income tax credit or other refundable tax credit	1,007	3.5
Transferred to social services block grant	927	3.2
Pregnancy prevention	919	3.2
Transportation and supportive services	543	1.9
Two-parent family formation and maintenance	310	1.1
Nonrecurrent short-term benefits	261	.9
Individual development accounts	27	.1
Authorized under prior law	1,646	5.7
Administration and systems	2,451	8.4
Total	29,057	100.0

Source: Mark Greenberg and Hedieh Rahmanou, *TANF Spending in 2003,* (Washington, D.C.: Center for Law and Social Policy, February 2, 2005), data available at http://www.acf.dhhs.gov/programs/ofs/data/tanf_2003.html.

used 8.9 percent of these funds. Spending to support low-income working families included child care expenditures of 18.1 percent of these funds and transportation and other supportive services of 1.9 percent. Tax credits, which increase the financial reward to work by reducing income taxes by a percentage of earnings, were 3.5 percent. (When a tax credit is "refundable" as these are, a family receives a check from the government if its calculated tax liability is negative.)

"Other nonassistance" in Table 9–2 included a variety of expenditures, such as services for child abuse and neglect, substance abuse programs, domestic violence services, before- and after-school programs, and payments to food banks and homeless shelters.[27] Not all these expenditures were for families receiving cash assistance. Families not on welfare were also the beneficiaries of expenditures for child care, tax credits, pregnancy prevention and two-parent family formation and maintenance, transfers to the social services block grant, and "expenditures authorized under prior law," a poorly understood item.

When Congress restricted families' access to TANF cash assistance, it placed increased reliance on other income support programs, particularly federal programs, to provide a financial safety net for the poor. Poor families continued to be eligible for the federal food stamp program and, if they had earnings, the federal EITC. As fewer families received cash assistance, these two sources of support became more important pieces of the safety net. For example, a single parent with two children who worked throughout 2003 at a half-time job paying the federal minimum wage of $5.15 per hour would earn $4,942 after payroll taxes, too much to qualify for TANF in Alabama, Louisiana, Mississippi, Missouri, Nevada, and Texas. This family was eligible for food stamps worth $3,588 and an EITC of $2,141, giving it a total income of $10,671, or 69.9 percent of the federal poverty line. Similar families living in states paying higher TANF benefits would continue to receive TANF and would have a higher total income, although still below the poverty line in all but seven states.[28] In addition, children in all families with income below the poverty line were eligible for state Medicaid programs. These programs can play an important role in supporting poor families in the new world of time limits on welfare. Unfortunately, due to lack of information, feelings of stigma, or a desire to avoid the hassles of the welfare system, not all eligible families participate in them.

Impacts on People

TANF raised the specter of soaring poverty among single mothers and their children as time limits and work requirements forced them off welfare. These fears prompted a flurry of studies to examine the well-being of low-income mothers with children and families leaving welfare. Because these studies cover only a few years, and hence have difficulty in separating the effects of policy changes from the effects of economic changes, the overall picture is still blurry. But the broad outline is that, as of 2003, the latest year for which data are available, TANF had not devastated these families.

In 1993, before caseloads began to fall, 46.1 percent of families with children under eighteen years headed by women were poor according to the surveys conducted by the Census Bureau. To the surprise of many, the rate of poverty among these families did not increase but declined sharply to 33.0 percent in 2000.[29] The percentage of single mothers who were employed rose sharply, particularly mothers with a child under age three, whose employment rate rose from 35.1 percent in 1993 to 59.1 percent in 2000.[30] The 2001 recession reversed these trends somewhat, with the employment rate falling and the poverty rate climbing to 35.9 percent in 2004, but neither measure was close to its earlier level. Tempering this good news were data showing that the poorest of these families, those whose incomes rank in the lowest fifth of the incomes of all single-mother families, experienced a drop in income of about 10 percent since 1994.[31]

Questions about the well-being of the people who left welfare led the U.S. Department of Health and Human Services to fund a set of studies about welfare "leavers." They found the experience of leavers was highly varied, reflecting differences in their abilities, their family situations, and their eligibility for other government assistance. The majority of adults found work.

A review of fifteen leaver studies showed that about 60 percent of adults were employed at some point during the first thirteen weeks after leaving the program.[32] But because many were not employed for all thirteen weeks or were not working full time, their mean earnings during this calendar quarter were low, varying among the studies from a low of $1,900 to a high of about $3,400, the latter amount being near the poverty level.[33] Unstable employment was common, so although more than 70 percent of people leaving welfare began to work at some point during their first year off welfare, only 40 percent worked in all four quarters of the year.[34] Surveys of leavers found that mean hourly wages in the states ranged from $7.50 to $8.74, but a substantial minority had earnings closer to the minimum wage of $5.15 an hour.[35]

A 1999 survey of people leaving welfare between 1997 and 1999 found that 44 percent had no recent employment. Among these leavers, 10 percent had no income from work but had income from other sources, including a disability program (1.5 percent) and a spouse or cohabiting partner (8.6 percent). Almost 22 percent of these leavers had returned to TANF, which is a lower recidivism rate than had been the norm under AFDC. Another 19 percent had none of these sources of income, and although 7 percent had worked recently, the remaining 12 percent had not worked in the past year. Among these 19 percent, 50 percent were in poor physical or mental health, 19 percent had a disabled child, and 8 percent had a child under age one.[36]

A third group of studies tracked families over time to examine the change in income experienced when the mother became employed. They found that a family's real income increased by less than the increase in the mother's earnings. Because TANF and food stamp benefits are scaled to income, these benefits decreased as earnings increased. The study in Michigan found that families' incomes increased by 63 percent when a mother left welfare for work. But studies in the three other sites, using a slightly different methodology, found that, ignoring the Earned Income Tax Credit and state taxes, families' incomes increased only 14 percent and that 72.5 percent of families were poor. When the EITC and taxes were taken into account, families' incomes increased 26 percent and the poverty rate decreased to 52.5 percent, illustrating the importance of the EITC.[37]

These studies show that basic dilemmas in designing a system of payments to poor families have continued with TANF. Time limits on welfare provide an incentive to a single parent to work and seek child support from an absent parent, but families without income from these sources are threatened with deep poverty. Disregards of earnings in calculating payments also encourage work, but the more generous the disregard, the more a parent must earn in order to leave welfare. Parents who stay on welfare and use welfare to supplement their low earnings experience less poverty, but they run into their state's time limit. Liberals argue that poverty reduction should be an explicit goal of the program, whereas conservatives place greater weight on the virtue of strong incentives for recipients to work.[38] TANF emphasized work over poverty reduction, but the compromise between these goals is not carved in stone.

Looking to the Future

Even the staunchest critics of TANF now acknowledge that the law has produced successes.[39] More low-income single mothers are working and the effects on the well-being of families have been surprisingly benign. Many welfare scholars give a broadly positive assessment to TANF, and although they examined the program in its early years and could reach different conclusions in the future, they have not recommended major reforms.[40] More grave problems, particularly the threat of terrorism and the war in Iraq, have eclipsed welfare as a policy issue. In public opinion polls asking people to identify the most important problem facing the nation, between 6 and 8 percent named welfare in the 1990s, but only 1 percent named welfare in 2001.[41]

Federal Reauthorization of TANF

PRWORA authorized the TANF block grant through fiscal year 2002, requiring Congress to reauthorize the program by October 1, 2002. To begin the reauthorization process, the Bush administration submitted a proposal in early 2002 that declared the results of TANF to be "nothing short of spectacular" and maintained the basic outlines of the program.[42] The proposal set the TANF block grant at $16.6 billion, the same amount as the 1996 law, and held states to the same Maintenance of Effort requirement. Funding for child care was also the same. Several features of the administration's proposal raised serious opposition.

Attracting the most criticism were the work participation rates to be met by the states. The 1996 law required states to achieve a work participation rate of 50 percent by 2002, a requirement that most states met by claiming the caseload reduction credit. To be counted as participating, a recipient needed to be engaged in a work activity for a minimum of thirty hours per week, or twenty hours if a parent of a child under six. The administration's plan increased the work participation rate to 70 percent by 2007 and counted toward the participation rate only recipients who worked for forty hours per week. Furthermore, the plan would eliminate the caseload reduction credit by 2005.

Critics viewed these features of the administration's plan as both unrealistic and undesirable. In order to achieve a rate of 70 percent, states would need to impose a universal work requirement, since a steady portion of recipients are unable to participate for transitory reasons like illness, waiting for a program to begin, or arranging for child care. But health and mental health problems of adults or their children make a universal work requirement unrealistic. In addition, a 70 percent rate would be unrealistic without significantly more money for child care. Experts also argued that a 70 percent rate is undesirable because it would limit the states' ability to adopt programs that research shows are most effective.[43] Finally, critics argued that the president was making excessive demands on welfare recipients. The Census Bureau defines a full-time worker as someone who usually works a minimum of thirty-five hours per week. Should single mothers, especially mothers with young children, be expected to work a minimum of forty hours a week?

The level of funding in the president's proposal was another point of contention. Funding the block grant and child care at their 1996 levels did not adjust for the inflation since 1996, which would reduce the real amount of federal funds. Although the decline in caseloads lessened the need for expenditures on cash assistance, funds were still necessary for expenditures on child care, transportation, the EITC, and the other supports listed in Table 9–2, which undergirded the decline in caseloads. Indeed, many argued for increases in these expenditures, pointing to the lack of funding for child care for the working poor.

The House Ways and Means Committee approved a bill containing many of the provisions of the administration's proposal and sent it to the floor of the House, where it passed in May 2002. The bill then went to the Senate Finance Committee, which passed it in July after softening the participation requirement and substantially increasing funding for child care. But with Congress preoccupied with homeland security and a war resolution, the bill was not brought to the Senate floor for a vote. Instead, Congress passed a three-month extension of funding for TANF. Variations on this scenario have been repeated each year since then, and as of summer 2005, the full Senate has yet to vote on a bill. Welfare reform was not a big issue in the 2004 presidential campaign and has not been a priority for President Bush in his second term. Welfare reform may have lost steam as a way to generate political capital.

More Waivers and Block Grants on the Horizon?

Citing the success of TANF, the administration's reauthorization proposal would allow states to seek "program integration waivers" for integrating funding and program rules across assistance and workforce programs. Called a "superwaiver," the president and the governors would have authority to override federal rules in programs such as TANF, food stamps, job training, unemployment insurance, federal housing programs, and federal adult and post secondary education programs. States could seek waivers to reduce the bewildering variety of eligibility criteria, target groups, and other rules and definitions that complicate efforts to serve clients with a well-integrated set of services.

Proposals to create additional block grants have also been made by the administration and members of Congress. Their proposals would transform the federal funding streams for food stamps, Medicaid, Head Start, job training, housing vouchers, and several other programs into block grants.[44] Block granting food stamps and Medicaid, which are currently entitlement programs, would be a particularly drastic step.

Whatever the merits of these individual proposals, the states' response to TANF has given policymakers in Washington more confidence in the idea of devolving additional authority to them. As this comment by a Washington think tank indicates, the distrust of the states that helped centralize welfare policy has diminished:

> The foes of superwaivers have valid reasons to be uneasy. But as practically everyone agrees, none of the states today resembles the antediluvian polities—governed by reactionary governors, malapportioned legislatures, feeble bureaucracies, and passive courts—that existed in some regions of the country through the first half of the twentieth century. Few, if any, American state governments today seem prone to subvert rather than support the nation's safety net.[45]

Conclusion

Although states may not be subverting the nation's safety net, their efforts to achieve a stated purpose of TANF, "to end the dependence of needy parents on government benefits by promoting job preparation [and] work," came at its expense. Time limits, sanctions for failure to comply with work requirements, and the erosion of cash benefits by inflation all served to increase the incentive to work by weakening the safety net. The stringency of states' policies varied greatly, but all states promoted work in their TANF program and, in doing so, made welfare a less certain prospect for poor families.

As states toughened their work incentives, they increased their spending on employment and training services to help people prepare for work and find jobs. Expenditures to finance the child care and transportation that parents need in order to work increased as well, even surpassing expenditures on cash assistance in some states. In addition, some states devoted funds to substance abuse programs, domestic violence programs, and other services for people with problems that interfered with their ability to hold a job. With the decline in expenditures for cash assistance, the Maintenance of Effort requirement created a pool of funds available to pay for these services. Although states varied in the breadth and depth of services provided, the time limits and work requirements in TANF generally made them more willing to spend money on services that help poor families cope with these new rules.

The combination of work incentives and services to support work deterred applicants from coming onto welfare and moved recipients off welfare, producing a sharp decline in caseloads. The majority of welfare leavers found jobs, but their wages were generally low and their work was often intermittent, leaving many in poverty. Medicaid, food stamps, the EITC, and child care subsidies became relatively more important sources of income and were critical to their well-being. Families staying on welfare received benefits that varied widely from one state to another, and even generous states paid too little to lift them out of poverty. All in all, more single mothers were working and fewer were receiving welfare, but as a group their economic well-being improved only modestly.

TANF has given states more control over their welfare policies than at any time since the 1960s, freeing them to design a diverse array of programs. As long as states have sufficient funds to maintain their current programs and the well-being of poor families remains stable, little pressure for a greater federal role will develop. But if the well-being of poor families begins to deteriorate and funds appear inadequate to serve them, the balance of control between the federal government and the states may shift once again.

Notes

1. PROWRA: PL 104-193, signed August 22, 1996; TANF: Social Security Act, Title IV, Part A, codified at 42 U.S.C. 601 et seq.
2. Richard A. Musgrave, *The Theory of Public Finance* (New York: McGraw-Hill, 1959), 181–182.
3. Michael A. Bailey, "Welfare and the Multifaceted Decision to Move," *American Political Science Review* 9, no. 1 (February 2005): 125–135.
4. Paul E. Peterson and Mark C. Rom, *Welfare Magnets* (Washington, D.C.: Brookings Institution, 1990); Scott W. Allard, "Revisiting *Shapiro:* Welfare Magnets and State Residency Requirements in the 1990s," in *Welfare Reform: A Race to the Bottom?* ed. Sanford F. Schram and Samuel H. Beer (Washington, D.C.: Woodrow Wilson Center Press, 1999).
5. Expenditure data for all programs except TANF, Medicare and Medicaid, and the EITC are from the *2004 Annual Statistical Supplement to the Social Security Bulletin*, http://www.ssa.gov/policy/docs/statcomps/supplement/2004. TANF data are from http://www.acf.dhhs.gov/programs/ofs/data/tanf_2003.html. Medicare and Medicaid data are from the *Health Care Financial Review, Medicare and Medicaid Statistical Supplement, 2003*, http://www.cms.hhs.gov/review/supp/2003. EITC data are from the Internal Revenue Service, *Statistics of Income*, http://www.irs.gov/taxstats.
6. National Association of State Budget Officers, *2003 State Expenditure Report* (Washington, D.C.: National Association of State Budget Officers, 2004).
7. *Goldberg v. Kelly*, 397 U.S. 254, at 262 (1970).
8. Michael B. Katz, *In the Shadow of the Poorhouse: A Social History of Welfare in America* (New York: Basic Books, 1986).
9. Judith Gueron and Edward Pauly, *From Welfare to Work* (New York: Russell Sage Foundation, 1991).
10. Ibid.; Robert Moffitt, "Incentive Effects of the U.S. Welfare System: A Review," *Journal of Economic Literature* 30 (March 1992): 27–31.
11. Lawrence M. Mead, *Beyond Entitlement* (New York: Free Press, 1986); National Governors' Association, *Making America Work: Productive People, Productive Policies* (Washington, D.C.: National Governors Association, 1987); and Michael Novak and others, *The New Consensus on Family and Welfare* (Washington, D.C.: American Enterprise Institute for Public Policy Research, 1987).
12. Richard P. Nathan, *Turning Promises into Performance* (New York: Columbia University Press, 1993).
13. Interview with author.
14. Bill Clinton, *My Life: The Presidential Years* (New York: Vintage Books, 2005), 720.
15. 42 U.S.C. 601(a).
16. 42 U.S.C. 601(b).
17. Because states qualify for 75 percent if they meet the minimum work participation rate, a 75 percent Maintenance of Effort is the norm.
18. 42 U.S.C. 603(a)(4) and 42 U.S.C. 603(a)(2), respectively. The law does not define "high performance."

19. 45 CFR 260.31.
20. U.S. Department of Health and Human Services, Administration for Children and Families, *Temporary Assistance for Needy Families Program (TANF) Sixth Annual Report to Congress* (Washington, D.C.: Department of Health and Human Services, 2004), 104–105.
21. Ibid., 103–104.
22. The $120 included $30 as a work incentive and $90 to cover work expenses.
23. U.S. Department of Health and Human Services, Administration for Children and Families, Office of Family Assistance, TANF Program Information Memorandum no. TANF-ACF-IM-2004-03, Washington, D.C., December 22, 2004, table 6c.
24. U.S. House, Committee on Ways and Means, *2004 Green Book*, March 2004, 7–37 to 7–39.
25. Deborah A. Orth and Malcolm L. Goggin, *How States and Counties Have Responded to the Family Policy Goals of Welfare Reform* (Albany, N.Y.: Rockefeller Institute of Government, 2003).
26. Mark Greenberg and Hedieh Rahmanou, *TANF Spending in 2003* (Washington, D.C.: Center for Law and Social Policy, 2005), 6.
27. Ibid., 7.
28. House Committee on Ways and Means, *2004 Green Book*, 7–45 to 7–47.
29. U.S. Bureau of the Census, "Historical Poverty Tables-Current Population Survey," table 4, http://www.census.gov/hhes/poverty/histpov/hstpov4.html.
30. House Committee on Ways and Means, *2004 Green Book*, L-10.
31. Ibid., L-18.
32. Gregory Acs and Pamela Loprest, *Leaving Welfare: Employment and Well-Being of Families that Left Welfare in the Post-Entitlement Era* (Kalamazoo, Mich.: W. E. Upjohn Institute for Employment Research, 2004), 27.
33. Ibid., 32.
34. Ibid., 41.
35. Ibid., 35–36.
36. Ibid. 59–68.
37. Robert Moffitt and Katie Winder, "Does It Pay to Move from Welfare to Work? A Comment on Danziger, Heflin, Corcoran, Oltmans, and Wang," *Journal of Policy Analysis and Management* 24, no. 2 (Spring 2005).
38. Ron Haskins and Wendell Primus, "Welfare Reform and Poverty," in *Welfare Reform and Beyond: The Future of the Safety Net,* ed. Isabel V. Sawhill and others (Washington, D.C.: Brookings Institution Press, 2002).
39. Wendell Primus, Testimony before the Subcommittee on Human Resources of the House Committee on Ways and Means, April 11, 2002, http://waysandmeans.house.gov/legacy.asp?file=legacy/humres/107cong/4-11-02/4-11prim.htm.
40. Sawhill and others, *Welfare Reform and Beyond,* and Rebecca Blank and Ron Haskins, eds., *The New World of Welfare* (Washington, D.C.: Brookings Institution Press, 2001).
41. Greg M. Shaw and Robert Y. Shapiro, "Cooler Passions: Welfare Reform Five Years Later," *Public Perspective* 13, no. 2 (March-April 2002).
42. "Working Toward Independence," February 26, 2002, press release, http://www.whitehouse.gov/news/releases/2002/02/welfare-reform-announcement-book.html.
43. Mark H. Greenberg, Testimony before the Subcommittee on Human Resources of the House Committee on Ways and Means, March 7, 2002, http://www.clasp.org/publications/Testimony_of_Mark_Greenberg_3-7.pdf.
44. Kenneth Finegold, Laura Wherry, and Stephanie Schardin, *Block Grants: Historical Overview and Lessons Learned,* New Federalism Series A, no. A-63 (Washington, D.C.: Urban Institute, 2004).
45. Pietro S. Nivola, Jennifer L. Noyes, and Isabel V. Sawhill, *Waive of the Future? Federalism and the Next Phase of Welfare Reform,* Welfare Reform and Beyond Policy Brief 29 (Washington, D.C.: Brookings Institution Press, 2004).

10

State Health Policy
Joel C. Cantor

Broadly conceived, much of what state governments do concerns health policy. Education agencies determine health and physical education curricula and establish requirements for school nurses; transportation agencies concern themselves with traffic safety; and the connection between the child protective services, environmental protection, and policing functions of state government and health is also clear. The state judiciary also has a substantial role in health policy in that state courts adjudicate civil claims with the aim of compensating and deterring personal injury torts.

More narrowly, state health policy can be seen as those government actions specifically directed at protecting or promoting health or reducing the harm caused by illness. The Institute of Medicine of the National Academy of Sciences enumerated "essential public health services."[1] These basic government health policy functions are shown in Table 10–1 along with specific examples of state government activities. States operate in two broad domains of health policy: population health services and personal health care services. Personal health services are face-to-face encounters between health care providers and their patients, whereas population health services encompass all other health-related activities. Population health services include many of the functions of public health departments, such as restaurant sanitation inspection, disease outbreak investigation and control, and antismoking media campaigns.

Spending on population health services pales compared with that on personal health services, and financing health care services is a long-standing conundrum for state policymakers. In 2003 the nation spent $1.7 trillion on population and personal health services, which translates to $5,670 per person, or 15.3 percent of the gross domestic product.[2] Of this amount, only $53.8 billion, or 3.2 percent of total national health expenditures, was spent by government on population health services; the remainder went for personal health care services, administrative costs, research, and construction of health care facilities. Moreover, the health sector is among the fastest growing in the U.S. economy, more than doubling as a percentage of gross domestic product between 1970 and 2003.[3]

States play a central role in financing and administering population and personal health services.[4] In 2003 state and local spending on health stood at $224 billion, 29.3 percent of government spending in this sector. But this number, which represents only state and local revenue commitments, does not

Table 10–1 Essential Public Health Services

Public health functions	Examples of state activities
1. Monitor health status to identify problems	• Vital records (e.g., birth and death reporting) • Mandatory reporting of sexually transmitted diseases • Surveys of behavioral risk-factor prevalence
2. Diagnose and investigate health problems and health hazards	• Epidemic outbreak investigation • Restaurant health inspection • Workplace accident investigation
3. Inform, educate, and empower people about health issues	• Anti-smoking media campaign • Family caregiver information hotline • Managed care patient bill of rights
4. Mobilize community partnerships to identify and solve health problems	• Minority health task force • Bioterrorism readiness planning • Grants for local maternal and child health programs
5. Develop policies and plans to support individual and community health efforts	• Clean indoor air act banning smoking • Creation of "health enterprise zones" where health professionals are eligible for education loan forgiveness • Establishment of community-service standards for state-licensed nonprofit health insurers and hospitals
6. Enforce laws and regulations that protect health and ensure safety	• Civil rights enforcement requiring trained medical interpreters in health care settings serving immigrants • Hospital and clinic health and safety inspection
7. Link people to needed personal health services and ensure the provision of health care when otherwise unavailable	• Reimbursement for hospital charity care • Medicaid and child health insurance for low-income populations • Grants to community health centers
8. Ensure a competent public health and personal health care workforce	• Legislation defining training requirements and scope of practice for the health professions • Establishment of continuing education requirements for health professionals
9. Evaluate effectiveness, accessibility, and quality of personal and population-based health services	• Program evaluation studies • Community health surveys
10. Conduct research to attain new insights and innovative solutions to health problems	• Financing health professional schools • Grants for scientific investigation

Source: Adapted from Institute of Medicine, *The Future of the Public's Health in the 21st Century* (Washington, D.C.: National Academies Press, 2003), 99.

fully capture the role of states. With the exception of the federally operated Medicare program, which funds care for seniors and the long-term disabled, much of the remaining $259 billion in federal spending flows through states, including $159 billion (an additional 20.8 percent of all government health spending) in federal Medicaid expenditures, which help states finance care for many low-income and disabled individuals.

Medicaid looms large in state budgets. In fiscal year 2003 Medicaid represented 21.4 percent of total state spending, roughly tied with elementary and secondary education (21.7 percent) as the largest spending item.[5] Medicaid holds second place in spending of state general revenue (16.5 percent) after elementary and secondary education (35.5 percent), but it represents the biggest state expenditure of federal funds (43.5 percent).[6] Medicaid represents challenges for states not only because of its high cost but because the program is an entitlement, that is, it guarantees benefits to all who meet eligibility criteria regardless of the availability of funds, leaving states little control over spending. In fiscal year 2003, for example, Medicaid spending exceeded budgeted amounts in half of the states, a total of $3.6 billion beyond what states had budgeted.[7]

In this chapter the context, recent developments, and current challenges of state health policy are discussed. The following section lays the groundwork for this discussion by describing variations among states in health problems and capacity to address those problems. Next is a brief overview of the emergence of state and federal roles in health policy over the last century. Recent developments in state health policy are examined in detail, including a decades' long effort by states to address the gap in health insurance coverage. Funding of personal health care services has dominated state health policy discourse and is therefore the principal focus in this chapter. However, the chapter also examines two other recent themes in state policy to illustrate state responses to other health challenges: the state use of revenue from the national tobacco settlement and the potential conversion of state-chartered, nonprofit Blue Cross Blue Shield health plans to profit-seeking health insurance companies, and state efforts to promote embryonic stem cell research. The chapter closes with a discussion of the future of state health policy and state-driven health reform.

State Capacity to Meet Health Care Needs

Health and health care needs vary greatly among the states.[8] Not surprisingly, states with lower average incomes and higher rates of poverty also experience the greatest burden of population illness. For instance, Mississippi, the state with the second lowest median household income ($31,886), has an infant death rate (10.5 per 1,000 live births) that is more than twice the rate in New Hampshire (under 4 per 1,000 live births), the state with the third highest median income ($55,116). Adult diabetes prevalence ranges from nearly 10 percent in Alabama and Mississippi, two low-income states, to about 5 percent in Alaska, Colorado, Minnesota, and Utah, which all rank in the top quarter of the median income distribution among the states. Important risk factors for future disease, such as smoking, physical inactivity, and obesity, follow similar patterns across states. In Kentucky, Louisiana, and Nebraska, for example, only about a third of adults meet recommended standards for regular physical activity compared with over 55 percent of adults in Vermont and Washington State.

States with a greater burden of sickness also have higher shares of their population with no health insurance coverage, and many lag in other measures of health system performance.[9] In one thirteen-state survey, respondents in the four states with the highest uninsured rate were about 60 percent more likely to report that their general health was only "fair or poor."[10] Specific health performance measures follow a similar pattern. For example, rates of potentially life-saving flu vaccine given to the elderly vary from a low of about 55 percent in Kentucky and Louisiana to over 70 percent in Wisconsin and Minnesota. Moreover, hospital and health system performance is comparatively low in many states that have low per capita income and a high prevalence of disease and risk factors. For example, Louisiana, Mississippi, and Texas rank at the bottom of a recent study of twenty-two health care quality indicators for the Medicare population.[11]

Clearly, the ability of state governments to address health insurance and system performance problems depends on their fiscal capacity. High rates of medical uninsurance, high disease burden (which makes coverage more costly), poor system performance, and low income create formidable barriers to financing effective policy solutions in the states experiencing the greatest problems.[12] The problem of fiscal capacity may be further exacerbated as the high-need states are also likely to have the greatest difficulty sustaining bureaucratic expertise or political capacity to address complex health problems.[13]

Despite the significant variation and clustering of health care challenges among the states, the United States relies heavily on the states to address the health care needs of the most vulnerable populations. Although the shape of federalism in U.S. health care policy remains a matter of public policy discourse, the underpinnings of the current system were established early in the twentieth century as modern medical care came of age.

The Evolution of Federalism in Health Policy

Contemporary roles of the federal and state governments in health care have evolved over a period beginning in the 1930s. Early investments of the U.S. government in the health arena were driven by the promise of medical advances. In turn, medical innovation, spurred in large part by public spending, created political demand for government support of access to new medical treatments. This section outlines the development of government policy over nearly a century, supporting medical innovation and building institutions to pay for health care services.

Defining Federal and State Roles

The successes of medical treatment early in the twentieth century and a rising political coalition that saw public investment in health care as a vital economic engine, particularly after World War II, drove policies that established a significant role for government in health care.[14] Early public investments promoted medical advancement and expansion of the health care delivery system. The National Institutes of Health and National Cancer Institute, established in 1931 and 1937, respectively, marked the large-scale entry of the national government into this area. After World War II the Hill-Burton Act of 1946 began an infusion of federal dollars that greatly expanded hospital capacity in local communities throughout the United States.

The national government led early public-sector efforts in health care, but states also played a central role in advancing health science and delivery. In a convergence of state health and education policy, states established fifteen new medical schools and expanded others in the 1950s and early 1960s.[15] The Hill-Burton debate raised questions about the ability of families to pay for care delivered through the growing health care infrastructure, but in the end, publicly sponsored health insurance coverage was put off for another day.[16]

States and the Creation of Private Insurance

In the absence of a national initiative providing health coverage, state legislatures facilitated the growth of private health insurance in the early 1930s. Most states established Blue Cross plans starting in that decade, financed by hospitals and, in some cases, community philanthropies. Despite a debate among proponents of Blue Cross plans about whether they were primarily insurance companies intended to ensure stable financing of care or whether they were "community-minded consumer cooperatives," almost all state legislatures conferred on them privileged tax status and other benefits to promote their growth.[17] Later, in 1942, the federal War Labor Board gave labor unions and employers the right to collectively bargain for health benefits without violating wage stabilization rules. This and the exemption of employer payments of health coverage from the federal income tax prompted the spread of commercial, employer-sponsored coverage.[18]

Public Coverage

Notwithstanding serious proposals, the idea of government-sponsored health insurance gained little traction through the early 1960s. Nevertheless, the growing difficulty with which local public hospitals were shouldering the burden of care for the indigent, and the looming possibility of financial ruin of retirees (and, notably, the burden on their adult children), gave rise to new demands for a public strategy to finance coverage. Consequently, health care became an important part of President Lyndon B. Johnson's Great Society programs. In 1965 Congress enacted two public health insurance programs: Medicare for the elderly and long-term disabled and Medicaid for the poor.

Medicare was to be financed and run by the federal government with benefits modeled on private health insurance of the time, covering mainly acute illness care provided by physicians and hospitals. To avoid supplanting the role of states in providing care for those who would be public wards, Medicaid was designed as a joint state-federal program. Originally, federal law encouraged states to set high eligibility limits in Medicaid, based on income, but this provision was repealed during the early years of the program.[19] Thus, early on, the vision of a broad Medicaid program covering low-income populations was substituted for a program linked to welfare eligibility and focused on the most "deserving" poor. In addition to covering acute care services for children, pregnant women, and other groups, the program provided coverage for medical and long-term-care needs of the low-income elderly and disabled. As the only public reimbursement program for expensive chronic and custodial care, Medicaid became the principal source of financing nursing homes and related services.

Both Medicare and Medicaid were created as entitlement programs, with guaranteed benefits for all who met eligibility criteria. To overcome the objections of physicians and hospitals, all qualified health care providers would be entitled to participate in the programs under reimbursement provisions that clearly favored the providers. For Medicaid, entitling providers ensured continued political support for the program, even though its intended beneficiaries were largely the disenfranchised poor.

Developments in State Health Services Financing

Today, a significant role of government in paying for health services is well established, but large gaps in health care access remain. This section addresses the challenges faced by states as they have sought to extend government-sponsored health coverage to vulnerable populations and to encourage private coverage for others. The opportunities and challenges for state policymakers of working within the framework of major federal government health care financing initiatives are described. Finally, state responses to economic forces affecting private health insurance are discussed.

Medicaid Today

Table 10–2 illustrates the distribution of Medicaid expenditures (including both state and federal shares) by type of services covered. One-third of Medicaid spending in 2003 was for nursing homes, home health care, and related community-based long-term-care services for the elderly and other disabled populations. Mental health facilities (primarily psychiatric hospitals) and long-term-care facilities for people with developmental disabilities (called Intermediate Care Facilities for the Mentally Retarded) accounted for an additional 6.3 percent of Medicaid spending nationally. Because these long-

Table 10–2 Medicaid Expenditures by Type of Service, Fiscal Year 2003 (millions of dollars)

Service	Expenditures ($)	Expenditures (%)
Acute care	155,518	58.3%
Hospital inpatient	36,130	13.5%
Physicians, lab, X-ray	9,850	3.7%
Outpatient[a]	17,736	6.6%
Prescription drugs	26,603	10.0%
Managed care	40,328	15.1%
Other	24,871	9.3%
Long-term care	97,026	36.4%
Nursing homes	45,137	16.9%
Home health and personal care[b]	35,063	13.1%
Intermediate care facilities for the mentally retarded	11,916	4.5%
Mental health facilities	4,910	1.8%
Total spending	266,817	100.0%

Source: Adapted from Kaiser Commission on Medicaid and the Uninsured, *Medicaid Spending and Enrollment: State and National Data Update* (Palo Alto, Calif.: The Henry J. Kaiser Family Foundation, 2005), http://www.kff.org/medicaid/kcmu031104pkg.cfm.

Note: The balance of spending, not shown in this chart (6.3% of total spending), was distributed to states through "disproportionate share" payments, which are discussed below.

a. Includes hospital outpatient departments and other ambulatory facilities.

b. Includes home nursing and personal care support services and other home and community-based services, such as medical day care.

term-care populations suffer disproportionately high levels of acute illness, they also account for a very large share of the 58.3 percent of Medicaid spending for acute care.

The high level and complexity of the health needs of Medicaid beneficiaries and their limited financial resources mean that service limitations or cost-sharing requirements could raise insurmountable barriers to care for many. Thus, the range of services covered by Medicaid is quite comprehensive, and federal rules permit only very limited cost sharing by patients.

Table 10–3 shows the range of services covered by Medicaid. Services shown in the "Optional coverage" section of the table are those that are eligible for federal matching funds but are not required by federal rules. Many of these services, including prescription drugs, facilities for the mentally retarded, and personal care services, are, in fact, offered by virtually all states. States may elect to offer "medically needy programs," which cover persons who are categorically eligible (for example, pregnant women, the elderly, or the disabled) but whose income is too high. Under guidelines concerning the

Table 10–3 Summary of Coverage under Federal Medicaid Rules

Coverage	Service
Mandatory coverage	• Inpatient hospital services • Outpatient hospital services • Physician services • Medical and surgical dental services • Nursing facility services for those 21 or older • Home health care for persons eligible for nursing facility services • Family planning services and supplies • Rural health clinic services • Laboratory and X-ray services • Pediatric and family nurse practitioner and nurse-midwife services (to the extent authorized under state law) • Federally qualified health center services that are covered in other settings • Early and periodic screening, diagnosis, and treatment services for those under age 21
Optional coverage	• Clinic services • Nursing facility services for individuals under age 21 • Intermediate care facility and mentally retarded services • Optometrist services and eyeglasses • Prescribed drugs • Tuberculosis-related services • Prosthetic devices • Dental services • Home and community-based care services to certain individuals, including personal care, respite care, adult day health services, homemaker services, home health aide, case management and related services • Otherwise ineligible women with breast or cervical cancer or precancerous conditions
Medically needy	• Prenatal care and delivery services for pregnant women • Ambulatory services to children and individuals entitled to institutional programs services • Home health services to individuals entitled to nursing facility services • Comprehensive services for persons in facilities for the mentally retarded and mentally ill

Source: Data from U.S. Department of Health and Human Services, Centers for Medicare and Medicaid Services, *Medicaid Services,* http://www.cms.hhs.gov/medicaid/mservice.asp (accessed September 16, 2005).

medically needy, persons are deemed eligible once their family income less out-of-pocket medical costs for qualified health care reach the state's eligibility threshold. Medically needy programs are complex, and states may exercise this option selectively for different Medicaid eligibility categories. As of 2001 all but sixteen states had some form of medically needy program.[20]

Medicaid's means testing sets strict limits both on the income and assets for eligibility. Although the federal government requires coverage of certain

Figure 10-1 Health Insurance Coverage of the Non-elderly, by Source of Coverage and Federal Poverty Level, 2003

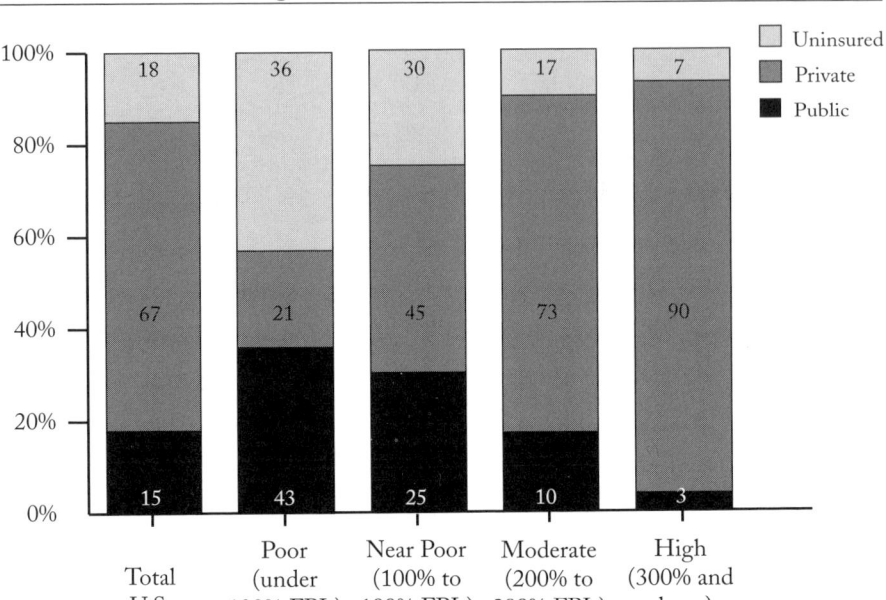

Source: Kaiser Commission on Medicaid and the Uninsured, *The Medicaid Program at a Glance* (Palo Alto, Calif.: The Henry J. Kaiser Family Foundation, January 2005), http://www.kff.org/medicaid/upload/The-Medicaid-Program-at-a-Glance-Fact-Sheet.pdf. Used with permission.

Note: "Public" includes Medicaid, the State Children's Health Insurance Program, and military-related coverage. "Private" includes employer-sponsored and direct-purchase coverage. FPL = federal poverty level.

populations and services, federal rules permit discretion in the extent to which states may elect to cover others. Because of the latitude that states are afforded and the categorical nature of eligibility rules, Medicaid leaves many low-income people uninsured. Figure 10–1 shows that only 43 percent of the non-elderly poor, that is, those living below the federal poverty level ($14,680 for a family of three in 2003), are covered by public programs, primarily Medicaid. Just slightly more than one in three Americans living in poverty has no health coverage. The proportion of those with public coverage declines as income rises, with only about one in four of the near poor (between 100 percent and 199 percent of poverty) covered by Medicaid or another public program.

The federal government matches state funding according to a formula that takes into account state per capita income; the matching funds range from 50 percent to 77 percent of costs and average about 57 percent. Combined state-federal Medicaid spending accounted for about 17 percent ($268.6 billion) of the $1.6 trillion in spending on health services and supplies in 2003, slightly less than Medicare ($283.1 billion) but more than consumer out-of-pocket payments to providers of care ($230.5 billion).[21] The role of Medicaid varies greatly by type of service, covering 46 percent of all nursing home spending and between 12 percent and 19 percent of professional services, hospital care, and prescription drugs. This makes states, which establish reimbursement policy for Medicaid, major players in shaping health services delivery, especially long-term-care services.

The complex eligibility and benefit structure of Medicaid leads to a diverse enrolled population. Two eligibility groups account for the greatest share of Medicaid costs: the elderly (9 percent of beneficiaries and 26 percent of costs) and the disabled (16 percent of beneficiaries and 43 percent of costs). Other groups constitute a larger share of beneficiaries but a much smaller share of costs, including other adults (27 percent of beneficiaries and 12 percent of costs) and children (48 percent of beneficiaries and 17 percent of costs).[22]

Because long-term-care services are expensive and are used over long periods, Medicaid generally covers all the elderly in need of these services who live long enough to "spend down" to eligibility thresholds. In effect, the state-federal funded Medicaid program provides universal coverage for long-term care with "a deductible that is equal to a person's lifetime savings and a coinsurance rate equal to a person's monthly income."[23]

The State Children's Health Insurance Initiative

In 1993 and 1994 the nation debated President Bill Clinton's proposed Health Security Act, which would have created a complex blend of federal coverage mandates and new public subsidies for health insurance to achieve near-universal coverage. Although the Clinton plan ultimately failed to gain approval in Congress, policymakers appeared to understand voter anxiety about the dependability of the current public-private patchwork of the health insurance coverage system. With liberals' newfound willingness to accept incrementalism in health reform and conservatives' reluctance to create new federal entitlements, states and children emerged as the common political ground for the expansion of the government's role in health care. In 1997 the State Children's Health Insurance Program (SCHIP) was enacted as part of the federal Balanced Budget Act; it was the first major expansion of publicly funded health coverage since 1965.

SCHIP was structured like Medicaid, as a federal-state partnership, but with some important differences. First, from a federal perspective, SCHIP is not an entitlement. That is, federal expenditures on the program are capped regardless of the number of children who are eligible. States may choose to entitle groups of beneficiaries, but they are responsible for full program costs after federal allotments are exhausted. Second, states are given much broader latitude in structuring eligibility and benefits. States are permitted, for example, to impose greater beneficiary cost sharing. Finally, states receive enhanced federal matching funds, up to 85 percent of costs in low-income states.

Although recruitment and retention of children in SCHIP has proved challenging, during the first quarter of federal fiscal year 2005, 4.3 million children were enrolled in the program.[24] It is difficult to estimate how much public child health insurance programs have reduced the number of uninsured children, but it is clear that these programs have not fully met their potential; roughly 10 million children remain uninsured, and about two-thirds of those eligible are not enrolled in Medicaid or SCHIP.[25]

SCHIP has been a very popular program among policymakers.[26] Clearly, that it is focused on children is one reason for its popularity, but there are other reasons as well. As noted, SCHIP is not a federal entitlement, making it more acceptable to conservatives. Another appealing feature to conservatives is the wide latitude given to states to contract with private health plans to deliver care. At the same time, the policy autonomy SCHIP offers to states coupled with favorable federal matching rates make it very popular among governors and state legislatures.

Medicaid and SCHIP as State Policy Tools

Since their establishment, Medicaid and SCHIP have been the main vehicles by which states can extend public coverage to their low-income populations. The first major Medicaid eligibility expansions began in the 1980s through a series of amendments to the Medicaid law under the leadership of Rep. Henry Waxman (D-Calif.). Through these incremental expansions, states were required to increase income eligibility thresholds for pregnant women, children, and other vulnerable populations.

A second wave of Medicaid eligibility expansions took place during the Clinton administration under provisions of the Social Security Act that permit experimental initiatives to test innovations in benefit and eligibility design under waivers of federal rules affecting Medicaid and SCHIP. Although these "Section 1115 waivers" require federal budget neutrality, the federal government has considerable latitude in deciding whether to approve state waiver applications.

Thirteen states were early innovators in using Section 1115 waivers starting in 1993.[27] These waivers, drawing on savings projected to come from transitioning large numbers of Medicaid beneficiaries into private managed care plans, brought previously ineligible populations into Medicaid programs. Significant savings from managed care did not materialize, however, and many states experienced serious fiscal strains in maintaining their coverage expansions. Despite these early experiences, federal waiver authority continues to afford states opportunities to innovate. In recent years, new Medicaid and SCHIP waiver authority has been created under federal statute.

Waiver-based coverage initiatives of some states have been bold, in some cases aiming for "universal" coverage. These state experiments have demonstrated how the structures of federalism in health care could serve as the foundation for addressing the problem of the uninsured in the United States. In many ways, states have taken "two steps forward and one step back" in their coverage initiatives. Oregon and Tennessee provide case examples of states that, building on their Medicaid programs, pursued sweeping health system reforms that have not been sustainable.

In 1994, under the leadership of Oregon's then physician-governor John A. Kitzhaber, Oregon began implementing a plan for near-universal coverage. The plan would have three interdependent parts: a budget-neutral expansion of Medicaid coverage to new populations financed by a reduction in the scope of benefits for current enrollees, a mandate that employers either provide basic health coverage to their workers or pay a new payroll tax (called a "pay or play" mandate), and a state-financed pool to provide subsidized coverage for individuals who could not get coverage elsewhere.[28] The second two strategies were to be implemented after the necessary federal Medicaid waivers were in place for the first strategy.

The Oregon Medicaid strategy immediately garnered controversy. The state would use a formal process to rank Medicaid procedures by their cost and effectiveness, then limit coverage only to those that came above a line to be drawn depending upon the funds available. Initially, the federal government would not approve the waiver, but by 1994 the Section 1115 waiver was in place. By that time declining state tax revenues precluded implementation of the Medicaid portion of the strategy. Subsequently, the employer play or pay mandate and other plan components were repealed. Today, Oregon has significantly scaled back ambitions; it has no private coverage mandate, and its public coverage eligibility thresholds are lower than in many other states.[29]

Tennessee had even bolder plans than Oregon. In 1993 Tennessee dramatically expanded its public coverage under a Section 1115 waiver. This new program, called TennCare, would, at its peak, cover more than 400,000 previously uninsured people.[30] By 1995 higher-than-anticipated costs led Tennessee to freeze enrollment for most groups, and continuing fiscal stress through the early 2000s led to further reduced eligibility. TennCare, which once covered children up to 400 percent of the federal poverty line, now covers only children and adults without access to employer-sponsored coverage up to twice the federal poverty standard and the "medically uninsurable" (that is, those rejected by private insurers) up to the poverty line. Finally, in April 2005, Tennessee announced that it would close enrollment to most of the remaining TennCare populations, effectively retrenching to the modest Medicaid program the state had in place prior to this bold reform.[31]

A few states have been more successful than Oregon and Tennessee in building health coverage initiatives for low-income populations.[32] Minnesota, for example, created a state-funded health coverage initiative in 1992 called MinnesotaCare. Taking advantage of federal waiver authority and new funds available through SCHIP, MinnesotaCare now covers a full range of services for parents and children up to 275 percent of the federal poverty level and other adults up to 175 percent of poverty.

New Jersey is another state with broad public coverage eligibility. Under SCHIP, New Jersey covers all children up to 350 percent of the federal poverty level, the highest income eligibility in the nation (briefly Tennessee held the distinction of most generous eligibility for children). Beginning in 2000, under federal waivers, New Jersey became one of only a handful of states to cover adults in its SCHIP program. In addition, New Jersey used its own funds (without federal matching funds) to extend coverage to adults without children up to the poverty line. Because of a state revenue shortfall, however, New Jersey froze enrollment of adults in its SCHIP program in September 2001, but those who had enrolled prior to the freeze remain eligible for coverage.

Undeterred Innovators

Despite a frustrating history of state coverage initiatives, some governors and state legislatures seem undeterred. Among the boldest new initiatives is Maine's Dirigo health plan, which began phased implementation in 2003. Dirigo, Latin for "I lead," seeks to control health care costs, improve quality, and achieve major coverage expansions.[33] Maine will finance the program with state general revenue in the first year *only*; later financing will come from within the state's existing health care budget and enhanced federal matching funding on premiums collected from employers. The planned reallocation of state health spending will take place only if expanded coverage under Dirigo leads to reduced charity care and bad debt and other savings to providers. Dirigo is ambitious, potentially extending public coverage for most people up to 125 percent of the poverty line and for parents up to 200 percent of poverty (children up to this level are already eligible through the state's SCHIP initiative) and providing subsidies for coverage for those up to 300 percent of poverty. Time will tell whether Maine will be able to capture the requisite revenue streams from system savings and federal matches of employer contributions.

In tight fiscal environments other innovative states are looking to budget-neutral solutions to expand coverage at the margin. For example, New Jersey legislators have proposed to require insurers to offer coverage for adult dependents in group plans up to age thirty. Currently, these plans are required to cover dependants only to age nineteen or age twenty-three for students. This proposal, which does not involve any state revenue or require contributions from employers, could potentially make group coverage available to more than a third of the uninsured in that state.

Another state-revenue-neutral proposal, by Gov. Mitt Romney of Massachusetts, would permit firms that do not offer coverage or that employ some workers who are ineligible for coverage (for example, part-time workers) to make pretax deductions of the full cost of coverage from workers' paychecks. This plan would save workers between 15 and 30 percent of the cost of coverage, depending on their marginal federal tax rate, but would not involve state revenue or require employer financial contributions.[34]

Tensions in the Federal-State Partnership

In the decades since Medicaid was established, something of an arms race has ensued as states have sought ways to obtain federal Medicaid matching funds and the federal government has responded by tightening matching rules. States have long sought to shift state-sponsored programs, such as home health care services and state-funded coverage programs, into Medicaid.[35] In the most controversial Medicaid maximization strategies, states have increased federal Medicaid payments without contributing any new state revenue. In the mid-1980s, many states began collecting taxes and donations from providers of Medicaid services, effectively recycling funds to obtain additional federal matching revenue. Most often, the providers were reimbursed fully by the states for the new taxes or donations they contributed. By 1992 thirty-nine states had provider donation and tax schemes.[36] Although most states used the additional federal revenue to enhance health care, some used it to supplant other state funding.

The monies involved in state efforts to maximize federal Medicaid payments have been significant. Medicaid "disproportionate share hospital" programs have been a prime battleground in the federal matching fund conflict. Under these programs, states receive enhanced federal funding for Medicaid services delivered through hospitals that serve large numbers of uninsured patients. As part of their strategies to maximize federal Medicaid payments and without delivering any additional services to Medicaid beneficiaries, states changed their hospital reimbursement formulas to increase their federal disproportionate share hospital payments. As a result, federal disproportionate share payments rose from $1.4 billion in 1990 to over $17 billion in 1992.[37] Subsequently, the federal government significantly tightened its guidelines for the disproportionate share hospital program.

Regulating Private Insurance

As states concentrated on developing Medicaid programs to fund care for low-income and institutionalized populations, the power of major national corporations ensured that states would not use employer-sponsored health insurance to advance their coverage policy goals. Specifically, the federal Employer Retirement and Income Security Act (ERISA) of 1974, created in response to the need for regulation of pensions, preempted states from regulating employer benefit plans.[38] Although it removed one of the potentially most potent policy tools for states to ensure health insurance coverage for the majority of their residents—requiring employers to offer and finance health benefits—ERISA does permit states to regulate the "business of insurance." The implications of this vague provision of federal law have increased the complexity of state policy development. For instance, it was initially unclear how states could create tax incentives for employers to offer health coverage. Under U.S. Supreme Court decisions, permitted state roles have become clearer. For example, states can, under some circumstances, require medical providers to collect taxes from patients in employer-sponsored health plans in order to raise funding for care for the uninsured. But working around ERISA requirements to achieve state policy goals has proved complex and difficult to sustain.[39]

In recent decades, state health insurance market regulation has been an area of active policy debate. Although states may not regulate employer health benefit plans that are "self-funded" (that is, where the employer acts as insurer by bearing financial risk), most medically uninsured individuals are employed by or are dependants of employees of small firms that are not in a position to bear the financial risk of self-funding health benefits. Thus, states bear responsibility for ensuring that private health insurance markets function well for the population most at risk of being uninsured.

In this role, states face a dilemma. In unregulated small-group (businesses with fifty or fewer employees) and individual (individuals and families who purchase coverage directly from an insurer rather than through their employer) health coverage markets, insurers prefer to charge premiums based on health risk, impose waiting periods, not cover preexisting conditions, or deny coverage entirely for high-risk groups or individuals. Thus, constituents with serious health needs and providers eager to have their services covered demand that state legislators impose regulations requiring insurers to cover a broad range of services, guarantee access to and renewability of coverage, and limit the extent to which they may charge higher premiums to customers with greater health risks. At the same time, insurance interests seeking profit and employer interests seeking to avoid costs strongly resist such regulations. As a result, state legislators have enacted laws that are in apparent conflict, mandating coverage-specific benefits or classes of providers while creating "bare bones" health plans with limited benefits and high cost-sharing.

State health insurance regulations exert strong influences on the composition of the insured market.[40] States not requiring insurers to cover populations with high expected medical costs have health insurance markets that serve mainly healthy populations; states with more restrictive regulations do a better job of ensuring access to coverage for higher-need populations but at a higher cost. The tradeoff inherent in state insurance regulation presents a difficult political balancing act for policymakers, but it also presents complex technical challenges with risks of unintended adverse consequences. For example, in 1993, regulations in New Jersey that were intended to ensure access to coverage for older individuals led to a market that now covers less than half of the state's maximum enrollment with premiums that have grown more rapidly than coverage in other markets.[41]

The Impact on the Uninsured: Bailing a Leaking Boat

Have state and federal health care coverage initiatives made much difference? There are countervailing trends in health insurance coverage. Employer-sponsored health insurance is on the decline. The rising cost of health care has outpaced growth in worker compensation (which includes the cost of wages plus benefits), leading to fewer workers with coverage through their jobs.[42] Expanded public program eligibility has compensated for erosion in employer coverage to a degree, but over a long period, the proportion of the non-elderly population without coverage has grown.

Underlying this trend is a change in the composition of the uninsured.[43] The average income of people with employer-sponsored coverage, still the main source of private health insurance, is rising. Low-wage workers are disproportionately likely to work for an employer that does not offer coverage or to face high out-of-pocket premium costs and consequently forgo coverage. As health insurance costs have risen, the income level at which coverage is affordable also rises. Eligibility for public coverage has grown from the bottom of the income distribution. Consequently, the risk of going without coverage is creeping up the income distribution. Of course, as uninsurance becomes more of a middle-class problem, voter demand for health reform will grow.

With SCHIP, public program eligibility for children rose to unprecedented levels. Since many children living in poverty were already eligible for Medicaid, states concentrated SCHIP expansions on children in near-poor families. Between 1979 and 2001, the proportion of children living at or below the federal poverty level without health coverage remained about 30 percent, whereas the proportion of near-poor children (between 100 percent and 199 percent of poverty) declined from over 60 percent to less than 40 percent.[44] Children in states with the highest uninsured rates gained the most from SCHIP; child coverage in southern states grew by 36 percent following SCHIP implementation, whereas coverage of children in comparatively well-off New England and the Middle Atlantic states grew by 15 percent and 7 percent, respectively.[45]

The Future of State Health Policy

Recent developments provide clues to the future of state health policy. This section begins with a discussion of how states are confronting significant growing tensions between providing access to care and paying for public coverage initiatives. In addition, lessons from two examples of state responses to unexpected health-related revenue windfalls provide a rich source for understanding the impulses of state policymakers. Finally, this section draws on developments in human stem cell research to argue that promoting medical innovation, an early theme in health policymaking, remains on the public agenda.

Growing Health Care Costs and State Budgets

The growth of health insurance coverage, initially lax reimbursement policies in both public and private health insurance, and unrelenting progress in medical technology have been costly.[46] Health expenditures in the United States have outpaced growth in the economy overall for decades, with health spending growing from 7.0 percent to 15.3 percent of the U.S. gross domestic product between 1970 and 2003.[47] The public sector has absorbed a disproportionate share of the increase. In 1965, the year before Medicare and Medicaid were implemented, the public sector share of total national health expenditures stood at less than one-fourth. By 2003 public programs financed 45.6 percent ($765.7 billion) of national health spending ($1.68 trillion). States and localities provided just under a third of public health spending in 2003. Official projections suggest that under current law total public sector spending will reach 50 percent of national health expenditures by 2014.[48]

Underlying changes in the U.S. economy affecting state tax revenue collections also has had a major influence on state budgets.[49] Changes in annual state tax collections had ranged from increases of more than 10 percent to declines of 1 percent or less from the mid-1950s through 2001, but a remarkable turnaround was evident beginning in fiscal year 2002 with a decline in state tax revenue of more than 5 percent.[50] Medicaid represents about one in five dollars in state spending, and total health spending at the state level is about 30 percent of annual state outlays.[51] Medicaid is also one of the fastest growing components of state spending, up 13 percent in 2002 and 8 percent in 2003. As state policymakers seek to avoid tax rate increases, health programs have become a prime target for savings.

Medicaid spending is driven, in part, by enrollment increases, which can be substantial during periods of economic downturn, the same periods when state revenue growth is most likely to decline. Nationwide Medicaid enrollment increased by 8.6 percent and 6.2 percent in fiscal years 2002 and 2003, respectively. But the cost of services and the degree of use per beneficiary are also important drivers of cost increases, with more than half of the $15.7 billion *increase* in total Medicaid spending between 2001 and 2002 attributable to growth in outlays per beneficiary.[52] The federal government forecasts continued annual Medicaid spending growth as high as 8.5 percent from 2004 to 2014.[53]

The clash between declining state revenues and growing health care costs has provoked broad cost containment efforts among the states. Table 10–4, based on a 2004 survey of state Medicaid directors, shows a trend toward a wide breadth of state efforts to reign in program costs. Even with these cost control efforts, the sense of fiscal crisis in Medicaid continues, with options for deep cuts under consideration in Washington, D.C., such as significantly reducing the scope of federally mandated benefits or capping federal Medicaid spending (effectively reversing the entitlement nature of Medicaid).[54]

Medicaid cost containment has focused on short-term savings, but there is a natural limit to how much can be saved through measures such as provider payment reductions (if payments drop too low, few providers will be willing to serve Medicaid patients). The majority of costs for public health coverage programs are attributable to beneficiaries with serious, long-term illnesses, such as

Table 10–4 State Medicaid Cost Containment Strategies, Fiscal Years 2002–2004

	Number of states		
Strategy	Actual, 2002	Actual, 2003	Planned 2004[a]
Control prescription drug costs	31	46	44
Reduce or freeze provider payments	22	50	49
Reduce or restrict eligibility	8	25	18
Reduce benefits	9	18	20
Increase patient cost sharing	4	17	21

Source: Adapted from Vernon Smith, "State Responses to Fiscal Pressures: State Medicaid Spending Growth and Cost Containment" (Palo Alto, Calif.: Kaiser Family Foundation, 2003), http://www.kaisernetwork.org/health_cast/uploaded_files/SmithSlides.pdf.

a. As of January 2004.

mental illness like schizophrenia and chronic medical conditions, including diabetes. A significant challenge for achieving long-term cost control for these populations is finding ways to manage care to avoid acute exacerbations leading to expensive hospitalizations and emergency department use. But the return on investment of such strategies, sometimes called "disease management," may not come in the short one-year time frame that state budgets dictate. Despite potential cost savings and improvements in patient outcomes, these interventions require considerable technical expertise and up-front financial investment, two resources that states have difficulty garnering.

State Responses When Fiscal Constraints Are (Sort of) Eliminated

If states did not face severe fiscal constraints in creating coverage options, would they have the political will and technical ability to craft lasting solutions? Recent, natural experiments in health-related fiscal windfalls offer opportunities to consider this question. In late 1998 the attorneys general of forty-six states entered into a "master settlement agreement" with the tobacco industry, which had been forced to compensate states for harm caused by its deceptive marketing practices.[55] Under the agreement, the forty-six participating states would share an estimated $206 billion over the initial twenty-five years of the agreement, the largest settlement of its kind.[56] States would be free to spend the funds as they saw fit, but many constituencies saw state health policy priorities as having been first in line for use of the windfall.

In 2000 state legislatures began developing plans for the tobacco settlement funds. Economies in most states were still strong in 2000, but settlement allocations made in subsequent years would be under the cloud of an economic downturn and declining state revenues. The ways in which governors and state legislatures used the tobacco windfall in this context reveals much about the priorities that states have overall and in the health policy arena specifically.

Initially, states used master settlement agreement funds for bold new health care and other initiatives. Typical of states focusing on health priorities, Colorado committed half of the current year and future funds to a health care trust fund for service expansions and allocated remaining funds to their SCHIP program, long-term care services, substance abuse treatment, smoking prevention, and literacy initiatives. In fiscal year 2001, 45.2 percent of the funds in all the affected states went for health care services, long-term care, tobacco programs, or related health priorities. In that year, an additional 29.0 percent of the revenue was allocated to endowments or reserve funds held for future state needs. The balance of the funds (16.2 percent of the funds), was allocated to education (4.2 percent), children and youth programs (4.2 percent), transitional aide for tobacco farmers (3.0 percent), and other priorities (16.0 percent).

But the economic downturn that followed these initial decisions changed the priorities of state decision makers. Although allocations to health-related priories declined only modestly by fiscal year 2004 (to 41.1 percent of the tobacco funds), states pulled back almost entirely from funding reserves and endowments. In fact, states began to draw down funds that they had already allocated to reserves. Funds allocated to other priority areas also declined, with states using more of the current-year funds to balance their budgets. Eight states (California, Connecticut, Massachusetts, Minnesota, New Mexico, New York, Tennessee, and Wisconsin) allocated all their tobacco funds in 2003 to make up for revenue shortfalls in their general funds.

Moreover, states began to borrow funds to pay for current programs by using the anticipated revenue from the tobacco settlements as a revenue stream to pay off their debt. State budget pressures in fiscal year 2002 led eight states to issue bonds to draw down all or part of the next twenty years of expected tobacco settlement revenue. Thirteen more states were expected to use this strategy in 2003, but a court decision that raised questions about the future ability of bond holders to collect led to higher interest rates and all but one state (New York) decided against the strategy in that year.

The tobacco settlement offers a case study of state priorities. Health advocates, because of their relationship to tobacco-related costs to the states (for example, Medicaid payments for treatment of smoking-related illness), argued that the funds should be used for health programs. Anti-tobacco advocates also laid claim to the funds, making similar arguments. Initially, governors and state legislatures agreed, but as the need to fill yawning gaps in state budgets grew, and the choice of cutting popular state programs or raising taxes became a reality, their commitment waned.

A second example of state responses to health-related revenue windfall provides another test of states' willingness and capacity to address health priorities. In the 1990s the number of nonprofit health insurance companies, mainly Blue Cross Blue Shield plans, seeking to convert to shareholder-owned, for-profit entities began to grow.[57] During this period, nonprofit plans sought conversion to give them access to market capital and to improve prospects for mergers and acquisitions so they could attain price leverage over providers. But as discussed above, state-based Blue Cross Blue Shield plans were frequently created under special state authority, and in any case, the law requires that the assets of such nonprofit entities remain devoted to their charitable mission. As the largest health insurers in many of the affected states, and sometimes as the insurer of "last resort" for people without other access to coverage, Blue Cross Blue Shield conversions collected considerable attention.

Early Blue Cross Blue Shield conversions were permitted to go forward by state regulators without close scrutiny of the value of assets that would remain for charitable purposes, but as state legislatures, insurance regulators, and attorneys general gained experience, they quickly began requiring fair market valuation of assets.[58] In most cases, plan conversions led to the creation of charitable trusts, with the boards of directors appointed under state conversion statutes. The disposition of charitable assets from conversions is determined by the boards, thus the process by which trustees or directors are selected is important. Some states have structured independent conversion foundation boards, but recently the way that some states have structured Blue Cross Blue Shield conversions has led to questions about whether the resulting foundation assets will be spent for the intended charitable purposes.[59] Under 2002 enabling legislation, for example, New York regulators allocated most of the proceeds from the conversion of Empire Blue Cross Blue Shield to a fund to provide raises to health service union members. This arrangement was made with little public scrutiny in a contentious election year in which the main hospital workers union endorsed the incumbent governor. The decision to use the conversion funds in this manner has been challenged in the courts by consumer advocates, but it illustrates how state health policy priorities can be overshadowed by political imperatives.

The Health Care Innovation Imperative Revisited

This chapter began with the argument that the American government's first large expansion into health in the twentieth century was not through health insurance initiatives but through efforts to promote medical innovation. Surely, the National Institutes of Health's multibillion dollar budget makes the federal government, in partnership with private industry, a primary mover in medical technology. But recent events demonstrate that even today states are seeking to be players in high-stakes medical innovation.

In the late 1990s, advances in research on embryonic stem cells raised the prospect of promising new medical interventions to prevent or treat some of the most debilitating and common conditions, including juvenile diabetes, spinal cord injuries, Alzheimer's disease, and Parkinson's disease.[60] Despite its scientific promise, however, provisions attached to National Institutes of

Health appropriation bills since 1995 by antiabortion members of Congress have precluded federal funding of this work. In August 2001 President Bush, seeking a compromise, announced that he would advocate for federal funding of research using existing lines of stem cells, which would not require the use of new embryos.

At the federal level this promising new area of biomedical research seems to have stalled, although it has had proponents of all political stripes, including the former first lady Nancy Reagan and the late actor Christopher Reeve, as well as politically powerful opponents, who object to research on human embryos. Meanwhile, the debate is also playing out in the states. As of 2003 thirty states had enacted laws affecting stem cell research.[61] The majority of these laws ban or limit research using embryos, but laws in other states explicitly promote work in this area.

California, Illinois, New Jersey, New York, and other states are actively competing to create stem cell research enterprises. In 2004 New Jersey became the first state to appropriate funds specifically for embryonic stem cell work, and California then jumped into the fray with the passage of Proposition 72, which provides $3 billion over ten years.[62] Legislatures in other states, including Ohio and Pennsylvania, are debating investments in this area.[63]

In the face of anticipated limitations in federal support, substantial investments in stem cell research in financially strapped states are markers of the demand for continued public investment in medical progress. Like the discussions that led to the entry of the federal government into biomedical research financing nearly a century ago, the debates in the states focus not just on the potential for improved health (which, of course, will accrue to many beyond the states' borders) but on the economic development potential of attracting cutting-edge research. Jobs would be created, the argument goes, as biomedical research enterprises are attracted to the places where this controversial science is tolerated and encouraged. Moreover, if and when the National Institutes of Health is again free to provide support (presumably billions of dollars) for stem cell research, states with a head start would have the talent and infrastructure to compete successfully.

Conclusion

Health and health care push the limits of state fiscal and public management capacity. Most obviously, health care is among the most rapidly growing sectors of the economy and one of the largest components of state expenditure. Compounding the challenge of fiscal capacity is the unequal distribution of needs: states with the least capacity face the largest burden of uninsurance and health needs. Health and health care also challenge the technical capacity of state bureaucracies. There are few simple solutions in health policy. State efforts to ensure access to affordable private markets, for example, require complex regulations with considerable potential for unintended consequences. In the public coverage area, states must be content with arcane and ever-changing federal Medicaid and SCHIP program guidelines. Moreover, rising costs and improvement in the quality of care for public program beneficiaries require that states address difficult medical management questions, such as how to improve the management of costly chronic conditions and reduce preventable use of emergency and inpatient hospital services.

Competing demands in other policy areas, including education, housing, and tax reform, raise questions about whether states have the political capacity to make health and health care policy a priority. Returns on investments in complex health improvement initiatives come well beyond the timeframe of state budgets and electoral cycles and are likely only to slow cost increases, not reverse them. Without taking a thoughtful, long view of health policy questions, policymakers are most likely to seek reduced health spending by cutting benefits for already disenfranchised populations.

The problems facing state policymakers in the health arena are not static, and middle-class voters are feeling a growing sense of insecurity about their health coverage. The strategy of providing coverage for the middle class through private insurance while shoring up coverage for the poor through state programs is growing more difficult to pursue as health costs grow faster than the ability to pay.

Whether states can, in the final analysis, devise sustainable approaches to addressing health policy problems is an open question. The barriers to state solutions are substantial. Certainly, no state can afford to make its economy uncompetitive by financially burdening the private sector with universal health care coverage. As well, constraints of the existing state-federal relationship—federal Medicaid and SCHIP rules and the preemption of state regulation of employment health (and other) benefit plans—blunt the prospect for bold state initiatives. The forces underlying health system problems lie well beyond the borders of any given state. Rapidly rising health care costs, for instance, are driven largely by advances in medical technology.

As formidable as they are, these constraints are not likely to stop state policymakers from seeking broad strategies. State policymakers will continue to respond to voter demands to address health policy problems, and the very federal framework that constrains state action may one day become the foundation for shared responsibility for addressing the problem of the uninsured and the challenges of improving population health.

Notes

1. Institute of Medicine, *The Future of the Public's Health in the 21st Century* (Washington, D.C.: National Academies Press, 2003), 98–100.
2. Cynthia Smith and others, "Health Spending Growth Slows in 2003," *Health Affairs* 24 (January–February 2005): 186.

3. Ibid.
4. Ibid., 188.
5. National Association of State Budget Officers, *State Expenditure Report, 2003* (Washington, D.C.: National Association of State Budget Officers, 2004), 4.
6. Ibid., 4–5.
7. National Association of State Budget Officers, *Medicaid and Other State Healthcare Issues: Current Trends* (Washington, D.C.: National Association of State Budget Officers, 2003), 1–7.
8. A rich compendium of state-specific health indicators are provided at Kaiser State Health Facts Web site, http://www.statehealthfacts.org (accessed April 18, 2005). Except where noted, the examples of state variations in health indicators in this section are drawn from this source.
9. Joel C. Cantor, Stephen H. Long, and M. Susan Marquis, "Challenges of State Health Reform: Variations in Ten States," *Health Affairs* 17, no. 1 (January–February 1998): 191–200; Stephen F. Jencks, Edwin D. Huff, and Timothy Cuerdon, "Change in the Quality of Care Delivered to Medicare Beneficiaries, 1998–1999 to 2000–2001," *Journal of the American Medical Association* 298 (January 15, 2003): 305–312.
10. Lisa J. Blumberg and Amy J. Davidoff, *Exploring State Variation in Uninsurance Rates among Low-Income Workers*, Issue Brief B56 (Washington, D.C.: Urban Institute, 2004). This finding is based on a widely used measure of general health that asks survey respondents to rate their health as "excellent, very good, good, fair or poor."
11. Jencks, Huff, and Cuerdon, "Change in the Quality of Care."
12. For an informative illustration of the relationship between poor state fiscal capacity and the problem of uninsured individuals, see M. Susan Marquis and Stephen H. Long, "Federalism and Health System Reform: Prospects for State Action," *Journal of the American Medical Association* 278, no. 6 (August 13, 1997): 514–517.
13. Lawrence D. Brown and Beth Stevens, "Expertise Meets Politics," in *To Improve Health and Health Care, 1997: Robert Wood Johnson Foundation Anthology*, ed. Stephen L. Isaacs and James R. Knickman (San Francisco: Jossey-Bass 1997), 78–108.
14. Daniel M. Fox, *Health Politics, Health Policies: The British and American Experience, 1911–1965* (Princeton: Princeton University Press, 1986), 37–51.
15. Ibid., 188–205.
16. Eli Ginsburg, *The Road to Reform: The Future of Health Care in America* (New York: Free Press, 1994), 60–86.
17. Irwin Miller, *American Health Care Blues* (New Brunswick, N.J.: Transaction Publishers, 1996), 27.
18. Eli Ginsburg, *Road to Reform*, 62.
19. Randall R. Bovbjerg, Joshua M. Weiner, and Michael Housman, "State and Federal Roles in Health Care: Rationales for Allocating Responsibilities," in *Federalism and Health Policy*, ed. John Holahan, Alan Weil, and Joshua M. Weiner, (Washington, D.C.: Urban Institute, 2003), 25–58.
20. Kaiser Commission on Medicaid and the Uninsured, *Medicaid Medically Needy Programs: An Important Source of Medicaid Coverage* (Palo Alto, Calif.: Kaiser Family Foundation, 2003).
21. Smith and others, "Health Spending Growth Slows in 2003," 188.
22. Kaiser Commission on Medicaid and the Uninsured, *The Medicaid Program at a Glance* (Palo Alto, Calif.: Kaiser Family Foundation, 2005).
23. James R. Knickman, "Private Long-Term Care Insurance: Alleviating Market Problems with Public-Private Partnerships," in *Health Economics and Health Services Research*, ed. Richard. Scheffler and Louis Rossiter, (Greenwich, Conn.: JAI Press, 1988), 135-148.
24. Centers for Medicare and Medicaid Services, FY 2005 First Quarter Ever Enrolled Data by State—Total SCHIP, http://www.cms.hhs.gov/schip/enrollment/chenroll0105.pdf, May 19, 2005 (accessed May 24, 2005).

25. Kaiser Commission on Medicaid and the Uninsured, *Enrolling Uninsured Children in Medicaid and SCHIP* (Palo Alto, Calif.: Kaiser Family Foundation, 2005), http://www.kff.org/medicaid/loader.cfm?url=/commonspot/security/getfile.cfm&PageID=5 1998.
26. Jennifer M. Ryan, *SCHIP Turns Five: Taking Stock, Moving Ahead*, Issue Brief 781 (Washington, D.C.: George Washington University, National Health Policy Forum, 2002).
27. Teresa A. Coughlin and Stephen Zuckerman, "States' Strategies for Tapping Federal Revenues: Implications and Consequences of Medicaid Maximization," in Holahan, Weil, and Weiner, *Federalism and Health Policy*, 145–178.
28. Lawrence D. Brown, "The National Politics of Oregon's Rationing Plan," *Health Affairs* 10, no. 2 (Summer 1991): 28–51.
29. John Holahan and Mary Beth Pohl, "Leaders and Laggards in State Coverage Expansions," in Holahan, Weil, and Weiner, *Federalism and Health Policy*, 179–214.
30. G. Gordon Bonnyman, "Stealth Reform: Market Based Medicaid in Tennessee," *Health Affairs* 15, no. 1 (Summer 1996): 306–314; Holahan and Pohl, "Leaders and Laggards in State Coverage Expansions."
31. Bureau of TennCare, State of Tennessee, press release, April 29, 2005, http://www.state.tn.us/tenncare/New percent 20Updates/EnrollmentPR042905.pdf.
32. See Holahan and Pohl, "Leaders and Laggards in State Coverage Expansions," for an excellent discussion ranking the scope of state Medicaid and SCHIP programs.
33. Jill Rosenthal and Cynthia Pernice, *Dirigo Health Reform Act: Addressing Health Care Costs, Quality, and Access in Maine* (Washington, D.C.: National Academy for State Health Policy, 2004), 1–8.
34. Commonwealth of Massachusetts, Executive Department, "Romney Launches Healthcare Reform in Massachusetts," press release, April 6, 2005, http://www.mass.gov/portal/index.jsp?pageID=pressreleases&agId=Agov2&prModName=gov2pressrelease&prFile=gov_pr_050406_healthcare_roll_out.xml.
35. Teresa A. Coughlin and others, "A Conflict of Strategies: Medicaid Managed Care and Medicaid Maximization," part 2, *Health Services Research* 34, no. 1 (April 1999): 281–293.
36. Leighton Ku and Teresa A. Coughlin, "Medicaid Disproportionate Share and Other Special Financing Programs," *Health Care Financing Review* 16, no. 3 (1995): 45–58.
37. Teresa A. Coughlin and David Liska, *The Medicaid Disproportionate Share Hospital Payment Program: Background and Issues* (Washington, D.C.: Urban Institute, 1997).
38. Patricia A. Butler, *ERISA Preemption Manual for State Health Policy Makers* (Washington, D.C.: AcademyHealth, 2000).
39. For examples of the influence of ERISA on state health policy, see Patricia A. Butler, *ERISA Update: The Supreme Court Texas Decision and Other Recent Developments* (Washington, D.C.: AcademyHealth, 2004); and Joel C. Cantor, "Health Care Unreform: The New Jersey Approach," *Journal of the American Medical Association* 270, no. 24 (December 22–29, 1993), 2968–2970.
40. Kisali Ilayperuma Simon, "What Have We Learned from Research on Small-Group Insurance Reforms?" in *State Health Insurance Market Reform: Toward Inclusive and Sustainable Health Insurance Markets*, ed. Alan C. Monheit and Joel C. Cantor (London: Routledge, 2004), 21–45; and Deborah Chollet, "What Have We Learned from Research on Individual Market Reform?" in Monheit and Cantor, *State Health Insurance Market Reform*, 46–64.
41. Alan C. Monheit and others, "Community Rating and Sustainable Individual Health Insurance Markets: Trends in the New Jersey Individual Health Coverage Program," *Health Affairs* 23, no. 4 (July–August 2004): 167–175.
42. Richard Kronick and Todd Gilmer, "Explaining the Decline in Health Insurance Coverage, 1979–1995," *Health Affairs* 18, no. 2 (March–April 1999): 30–37.

43. Ellen O'Brien and Judith Feder, *Employment-Based Health Insurance Coverage and Its Decline: The Growing Plight of Low-Wage Workers* (Menlo Park, Calif.: Kaiser Family Foundation, 1999).
44. Todd Gilmer, Richard Kronick, and Thomas Rice, "Children Welcome, Adults Need Not Apply: Changes in Public Program Enrollment across States and over Time," *Medical Care Research and Review* 62, no. 1 (February 2005): 56–79.
45. Ibid., 74.
46. Lax reimbursement is a function of the political power of medical providers. Recall that Blue Cross was largely a creation of the hospital industry and that Medicare and Medicaid reimbursement strategies were initially quite generous to gain cooperation from powerful interests, including doctors and hospitals. More recently, the outpatient prescription drug benefit added to Medicare in 2004 did not include price controls, garnering political support of the prescription drug industry.
47. Smith and others, "Health Spending Growth Slows in 2003," 186.
48. Stephen Heffler and others, "U.S. Health Spending Projections for 2004–2014," *Health Affairs* 5 (February 23, 2005): 77. Official government statistics on health expenditures arguably understate the government share because they do not include foregone revenue from the favorable tax treatment of employer health insurance spending or government spending on health benefits for its own employees. In 1998, for example, government covered 45 percent of national health expenditure according to the official statistics, but an alternative estimate including tax expenditures and public employee health benefits boosted this proportion to 56 percent. See Daniel M. Fox and Paul Fronstin, "Public Spending for Health Care Approaches 60 Percent," *Health Affairs* 19 (March–April 2000): 271–273.
49. See Chapter 7 of this book for a detailed discussion of fiscal challenges facing the states.
50. Kenneth Finegold and others, "Social Program Spending and State Fiscal Crises," *Occasional Paper 70* (Washington, D.C.: Urban Institute, 2003), 3.
51. National Association of State Budget Officers, *Medicaid and Other State Healthcare Issues: Current Trends*, 1–7.
52. Vernon Smith and others, *Medicaid Spending Growth Results from a 2002 Survey* (Menlo Park, Calif.: Kaiser Family Foundation, 2002).
53. Heffler and others, "U.S. Health Spending Projections for 2004–2014," 78.
54. Robert Pear, "State Proposing Sweeping Change to Trim Medicaid," *New York Times*, May 9, 2005, A1.
55. The discussion of the tobacco master settlement agreement in this chapter is drawn from Andrew McKinley, Lee Dixon, and Amanda Devore, *State Management and Allocation of Tobacco Settlement Revenue* (Washington, D.C.: National Conference of State Legislatures, 2003).
56. This settlement followed a similar agreement with the four other states valued at $40 billion.
57. Grantmakers in Health, *Assets for Health: Findings from the 2001 Survey of New Health Foundations* (Washington, D.C.: Grantmakers in Health, 2002).
58. Amy Tiedemann and others, *Sustaining the Charitable Mission of Horizon Blue Cross Blue Shield after Conversion to a For-Profit Corporation: Issues and Best Practices* (New Brunswick, N.J.: Rutgers University, Center for State Health Policy, 2003).
59. California, for example, used an open public process involving a broadly based search advisory committee that reviewed highly qualified candidates identified by a professional search firm. The slate of board members for the Blue Cross Blue Shield conversion foundation was then ratified by the California Department of Corporations. Once established, the board of the California Endowment is self-perpetuating, leaving political decision makers out of the picture.

60. American Association for the Advancement of Science, "AAAS Issue Brief: Stem Cell Research," http://www.aaas.org/spp,cstc/briefs.stemcells/index.shtml, August 16, 2004 (accessed May 23, 2005).
61. National Conference of State Legislatures, "State Embryonic and Fetal Research Laws," http://www.ncsl.org/programs/health/genetics/embfet.htm, no date (accessed May 23, 2005).
62. National Conference of State Legislatures, "The Use of State Funds for Stem Cell Research," http://www.ncsl.org/programs/health/genetics/esstatefunds.htm, no date (accessed May 23, 2005); and MSNBC.COM, "California Gives Go-Ahead to Stem-Cell Research," http://www.msnbc.msn.com/id/6384390/print/1/displaymode/1098, November 3, 2004 (accessed February 1, 2005).
63. *State Stem Cell Funding News* 1, no. 4 (May 11, 2005): 7.